TELEVISION BROADCASTING IN CONTEMPORARY FRANCE AND BRITAIN

TELEVISION BROADCASTING IN CONTEMPORARY FRANCE AND BRITAIN

Edited by Michael Scriven and Monia Lecomte

Berghahn Books
New York • Oxford

First published in 1999 by
Berghahn Books

© 1999 Michael Scriven and Monia Lecomte

All rights reserved.
No part of this publication may be reproduced in any form
or by any means without the written permission
of Berghahn Books.

Library of Congress Cataloging-in-Publication Data
Television broadcasting in contemporary France and Britain /
edited by Michael Scriven and Monia Lecomte.
   p.   cm.
   Includes bibliographical references and index.
   ISBN 1-57181-946-0 (hardback : alk. paper)
   ISBN 1-57181-754-9 (paperback : alk. paper)
      1. Television broadcasting--Great Britain.   2. Television
broadcasting--France.   I. Scriven, Michael, 1947- .
II. Lecomte, Monia.
PN1992.3.G7T445   1999
384.55'0941--dc21   98-8490
                                                                  CIP

British Library Cataloguing in Publication Data
A catalogue record for this book is available
from the British Library.

Cover design by Noir Café, Paris

Contents

List of Tables	vii
Acknowledgements	viii
Editorial Note	viii
List of Abbreviations	ix
Introduction	xiii

Part I: Regulatory and Political Structures

1. Television and the State
   Raymond Kuhn and James Stanyer — 2

2. Independent Regulatory Authorities
   Hervé Isar — 16

3. Two Conflicting Notions of Audiovisual Liberalisation
   Serge Regourd — 29

4. The Future of Public Broadcasting
   Jean-Claude Sergeant — 46

Part II: Programming Structures

5. Two Programming Models
   Régine Chaniac — 58

6. Cinema and Television: From Enmity to Interdependence
   Lucy Mazdon — 71

7. Quality, Culture and Education
   Susan Emanuel   83

Part III: The New Media

8. Satellite Television
   Peter Goodwin   94

9. Cable Television
   Jean-Claude Sergeant   107

10. Beyond Digital Television
    Patrick Vittet-Philippe   120

Part IV: The Challenge of Europe

11. Multimedia Multinationals: Canal Plus and Reuters
    Michael Palmer   140

12. The Europeanisation of Programming
    Alex Taylor   168

13. Broadcasters' Involvement in Cinematographic Co-productions
    Anne Jäckel   175

14. The European Union Audiovisual Policies of the U.K. and France
    Richard Collins   198

Select Bibliography   222

Notes on Contributors   227

Index   230

LIST OF TABLES

Table 5.1. Percentage audience share on French television   60
Table 5.2. Percentage audience share on British television   61
Table 9.1. Growth of cable television in France   111
Table 9.2. U.K. cable performance, 1991-6   115
Table 9.3. Major cable operators in 1996   117

Acknowledgements

The Editors wish to thank the Service Culturel of the Ambassade de France and the Institute of Romance Studies for their generous support of the one-day conference, 'French and British Television in the 1990s', which was held in London in March 1997, and which formed the basis of this book. As organisers of the conference and editors of the book, we would also like to thank everyone who participated in the collaborative process from which *Television Broadcasting in Contemporary France and Britain* has emerged. In particular, we thank all those colleagues from Britain and France whose varied yet complementary approaches to the subject made this interdisciplinary research project possible.

Michael Scriven and Monia Lecomte

Editorial Note

Chapters 2 and 3 have been translated from the French original by the editors.

List of Abbreviations

A2	Antenne 2
ACT	Association of Commercial Television
ADSL	Asymmetric Digital Subscriber Line
AFP	Agence France Presse
ANOC	Association des nouveaux opérateurs constructeurs de réseaux câblés
AP	Associated Press
ARD	Arbeitsgemeinschaft der offentlich-rechtlichen Rundfunk-anstalten der Bundersrepublik Deutschland
ATM	Asynchronous Transfer Mode
BARB	Broadcasters' Audience Research Board
BBC	British Broadcasting Corporation
BCC	Broadcasting Complaints Commission
BDB	British Digital Broadcasting
BFI	British Film Institute
BLIC	Bureau de Liaison de l'Industrie cinématographique
BMIG	British Media Industry Group
BSB	British Satellite Broadcasting
BSC	British Standards Council
BSkyB	British Sky Broadcasting
BT	British Telecom
CCE	Commission des Communautés européennes
CGE	Compagnie Générale des Eaux
CGV	Compagnie Générale de Vidéocommunication
CLT	Compagnie Luxembourgeoise de Télédiffusion
CNC	Centre national de la cinématographie

CNCL	Commission nationale de la Communication et des libertés
CNN	Cable News Network
COM	Communication de la Commission des Communautés européennes
CSA	Conseil supérieur de l'audiovisuel
CTA	Cable Television Association
DBS	Direct Broadcasting Satellite
DG	Directorate General
DGT	Direction Générale des Télécommunications
DOM-TOM	Département et Territoires d'Outre-Mer
DTH	Direct-to-Home
DVD	Digital Video/Versatile Disk
EBU	European broadcasting union
ECF	European Co-production Fund
ECU	European Currency Unit
EEC	European Economic Community
EFDO	European Film Distribution Office
EPC	European Publishers Council
EU	European Union
FIDO	Film Industry Defence Organisation
FR3	France Régions 3
FT	*Financial Times*
GATT	General Agreement on Tariffs and Trade
HACA	Haute Autorité de la Communication Audiovisuelle
HDTV	High Definition Television
IBA	Independent Broadcasting Authority
IFCIC	Institut de financement des industries culturelles
INA	Institut National de l'Audiovisuel
IT	Information Technology
ITA	Information Technology Agreement
ITC	Independent Television Commission
ITV	Independent Television
LCI	La Chaîne de l'Info
MEDIA	Mesures pour encourager le développement de l'industrie audiovisuelle
MSNBC	Microsoft Network and National Broadcasting Cooperation
M6	Métropole télévision 6
NDS	New Digital Services
NVOD	Near-Video-on-Demand
Oftel	Office of Telecommunications
OMC	Organisation Mondiale du Commerce
OMSYC	Observatoire mondial des systèmes de communication

List of Abbreviations

ONP	Open Network Provision
ORTF	Office de Radiodiffusion-télévision Française
PAF	Paysage audiovisuel français
PAL	Phase on Alternate Lines
PANS	Pretty Amazing New Services
PBS	Public Broadcasting Services
POTS	Plain Old Telephone Services
PPV	Pay-per-View
PSB	Public Service Broadcasting
PTT	Postes télégraphes et téléphones
RA	Radio Authority
RAI	Radiotelevisione Italiana
RFI	Radio France Internationale
RPI	Retail Price Index
RPR	Rassemblement Pour la République
RTE	Radio Telefis Eireann
RTF	Radio Télévision Française
RTV	Reuters Television
S4C	Sianel Pedward Cymru
SCRIPT	European Script Fund
SECAM	Séquentiel couleur à mémoire
SEPT	Société d'édition et de programmation de télévision
SFP	Société Française de Production
SLII	Service de Liaison Interministériel pour l'Information
SMATV	Single Master Antenna Television
SOFICA	Société de financement de l'industrie cinématographique et audiovisuelle
TDF	Télédiffusion de France
TF1	Télévision Française 1
TLM	Télé Lyon Métropole
TLT	Télé-Toulouse
TMB	Télé 8 Mont Blanc
TNT	Turner Network Television
TPS	Télévision Par Satellite
TSA	Taxe spéciale additionnelle
TSW	TV South West
TVE	Television Española
TVS	TV South
TWF	Television Without Frontiers Directive
VOD	Video-on-Demand
WRAC	World Radio Administrative Conference
WTN	Worldwide Television Network
WTO	World Trade Organisation
ZDF	Zweites Deutsches Fernsehen

Introduction

The origin of this book lies in a disagreement: two editors, one English, one French, in accord on the centrality and importance of television broadcasting to contemporary society and culture, yet frequently failing to see eye to eye on the respective merits and achievements of the audiovisual spheres on the two sides of the English Channel. This dissonance of interpretation was ultimately productive. Rather than leading to polemical and non-comprehending positions, it led over a period of time to a greater understanding not only of the cultural specificities of television broadcasting in France and Britain, but also to a growing awareness of the manner in which cultural stereotypes are created, shaped and maintained. An initial blindness and a desire to cling to national cultural assumptions and prejudices were progressively transformed into a beneficial process of comparative self reevaluation.

At the same time, the further we explored our field of enquiry, the more apparent it became that there is currently a dearth of genuinely comparative material on French and British television. The abundance of published books of a historical, theoretical, empirical or nation-specific character contrasts markedly with the virtual non-existence of sustained comparative analyses of the two broadcasting systems. Although serious work has been carried out by French and British media commentators on the structural development of the audiovisual sphere in both countries, systematic comparisons between the two are rare. The originality of this book resides principally, therefore, in its ambition to pursue a rigorously comparative approach to the major issues confronting television broadcasting in France and Britain today. The thematic, comparative approach adopted in the following pages is consequently the site of an instructive cross-national dialogue: within each chapter coexists a natural propensity to define audiovisual systems from the perspective of certain national affinities, and an attempt to perceive the other's systems in a manner that does not fall prey to the distortions of any particular nation-specific lens.

This originality of comparative perspective is enhanced further through the contrastive effect of the varied backgrounds and experiences of the contributors themselves: academic, professional, technocratic. Given the all-pervading presence of television broadcasting in contemporary society, we considered as editors that it was important to give expression not solely to the voice of the academic specialist, but also to the professional programme maker and to the technocratic legislator. The striking differences in style and tone of expression between these different voices constitute an important ingredient in the overall debate surrounding the role and impact of television on our daily lives.

The choice of France and Britain as exemplars of contemporary television broadcasting is also not arbitrary. Geographically close, culturally similar though quite distinct, France and Britain none the less symbolise two very different, occasionally diametrically opposed models of television broadcasting. Although it would be a reductive and oversimplified position to maintain that the French and British models of broadcasting constitute mutually exclusive archetypes, since the reality of the world is far more complex and ill-defined, their structural differentiation marks them out for special attention in the European context. It would not be an overstatement to claim that France and the U.K., precisely because of their very different traditions and perspectives, are the two major actors in the shaping of the European audiovisual sphere. Britain, with its celebrated duality of public service and private sector broadcasting, and France, with its increasingly successful commercial sector and a deep commitment to Europeanisation, constitute primary models for the analysis of the impact of globalisation and homogenisation of the media in the 1980s and 1990s. The key question to resolve is whether these two very different models of television broadcasting are sustainable as we move towards the twenty-first century.

Television Broadcasting in Contemporary France and Britain is organised in four distinct but interrelated parts. Part I, 'Regulatory and Political Structures', offers an account of the differing national contexts in which broadcasting is framed in the two countries. Raymond Kuhn and James Stanyer explore relations between television and the state, Hervé Isar offers a comparative account of indepen-

Introduction   xv

dent regulatory authorities, whilst Serge Regourd and Jean-Claude Sergeant examine privatisation and public broadcasting respectively. Part II, 'Programming Structures', is aimed at assessing the audiovisual environment in which programmes are conceived, produced and televised on both sides of the Channel. It would have been impossible to include within the scope of a single book all programming genres. Although many areas undoubtedly merit analysis (children's programmes, morning programmes, regional programmes, sports programmes, documentaries, information and news), the scope of such a study would have been too extensive for one publication. In part II, therefore, Régine Chaniac locates two quite distinct programming models, Lucy Mazdon probes the nature of the relationship between cinema and television, and Susan Emanuel evaluates programming from the perspective of 'Quality, Culture and Education'. Moreover, in addition to the specific issues raised in these three chapters, there are also references to a variety of programming genres in other chapters of the book (regional programmes in chapter 3, news output in chapter 11, European programmes in chapter 12).

Part III, 'The New Media', is focused on the far-reaching impact of technological change on television broadcasting. Peter Goodwin sets the scene with a comparative analysis of satellite developments in both countries, Jean-Claude Sergeant offers an explanatory account of the differences of approach to cable television in France and Britain, whilst Patrick Vittet-Philippe dramatically broadens the scope of enquiry with his account of digital television. Arguing that the digital revolution is synonymous with `the simultaneous collapse of traditional boundaries between industries and of existing borders between regions', he propels the discussion beyond television to a complex network of interactive IT services, and beyond France and Britain towards Europe. His stress on the European dimension provides an excellent bridging chapter to the fourth and final part. 'The Challenge of Europe', focused on the technological, industrial, cultural and political dimensions of programming and policy developments, therefore significantly broadens the three previous themes within the overall context of Europe. In the first chapter of part IV Michael Palmer emphasises, as does Patrick Vittet-Philippe, the global, international dimension of television broadcasting in his analysis of `Multimedia Multinationals'. Alex Taylor, a professional programme maker, provides first-hand insights into the 'Europeanisation of Programming'. This breezy contribution, highlighting the practical difficulties of producing media output with representatives of several nations, contrasts with the writing of those academics who wish to buttress cultural programming within the EU. European audiovisual collaboration is none the less taking place, as Anne Jäckel demonstrates in her assessment of the success of Franco-British television co-productions. In the final chapter, 'The European Union Audiovisual Policies of the U.K. and France', Richard Collins engages in a detailed and thought-provoking account of the contribution of both countries to the growing Europeanisation and globalisation of contemporary television broadcasting. As such, it constitutes an appropriate concluding synthesis to the entire book.

The future development of television broadcasting in France, Britain and Europe is difficult to predict. The digital revolution which is transforming the entire broadcasting infrastructure at an exponential rate previously unknown will profoundly and irreversibly modify the entire audiovisual environment. However, the behaviour of French, British and European consumers/citizens confronted with the choice of an ever-increasing number of channels and programmes is uncertain. What is clear, none the less, is that the role of television in its digitised and interactive form will play a crucial role throughout Europe at the turn of the century. The fundamental issues raised in this book will evidently continue to exercise the minds of professional commentators and programme makers, but more importantly will have a significant impact on the decision-making processes of governing élites at a national and European level, and on the daily lives of the public at grass-roots level. Who can deny that television broadcasting in France and Britain will become increasingly more influential and socially significant? Time alone will tell, however, what the cultural and political consequences of this growing televisual presence will be.

Michael Scriven and Monia Lecomte

PART I

REGULATORY AND POLITICAL STRUCTURES

CHAPTER 1

TELEVISION AND THE STATE

RAYMOND KUHN AND JAMES STANYER

The state in Britain and France has been intimately involved in the organisation of television throughout its implantation and routinisation as a mass medium of information and entertainment. In both countries television was initially managed as a state monopoly, funded from a licence fee whose level was (and remains) set by the government. For much of television's history the state strictly controlled market entry, with the result that the growth in the supply of television was slow and incremental. Britain and France had only three channels each by the start of the 1980s. In addition, the state imposed specific programming obligations on the output of television companies in line with national interpretations of public service values.[1]

There were important differences between the two countries in the state's relationship with television. In Britain the establishment of Independent Television (ITV) in 1955 to compete with the British Broadcasting Corporation allowed private interests to run a nationwide television network, organised in regional companies and funded from advertising (see chapter 3). The output of the BBC/ITV duopoly was subject to regulations drawn up by government and enforced by state-appointed regulatory authorities[2] (see chapter 2). In France state monopoly ownership of television persisted until the 1980s, though advertising finance was introduced in 1968 and greater competition for audiences became the norm after the creation of separate programme companies in 1974. Direct governmental interference in political information on British television was rare, but a mix of regulation and convention largely ensured that television's news agenda reflected the consensual mainstream of party politics. In France state control of key managerial and editorial appointments and overt ministerial interference in television news production were more common, with the result that political information on television was sometimes shamefully pro-government.[3]

During the 1980s both television systems began to enter a period of significant change, inspired by developments in new media technology such as fibre-optic cable and direct broadcasting by satellite (see chapters 8 and 9). In the 1990s digitalisation promised further to increase the amount of television programming available to households and, potentially at least, open up the market to new suppliers of programming and product (see chapter 10). The reality of multichannel television called into question the continued relevance of the state's regulatory role which had developed in conditions of scarcity of supply. Neo-liberals and pragmatists argued that consumers should be allowed to exercise their choice in a minimally regulated market, while traditionalists sought to defend public service values in the face of a technological and ideological pincer movement.

In a parallel and partly related development, state authorities faced more intractable problems than previously in structuring television's news agenda. Censorship and intimidation were less successful, journalistic deference to official sources less common and audiences more sceptical in the multichannel environment of the late 1990s. Ministers and their officials increasingly resorted to manipulating and seducing television's news professionals through an emphasis on image projection and attractive sound bites.[4]

This initial chapter examines some of the ways in which the state has tried to adapt to and manage the process of change in television regulation and agenda structuring. It shows how in both areas of activity the authorities in Britain and France now operate within more complex environments than previously. The ends and means of system regulation are a constant issue in media policy debates, while structuring television's news agenda is a daily process of negotiation and bargaining.

Regulating the television system

Since the early 1980s the nature and extent of state regulation has featured prominently in television policy debates in both Britain and France. Following the election of Thatcher's radical right-wing government in 1979, the British public service model of regulation was challenged by a market liberal discourse which reflected the rise of New Right ideas in governing circles. In particular, the principal embodiment of the public service tradition – the BBC – found itself under hostile attack[5] (see chapter 4) More generally, policy proposals which favoured easing conditions of market entry for new players (such as independent producers) and light touch regulation of television content found favour with key state actors in the policy-making process, including Prime Minister Thatcher herself[6] (see chapters 2 and 3).

Mitterrand's presidential election victory in 1981 acted as the catalyst for radical change in the structures and regulation of the French television system. The Socialists' 1982 legislation on audiovisual communication (*la loi Fillioud*) abolished the state monopoly which had come to be regarded as a symbol of right-wing government control of broadcasting. Europe's first terrestrial pay-tv station, Canal Plus, was established in 1984 and two off-air commercial channels, la 5 and TV6 (later renamed M6), were set up in 1986 at the personal instigation of the President. Following the conservative victory in the 1986 general election, the government led by Prime Minister Chirac introduced a new audiovisual statute (*la loi Léotard*) which included among its provisions the privatisation of the main public sector channel, TF1 (see chapter 3).

There have been specific national characteristics to the policy debate on television regulation. In Britain during the Thatcher premiership there was a strong ideological element, evidenced in the recommendations of the Peacock report with its belief in the primacy of market forces.[7] In France the initial liberalisation of the system by the Socialists was influenced by the desire to deliver on the 1981 electoral promise of change by introducing greater competition in the supply of programming.[8] Only the privatisation of TF1 can be said to have been part of an ideologically based programme.

There have also been certain common features. The first was the recognition by policy makers of the impact of technological change. In particular, the arrival of new media technologies challenged one of the traditional defences of state regulation – the frequency spectrum as a scarce public resource. Digital compression of signals via terrestrial, cable or satellite distribution systems finally kills off any defence of regulation on grounds of technical scarcity.

Second, technological convergence has made television part of a much wider multimedia revolution (see chapter 10). Boundaries between the previously discrete policy fields of broadcasting and telecommunications have become blurred. Traditional broadcasting players such as the established terrestrial television companies have been joined by new actors (including telecommunication giants British Telecom and France Télécom) wanting to enter the television market as network operators and/or service providers.

Third, internationalisation of television has become increasingly apparent. New media technology allows trans-frontier programme distribution across Europe, breaching previously well defended national borders. Powerful multimedia companies such as BSkyB and Canal Plus have emerged to grab a share of pan-European and global markets (see chapter 11). Meanwhile, the European Union (EU) has begun to carve out a role for itself as a supranational regulatory player, desiring the harmonisation of certain rules across its member states. The EU has also become a forum for intergovernmental bargaining (and conflict) as policy issues previously resolved at nation-state level fall victim to reverse subsidiarity (see chapter 14).

While these changes made policy making more complex for government ministers and state officials, in neither country was regulation of television abandoned. There was no equivalent in Britain or France of the radical deregulatory climate which prevailed in Italy and allowed Silvio Berlusconi to build up his control of the private sector of Italian broadcasting.[9] In Britain this was due in part to a social and political counter-mobilisation against the neo-liberal deregulatory thrust of government policy by defenders of public service values, including opposition political parties and broadcasting professionals. Significantly there was also division at ministerial level, institutionalised in a battle between the Home Office and the Department of Trade and Industry, over the extent of deregulation considered desirable. In France the anarchy of the Italian experience reinforced the technocratic inclination of policy makers to manage change from the top down.

Moreover, in both countries the state wanted to retain an influence on television content for social and cultural reasons. In Britain Conservative government ministers supported regulation against undesirable television programming, establishing the Broadcasting Standards Council to monitor the portrayal of sex and violence on television and patrolling the airwaves to protect British viewers from the output of continental adult channels. In France state actors, whatever their party political affiliations, continued to expect television to reflect national cultural and linguistic sensibilities. The French government fought long and hard during the GATT negotiations to protect its domestic audiovisual production industries.

Rather than a simple shift from public service regulation to deregulation, both Britain and France embarked on a protracted process of regulatory adjustment. In both countries the role of regulatory authorities became a key policy issue. In Britain the 1990 Broadcasting Act abolished the Cable Authority and the Independent Broadcasting Authority (IBA), replacing them with the Independent Television Commission (ITC) whose jurisdiction covered terrestrial, cable and domestic satellite television (except for the BBC). The ITC was given fewer formal powers than the IBA to regulate the output of commercial television, while the telecommunications watchdog,

Oftel, has recently challenged the primacy of the ITC in the regulation of digital television.

France took time to come to terms with the existence of regulatory agencies in the field of broadcasting, with no fewer than three separate agencies succeeding each other during the 1980s.[10] *La Haute Autorité de la communication audiovisuelle* (HACA) (1982-6) was attributed some functions previously performed directly by government, such as the appointment of the heads of public sector television companies. It was replaced in 1986 by *la Commission nationale de la communication et des libertés* (CNCL), which in turn gave way to *le Conseil supérieur de l'audiovisuel* (CSA) in 1989.

To a large extent the turnover of regulatory authorities in France was a legacy of the tradition of partisan politicisation of broadcasting, with the CSA's two predecessors being regarded by their opponents as too close to the government of the day. In an attempt to reinforce the legitimacy and political independence of the CSA, President Mitterrand proposed that its role be enshrined in the Constitution of the Fifth Republic. Though this was not implemented, the political success of the CSA may be gauged by the fact that it was retained by the conservative government of Edouard Balladur after 1993 and by President Chirac after 1995. Much later than in Britain and by a more tortuous route, France has acquired a regulatory agency which enjoys a high degree of political legitimacy (see chapter 2).

Three main issues have dominated the recent regulatory debate in both countries. The first is market entry. In neither Britain nor France has the state renounced its desire to control entry into its respective television system. The 1990 Broadcasting Act may have changed the rules for the allocation of ITV franchises by introducing a system of financial bids, but it was the Conservative government which drew up the rules and the ITC which implemented them. It was the government which gave the go-ahead for the launch of Channel 5, the last pre-digital terrestrial channel in Britain, and the ITC which awarded the franchise. Market entry to cable is also controlled by the ITC. In 1986-7 the CNCL awarded the privatised TF1 franchise to the Bouygues group and reallocated the franchises for channels five and six. The state not only authorised but financially backed the creation of a Franco-German cultural channel, Arte, at the beginning of the 1990s. In 1994 a new educational channel, La Cinquième, was set up by the state and funded from public money (see chapters 4 and 7). Finally, and in controversial circumstances, the government rather than the CSA renewed the TF1 franchise for the Bouygues group in 1996 without any competitor being allowed to make a rival bid.

It is clear that in both countries there has sometimes been disagreement between government and regulatory authorities over the rules of franchise allocation and the choice of successful franchise applicants. In France in particular this has often spilled over into conflict over appointments to top posts, such as that of Philippe Guilhaume as common head of the public sector television companies Antenne 2 (A2) and France Régions 3 (FR3) in 1989.[11]

Even more crucially, the capacity of the state, united or not, effectively to manage entry into national television markets has been made immensely more difficult by technological change. In Britain, for example, the ITC's chosen candidate to develop satellite television, British Satellite Broadcasting (BSB), was rudely pushed out of the marketplace by Rupert Murdoch's Sky channel in a remarkable entrepreneurial coup in 1990. In this case the regulatory authority was reluctantly compelled to accept the reality of Murdoch's commercial power as the newly named venture, British Sky Broadcasting (BSkyB), went on to gain a de facto monopoly in the distribution of satellite television programming to British audiences.[12] In France the state's desire to promote market entry for new programme providers on its hi-tech direct broadcasting satellite TDF1 was a dismal failure.[13]

The exploitation of digital television demonstrates some of the problems the state now encounters in the face of technological progress. In Britain the allocation of terrestrial digital multiplexes to established broadcasters such as the BBC was non controversial. In the competition for the remaining terrestrial digital franchise the winner was a consortium based around the ITV companies Granada and Carlton. BSkyB was originally part of this consortium, but under pressure from the ITC, itself influenced by European competition authorities, BSkyB was forced to withdraw its stake in the consortium. The possibility of the satellite company assuming a dominant position in the market for pay-television through its control of the decoding technology and programme rights was deemed of sufficient concern for it to be kept away from a stake in digital terrestrial television. However, if digital satellite television can be commercially successful, then BSkyB will remain a major player in the supply of programming to British audiences. The question remains open whether through regulation the state can continue to control entry into the broadcasting marketplace.

In France the government has backed away from the high prestige state-backed projects of the early 1980s and the practice of selecting national champions in key electronic sectors of the economy. Exploitation of digital television, which originally looked to be the monopoly of the first market entrant Canal Plus, has become the object of competition between the pay-tv company on the one hand and a consortium of other television companies including TF1 and France Télévision on the other. While there is a strong desire among state élites for a French company to be a powerful player in the European digital television market, the authorities have become less convinced of the desirability of trying to pick winners in advance. Regulation of competition to ensure a level playing field is now widely regarded as a more appropriate role for the state.

The second regulatory issue on the television policy agenda concerns ownership, both within the television sector and across different media. Here the challenge for British and French policy makers has been to reconcile the desirability of competition and choice at the national level with the need for companies to be able to compete successfully in European and global markets. The tension between the sociopolitical desirability of pluralism and diversity on the one hand and the economic arguments in favour of critical mass size and cross-media synergy on the other have been at the heart of the regulatory debate on ownership in both countries (see chapter 3).

In Britain a major cross-media ownership stake in both press and television was not possible under the terms of the 1990 Broadcasting Act which legislated for maximum press group holdings in broadcasting.[14] Three main sets of actors were involved in the policy debate on television ownership after 1990.

The first was Murdoch's News Corporation, which by the middle of the decade had built up a strong position in both the national newspaper industry and satellite broadcasting. Murdoch had been allowed to bypass the 1990 regulatory hurdles because the satellite television service BSkyB was considered by the authorities to be a non-domestic broadcaster, despite the fact that its programme output was aimed overwhelmingly at the British market.

The second set of actors was the British Media Industry Group (BMIG), which had been established in 1993 by Associated Newspapers, the Guardian Media Group, Pearson and the Telegraph group to campaign for a relaxation of the rules restricting newspaper holdings in television. As BSkyB's audience reach moved towards 25 percent of households by the middle of the decade, non-Murdoch owned national newspaper groups vigorously protested that the existing ownership rules effectively prevented their own cross-media expansion, while doing nothing to limit the growth of Murdoch's media empire. As well as campaigning for a change in the legislation, between 1990 and 1995 the major non-Murdoch press groups worked to build up their cross-media interests, but strictly within the prevailing regulations.

The third group consisted of major terrestrial commercial television companies who wanted to enhance their stake within the ITV network through mergers and take-overs. Their lobbying persuaded the government to relax ownership rules within the sector, prior to a fundamental review of television/cross-media ownership provisions being undertaken.

Following the publication of a White Paper in 1995,[15] the 1996 Broadcasting Act substantially liberalised media ownership regulations. In particular, numerical limits on the holding of television licences were abolished and a quota system based on audience share was introduced. The result of the various changes in ownership rules was that by 1997 the ITV network was dominated by three major groups based around Carlton, Granada and United Newspapers. The 1996 Act also allowed national newspapers with 20 percent or more of national circulation to take up to a maximum 20 percent interest in a licence to provide a terrestrial commercial service (either ITV or Channel 5). At current newspaper circulation rates both Murdoch's News Corporation and the Mirror Group were caught by this limit, while other press groups were not. In short, during the 1990s the British government liberalised television/cross-media ownership rules to the benefit of the major ITV companies and press groups (except News Corporation and the Mirror Group) in a strategy aiming to promote bigger media companies and at the same time prevent the Murdoch group from dominating media markets.

In France too the state has been actively involved in setting rules on permitted levels of ownership both within the television sector and across different media. Here also the decline of the domestic newspaper industry encouraged press groups such as Hersant to expand out of their core sectors and diversify into other media, including television. Perhaps surprisingly, many of these attempts at diversification by press groups ended in tears. In contrast, industrial and utility companies such as Bouygues, la Compagnie Générale des Eaux and la Lyonnaise des Eaux have built up important stakes in terrestrial and cable television over the past decade.

In the light of these changes, the French government sought to draw up an appropriate regulatory framework, while the Constitutional Council played a vital role in adjudicating on the constitutionality of proposed legislation. The current regulatory regime originated in 1986 when complex rules based on market share and potential audience size were introduced to apply to both single sector and cross-media ownership. These rules, already generous in scope, were further relaxed by *la loi Carignon* in 1994 to allow significant monomedia holdings and cross-media diversification.[16]

The third regulatory issue on the state's agenda in Britain and France concerns television content. In both countries it is clear that the era of a highly regulated public service television system is over. Television companies now operate under different regulatory constraints, with public sector companies such as the BBC and France Télévision the most highly regulated; cable, satellite and pay-tv channels (for example, BSkyB and Canal Plus) the least; and commercial terrestrial broadcasters (including ITV, Channel 5 and TF1) falling somewhere in between.

For much of the past decade the competitive pace in both countries has been set by commercial pay-tv broadcasters. BSkyB and Canal Plus have used their financial power based on viewer subscription to buy up attractive programme product such as feature films and sports rights. In contrast, with their commitment to balanced scheduling and investment in original national production, the public sector companies have had to make painful changes to their organisation (for example, the introduction of producer choice at the BBC and the regrouping of the two main French public channels into France Télévision) and defend the principle of licence-fee funding in difficult political circumstances. Whatever the status of content regulations, it is likely that for financial reasons public sector broadcasters will find it increasingly difficult to compete with commercial and subscription services in certain programme genres, as is evidenced in Britain by the controversial loss of sports transmission rights by terrestrial television to BSkyB.

Constructing the television news agenda

The state in Britain and France is closely involved in the complex task of television news management.[17] At the heart of the state the core executive in particular constantly seeks to influence what issues are featured on television and how these are covered by journalists. Policies have to be explained, promoted and defended on television as the authorities try to 'put their message across' to viewers and win public support. As the role of television has grown in the process of political communication, so the state has developed a variety of mechanisms and techniques for shaping television's news agenda.

At times the relationship between the state and the television news media has been strongly influenced by the authoritarian style of the regime. This was clearly the case during the de Gaulle presidency in France (1958-69) and the Thatcher premiership in Britain (1979-90). De Gaulle wanted to use television as a means of legitimising the new regime of the Fifth Republic against the backcloth of the Algerian war, while the Thatcher government wanted to build popular support for a new approach to economic management and welfare provision while also facing up to the threat of internal terrorism. Not surprisingly, censorship and associated repressive practices were very evident in the relationship between the state and television during these periods as strong leaders sought to impose their will on television for ideological purposes.[18] During the de Gaulle presidency the Ministry of Information exercised such close control of political information on television that the regime was described by one commentator as a 'telecracy' – government by television.[19] During the Thatcher premiership the government introduced a broadcasting ban to keep apologists for terrorism in Northern Ireland off British television screens, thus depriving them of the oxygen of publicity.[20]

However, in a liberal democracy such an approach to influencing television's news agenda is controversial and often counter-productive. Heavy-handed tactics by government ministers and state officials to control television news are in flagrant contradiction with established norms concerning the role of the media in a free society, are resented by television journalists as an unwarranted infringement in their professional domain and reduce the credibility of the medium and the message in the eyes of the public.

In any case the state does not always want to constrain the flow of information. It also wants to promote its policies and persuade the electorate of their effectiveness. In this respect censorship and repression are of limited value. Rather, in its routine, everyday attempts to structure television's news agenda the state in Britain and France has developed a vital role as a primary definer. The state is engaged in an institutionalised relationship with the television news media, which gives government ministers and state officials the opportunity to establish the initial framing of the topic in question. This interpretation then 'commands the field' in all subsequent treatment and sets the terms of reference within which all further coverage or debate takes place.[21]

The authority and legitimacy of the state mean that the media are accustomed to giving its representatives prominent coverage. To help ensure that the state's version of events dominates television coverage, the core executive in both Britain and France is helped by a range of support staff, including public relations personnel and media advisers, presidential and governmental spokespersons, press offices and information agencies. In Britain ministerial access to television journalists is routinised in the lobby system of attribution; in France presidential press conferences guarantee prime-time news coverage. Special events are staged largely for television consumption, while 'spin doctors' such as Peter Mandelson, Alastair Campbell and Jacques Pilhan are wheeled out to ensure that television covers the story from the official perspective. Timing of executive decisions can be made to ensure maximum television, and therefore public, impact. In sum, the state's version of events usually has little difficulty in finding a channel on British and French television.

The agenda-structuring role of the state for television news was particularly evident during the Gulf War. In their coverage of the conflict British and French television were not so much censored (though censorship did exist) as co-opted by the authorities into accepting the official perspective on the central issues of the war – the sovereignty of Kuwait and the upholding of international law.[22]

Yet though the state in Britain and France commands considerable institutional resources and authority to underpin its agenda-setting role for television news, its capacity to 'command the field' and set the terms of reference in which coverage takes place is certainly not unlimited. The state cannot impose its version of events at will. Indeed, evidence suggests that setting the agenda of television news is frequently fraught with difficulties.

The first problem faced by the state in its agenda-setting role is its lack of internal cohesion.[23] It is clear that in neither Britain nor France is the state a monolithic entity, acting with a unified will and a single sense of purpose. Policy disputes exist between state actors, as in the case of the handling of the Northern Ireland conflict.[24] In addition, there may be highly public ideological clashes, such as that between 'Euro-sceptics' and 'Europhiles' during the Major premiership. On the poll tax issue, television was able to exploit divisions within the ranks of the government and governing party regarding the new tax's merits and drawbacks.[25] In the French case the conflicts are sometimes based on party political divisions at the heart of the governing coalition. One obvious example of institutionalised political conflict at the very apex of the French state was the first period of *cohabitation* as President Mitterrand and Prime Minister Chirac engaged in a struggle to impose their respective political agendas on television in the run-up to the 1988 presidential contest. Following the 1997 general election result, the third experience of *cohabitation* may well see a similar prolonged battle between Gaullist President Chirac and Socialist Prime Minister Jospin.

Second, the counter-definitional role for television news of non-state actors as sources needs to be borne in mind. The state does not have a monopoly of resources or legitimacy. Television regularly uses other sources from a professional concern to cover an issue from different perspectives. These sources may challenge the state's attempt to frame an issue in a particular way and may generate counter-definitions. As a result, government ministers and state officials often find themselves competing against other discourses in their attempt to impose the official perspective. In the propaganda war which accompanied the armed conflict in Northern Ireland, for example, alternative (and occasionally even oppositional) discourses on terrorism received some coverage on British television alongside the normally dominant official perspective.[26] The pressure group Greenpeace has played a major role in shaping British television's coverage of environmental issues (such as the Brent Spar story in 1995). Greenpeace was also instrumental in mounting a strong definitional challenge to the French state's media defence of the nuclear tests in the South Pacific in the same year.[27]

Finally, emphasising the state's role as agenda setter tends to present television in a passive role. Yet television may frequently subject the state's attempted framing of events to critical scrutiny, taking the initiative 'in the definitional process by challenging the so-called primary definers and forcing them to respond'.[28] Investigative journalism is one way in which television may scrutinise the state's attempts at agenda construction. In Britain this has been especially true of programme genres outside of news such as current affairs, documentaries and drama. For instance, television current affairs programmes on the imprisonment of the Guildford Four and the Birmingham Six questioned the safety of the original convictions and contributed to the process which ended in the release of the defendants, much to the embarrassment of government ministers and members of the judiciary. Even in France, where the practice of investigative journalism is less well implanted in the professional journalistic culture, television has increasingly taken its cue from the print media and developed a tendency to act more as a public watchdog than a state transmission belt. The agenda-setting attempts of various ministers have failed to limit critical television exposure of malpractice and corruption, affecting Laurent Fabius (contaminated blood scandal) and Alain Carignon (financial irregularities) among others.

Conclusion

In the late 1990s the state in Britain and France remains a key actor in the regulation of the television system and the structuring of the medium's news agenda. However, technological change and internationalisation are expanding the provision of television, facilitating the emergence of new players in the market and bringing complex regulatory issues to the attention of policy makers. In the regulatory domain the state has often given the appearance of trying (and frequently failing) to keep up with the pace of change. In the agenda-setting process the expansion of channels makes old forms of control anachronistic, while other political actors have established their credibility as news sources. As a result, state élites have to negotiate and bargain with television journalists, winning coverage by using image friendly and media newsworthy tactics. Whether seeking to manage the evolution of the television system or construct television's news agenda, the power of the state to impose its will appears weaker than at almost any other period in the medium's history.

Notes and References

1. J. Blumler (ed.), *Television and the Public Interest*, London, Sage, 1992.
2. R. Negrine, *Politics and the Mass Media in Britain*, 2nd edn, London, Routledge, 1994.
3. R. Thomas, *Broadcasting and Democracy in France*, London, Crosby Lockwood Staples, 1976.
4. N. Jones, *Soundbites and Spin Doctors*, London, Cassell, 1995.
5. S. Barnett and A. Curry, *The Battle for the BBC*, London, Aurum Press, 1994; T. O'Malley, *Closedown? The BBC and Government Broadcasting Policy 1979-92*, London, Pluto, 1994; J. Seaton, 'Broadcasting in the Age of Market Ideology: Is it Possible to Underestimate the Public Taste?', *The Political Quarterly*, vol. 65, 1994, 29-38.
6. S. Brittan, 'The Fight for Freedom in Broadcasting', *The Political Quarterly*, vol. 58, 1987, 3-23.
7. Peacock Committee, *Report of the Committee on Financing the BBC*, Cmnd 9824, London, HMSO, 1986.
8. R. Kuhn, *The Media in France*, London, Routledge, 1995, 165-84.
9. G. Mazzoleni, 'Towards a "Videocracy"? Italian Political Communication at a Turning Point', *European Journal of Communication*, vol. 10, 1995, 291-319.
10. L. Franceschini, *La régulation audiovisuelle en France*, Paris, Presses Universitaires de France, 1995.
11. P. Guilhaume, *Un président à abattre*, Paris, Albin Michel, 1991.
12. P. Chippindale and S. Franks, *Dished! The Rise and Fall of British Satellite Broadcasting*, London, Simon and Schuster, 1991.
13. R. Kuhn, *The Media in France*, 204-28.
14. L. Ainsworth and D. Weston, 'Newspapers and UK media ownership controls', *Tolley's Journal of Media Law and Practice*, vol. 16, 1995, 2-9.
15. Department of National Heritage, *Media Ownership*, Cmnd 2872, London, HMSO, 1995.
16. For details see R. Kuhn, 'France', in V. MacLeod (ed.), *Media Ownership and Control in the Age of Convergence*, London, International Institute of Communications, 1996, 49-63.
17. B. Franklin, *Packaging Politics*, London, Edward Arnold, 1994; J. Gerstlé, *La communication politique*, Paris, Presses Universitaires de France, 1993.
18. R. Bolton, *Death on the Rock and other stories*, London, W. H. Allen, 1990; J. Bourdon, *Histoire de la télévision sous de Gaulle*, Paris, Anthropos/INA, 1990.
19. C. Durieux, *La Télécratie*, Paris, Tema, 1976.

20. L. Curtis and M. Jempson, *Interference on the Airwaves*, London, Campaign for Press and Broadcasting Freedom, 1993; D. Miller, *Don't Mention the War: Northern Ireland, Propaganda and the Media*, London, Pluto Press, 1994.
21. S. Hall, C. Critcher, T. Jefferson, J. Clarke and B. Roberts, *Policing the Crisis*, London, Macmillan, 1978.
22. P. Taylor, *War and the Media*, Manchester, Manchester University Press, 1992; D. Wolton, *War Game*, Paris, Flammarion, 1991.
23. P. Schlesinger and H. Tumber, *Reporting Crime*, Oxford, Clarendon Press, 1994.
24. D. Miller, 'Official sources and "primary definition": the case of Northern Ireland, *Media, Culture and Society*, vol. 15, 1993, 385-406.
25. D. Deacon and P. Golding, *Taxation and Representation: The Media, Political Communication and the Poll Tax*, London, John Libbey, 1994, 188.
26. P. Schlesinger, G. Murdock and P. Elliott, *Televising 'Terrorism'*, London, Comedia, 1983.
27. G. Derville, 'Media coverage of the "nuclear tests issue" in France: the single combat between the French authorities and Greenpeace', Paper presented at the European Consortium for Political Research workshop on New Developments in Political Communication, Oslo, 1996.
28. P. Schlesinger and H. Tumber, *Reporting Crime*, 19.

CHAPTER 2

INDEPENDENT REGULATORY AUTHORITIES

Hervé Isar

Comparisons between French and British regulatory authorities would appear at first sight to be of little interest. Analysis of the organisation of these authorities reveals no more than self-evident disparities since they are embedded in quite different political and socioeconomic environments. Beyond contextual and formal considerations, however, they have at least one thing in common: their function is to protect democracy from the excesses of political power, from the appetites of financial power and from the diversionary power of television. Consequently, although the structure and organisation of French and British regulatory authorities are effectively dissimilar, their functions remain comparable.

Regulatory authorities with different structures

The structure of regulatory authorities invariably discloses the political, economic and legal traditions of states. It is consequently vital to note these traditions at the outset in order to reach a complete understanding of the manner in which these authorities operate in France and Britain.

Political and economic traditions in long-time opposition

It needs to be noted initially that although the U.K. organised from the very beginning the independence of radio and television from those in power, France opted for more than forty years for dependency on government. Equally, although British liberalism rapidly allowed for the creation of a broadcasting duopoly consisting of public and private sectors, French 'colbertism' (centralised state economic system) maintained a monopoly until 1986. These 'nuances' have evidently had important consequences for the justification and timing of the creation of a regulatory authority. Thus, the Royal Charter of 17 December 1926, which established the British Broadcasting Corporation (BBC), made a point of entrusting radiotelephony to a public corporation separate from the state apparatus. Moreover, control was given to a Board of Governors whose prime function would be to ensure, from an independent position, that the company operated within the national interest.

The introduction of television in 1936 in no way modified this commitment to protect the BBC from political interference through the creation of a buffer authority. Nothing changed in 1954 when the Conservative government decided to open up the British audiovisual sphere to competition in order to offer free choice to viewers and a preferential space for advertisers. Indeed, when Independent Television (ITV) was created, the British legislator entrusted its establishment to an independent authority (ITA- Independent Television Authority) which, although very close to private operators, would also rapidly demonstrate its autonomy.

The creation of BBC2 in 1964, Channel 4 in 1982 and Channel 5 in 1997 had no impact whatsoever on the initial attitude adopted by the British government. Although the ITA disappeared in 1972 to give birth to the Independent Broadcasting Authority (IBA), which was in turn replaced in 1990 by the Independent Television Commission (ITC), there was no sign of political reprisals or attempts to take control of the institution.

It would evidently be naïve to believe that the independence of British television has never been in doubt. The Falklands episode or some of the interventions of the Thatcher government proved the contrary, but the principle of freedom has always prevailed. Besides, there has never existed in the U.K. a Ministry or a Secretary of State with specific responsibility for information or television broadcasting. Thus, the creation of regulatory authorities appears to be the consequence of the refusal of those in power to become directly involved in the administration of the audiovisual sector.

The French example is remarkably different. Although the French had to wait until 1945 to set up a state monopoly, they decided immediately and on a long-term basis to integrate audiovisual communications within the state apparatus. The Fourth Republic (1946-58) thus maintained the principle of state control, inherited for the most part from Vichy, which guaranteed total political ascendancy over Radio Télévision Française (RTF). The reform of 4

February 1959, initiated by a government led by General de Gaulle, responded to numerous criticisms by setting up a self-governing commercial and industrial public corporation (RTF). However, since this corporation was without a Board of Governors and was placed under the authority, not the supervision, of the Minister of Information, its political independence was explicitly denied by the legal text.

The Law of 27 June 1964, leading to the creation of the Office de Radiodiffusion Télévision Française (ORTF), appeared more respectful of legal categories and of the independence of the institution, since this public corporation was now granted a Board of Governors and placed under the authority of the Minister of Information. However, this statute was soon to show its limitations, and from April 1965, the government openly defended the practice of governmental interference.

The introduction of advertising in 1968 and the suppression of both the Service de Liaison Interministériel pour l'Information (SLII) and the Minister of Information did not really call into question the ascendancy of the political sphere over the corporation. The Law of 3 July 1972 sought to protect the corporation more effectively by establishing an Audiovisual Governing Board and a Chairman and Managing Director, who would in theory wield immense power and be nominated for three years. But the Governing Board, which had only an advisory power, was de facto incapable of guaranteeing any moral authority whatsoever. As for the supposedly irremovable Chairman and Managing Director, he was dismissed less than two years after his appointment because he proved to be too independent. The Law of 7 August 1974, which dismantled the ORTF and created in its place seven distinct bodies, three being television channels (TF1, A2, FR3), proved to be a slight improvement but the appointment of the main officials for radio and television remained within the power of the government.

In fact, it was not until after the Socialists gained power in 1982 and announced the end of the public monopoly that an independent regulatory authority, the Haute Autorité de la Communication Audiovisuelle (HACA) was finally set up. With responsibility for appointing the chairmen of the public channels and for guaranteeing the free flow of information, the HACA undoubtedly constituted a turning-point in the eventful history of French television broadcasting. Yet old instincts had far from disappeared. Thus, the Law of 30 September 1986, adopted by the new right-wing majority, the HACA, which was replaced by the Commission Nationale de la Communication et des Libertés (CNCL), whilst the return to power of the left in 1989 was symbolically marked by the disappearance of the CNCL replaced by the Conseil Supérieur de l'Audiovisuel (CSA). From then on, and despite changes of government, the existence of the CSA has not been seriously challenged and criticism against it has become less and less frequent.

It is therefore only recently that French television broadcasting has been operating in an acceptably independent manner in relation to the political sphere. Although the end of the state monopoly was heralded in 1982, it was only in 1986 with the creation, in a politically stormy atmosphere, of 'La Cinq' and 'La Six', together with the privatisation of TF1, that genuine competition between public and private channels emerged.

The new French regulatory authority has therefore an essential and symbolic dual role to play. On the one hand it seeks to protect public as well as private television channels from government interests; on the other, to administer, regulate and control an audiovisual sector subject to commercial interests that in France are still regarded with suspicion.

Little comparability between legal systems

For the French observer, the originality of the British legal system in its application to audiovisual communication is located above all in its flexibility and in its pragmatic evolution. It is indeed not infrequent for the drafting of a new law to be preceded by the publication of a report written by a specialist committee whose inspirational role is often significant. Moreover, the source of legislation appears to be divided insofar as the public sector is subject to the Royal Charter and the private sector is regulated by the Broadcasting Act. At the same time, the established legislative framework appears to be deliberately imprecise and the main body of detailed case law is for the most part the outcome of agreement between the various actors and not the result of the direct application of the law or of a decree. Consequently, custom, practice or convention are the important sources of legislation in British radio and television. Finally, British regulatory authorities are not necessarily separate from broadcasters, their judgements are rarely discussed and appeals are the exception.

This situation stands in marked contrast to the French legal system which remains centred on the mystique of the law, which alone is judged capable of expressing the general will. Indeed, the parliament takes centre-stage in the formulation of audiovisual Law and its interventions are numerous. Thus, the Law of 30 September 1986, which remains for the moment the key legal point of reference, has since its adoption been modified more than twenty-two times. Consequently, even though this frenzy of legislative activity has enabled the Conseil Constitutionnel to draft a genuinely constitutional statute for the freedom of audiovisual communication, it has also led the same Conseil to set significant limits to the regulatory powers which can be attributed to the regulatory authority. Henceforth, the legislator can entrust the Authority with enforcing the law on the strict condition that this authorisation concerns only those measures limited as much by their field of application as by their content, and in a framework laid down by the law or the regulations. In other words, the French regulatory authority only has at its disposal a power to regulate implementation and detail. The law and the regulation consequently remain the principal sources of French audiovisual Law, and it is with the utmost precision that the mission statements, methods, means and the limitations imposed on broadcasters are defined. Last but not least, the quibbling and undisciplined nature of the French temperament leads to decisions of the regulatory authority being systematically taken to appeal in the Council of State. The latter, being responsible for enforcing a complex and convoluted set of regulations, and denying all legislative power to the regulatory authority, is frequently forced to revoke these decisions, which weakens still further the institution.

Regulatory authorities with differing organisations

The organisation of the British regulatory system differs profoundly from the French system insofar as it is based on a multiplicity of authorities. Equally significant, however, is the method of appointing members to the authorities, as well as the composition of the authorities themselves.

Unitary French structure and plural British structure

In line with its centralising tradition, France has opted for a unitary structure in its regulation of the audiovisual sector. The creation of an administrative institution receiving neither orders nor instructions emanating from traditional administrative structures, certainly ties in with the recent modernising trend of French administration, but such originality comes to an end there. There is indeed no question that the authority has real regulatory power, nor are its powers fragmented. One authority alone presides over a given sector of activity. Its regulatory powers are strictly defined in writing and are exercised over all actors and activities concerned under the jurisdiction of a judge.

Apart from the transitory experience (1986-89) of the CNCL, which also had powers in the field of telecommunications, the French regulatory authority since 1982 has had sole power to regulate all audiovisual communication activities (radio, television, cable, satellite) and to control all broadcasters (public and private sectors). Moreover, its investigatory powers cover all aspects of audiovisual communication (technical, ethical, economic, etc.).

The British do not appear to be as concerned about the concentration and unity of regulatory powers. Several councils or bodies have general powers, but their regulatory power is applicable only to certain actors (private sector, public sector), others have general powers that are applicable to technically specialised sectors (radio) whilst others exercise their authority over the whole of radio and television but have a specialised remit (invasion of privacy, professional code of ethics). Thus, the Independent Television Commission (ITC), which replaced the IBA and the Cable Authority in 1990, is the central regulatory authority in the private sector for terrestrial, cable or satellite television. As for the Board of Governors, it is the autoregulatory authority for the BBC. It has a dual role. On the one hand, it selects and appoints the Chairman and Managing Director and the members of the Board of Directors. On the other, it keeps a close eye on the operation and production of public channels and checks that they are observing the Royal Charter. In fact, this Board is the guarantor of the BBC's independence and the guardian of the code of ethics of the public sector. The Welsh Fourth Channel Authority (Sianel Pedward Cymru or S4C) appears even more specialised since this authority has specific powers to monitor the Welsh Fourth Channel's respect for its broadcasting commitments. It constitutes a local example of self-regulation.

Other authorities have more specialised powers which cover the whole of radio and television. For example, the function of the Broadcasting Standards Council (BSC), established in 1988 and enshrined in the Broadcasting Act of 1990, is to exercise a moral imperative over all British public and private radio stations and television channels. Its principal mission is to note and examine complaints regarding the broadcasting of programmes considered by associations or viewers/listeners to be violent, indecent or disrespectful of good taste. In a similar vein, the Broadcasting Complaints Commission (BCC), set up in 1981 with powers comparable to those of the BSC, deals specifically with complaints concerning the invasion of privacy and keeps a check on the accuracy and impartiality of information. Finally, the Radio Authority (RA) created by the Broadcasting Act of 1990, with powers relatively similar to those of ITV, is the regulatory authority of the national and local commercial radio sector.

Minor differences in the composition and methods of appointment of members

The question of the composition and the methods of appointment of members of the regulatory authorities does not appear to be envisaged in the same way on the two sides of the Channel. In France, it unfailingly gives rise to controversy and discussion. In the U.K. it generates little passion. The issue of composition, which is closely linked to that of the appointment of members, is evidently of direct relevance to the independence of the institution itself. Consequently, the disproportionate amount of interest shown in the matter is explained above all by differences in sociopolitical environments.

In 1982 France unquestionably opted for a simple solution since the Haute Autorité consisted at that time of nine members appointed for a non-renewable period of nine years. Of these members, all of whom were appointed by a decree of the President of the Republic, three were proposed by the President of the National Assembly, three by the President of the Senate, and the other three – which included the President – by the Head of State. This composition, modelled on that of the Conseil Constitutionnel, was none the less severely criticised because it was regarded as excessively politically biased in favour of the government in power.

The new majority in 1986 therefore voted for a different system. The CNCL was composed of thirteen members appointed on a non-renewable basis for nine years. Six members were designated by the highest authorities of the State (President of the Republic, President of the Senate, President of the National Assembly), three were elected from the highest courts of Law (Council of State, Court of Appeal, Revenue Court), one by the Académie française and three were co-opted from the professions. The President was elected by the members of the CNCL from within its own ranks.

In 1989 the legislator decided that the system had not succeeded in guaranteeing the independence of the institution from those in political power, and returned to the 1982 system whilst reducing the length of the period of office. Since then the CSA has been composed of nine members appointed on a non-renewable basis for six years. The activities of the CSA are incompatible with any other elective mandate or public work, and all professional activities. Bound by professional secrecy, they cannot either directly or indirectly hold any position of responsibility, receive fees, nor hold shares in any company linked to the press, advertising, telecommunications or audiovisual sectors. Even though these appointments still have a significantly political slant, everything has been done to guarantee the independence of the institution.

The British are apparently much more pragmatic. They prefer to take on board criticism rather than to ignore it. The twelve members of the Board of Governors are therefore appointed for a maximum of five years by the Crown within the framework of the Royal Charter, but their appointment is monitored overall by the government. There is little distance between the ITC and the politically powerful since the members of the ITC (from nine to thirteen) are appointed on a renewable basis for five years by the Department of State for National Heritage. Moreover, the Home Office is often involved in these appointments. The same is true for the ten members of the Radio Authority, the eight members of the BSC and the five members of the BCC who are also appointed by the Department of State for National Heritage. This situation, which would appear as totally unacceptable in France, does not, however, seem to bother the British, who rightly or wrongly continue to perceive these different authorities as independent. It is none the less undoubtedly the case that it is not possible to legislate for independence. Governments do not last and traditions persist that can frustrate the most autonomous of regulatory bodies.

Regulatory authorities with numerous similarities of missions and means

De facto and de jure, the French and British regulatory authorities have a dual mission: on the one hand to avoid anarchy by guaranteeing the relatively harmonious operation of this sector of activity, and on the other hand to provide viewers with a minimum of quality programmes and to enforce public interest. Moreover, the means at their disposal are comparable since on both sides of the Channel, powers of control, authorisation, appointment, and publication of rules and sanctions have been granted to them. Although there are minor differences, the essentials remain the same.

Similar missions

The powers of the CSA are numerous and diverse, but the most important is undoubtedly the enforcement of the ethical principles underpinning French audiovisual communication. Thus, the modified Law of 30 September 1986 entrusts the CSA with the task of guaranteeing the independence and the impartiality of the public sector, of monitoring the quality and diversity of programmes and of publicly defending French language and culture. In addition, the CSA must guarantee the respect of plurality of expression of ideas and opinions in programmes on public channels and ensure that commercial channels respect honesty and pluralism in news and programming. Finally, it must in particular take care that programmes do not undermine the protection of children and teenagers.

Respect for these different principles, which numerous interventions by the CSA have specified, is also guaranteed by the British authorities. The origin of these principles is not necessarily always legislative or regulatory but the result is quite comparable. The BBC licence or the law charges the Board of Governors, the BSC and the ITC to ensure that programmes do not offend good taste and decency, do not incite crime or disorder, do not run counter to public sensibility. Moreover, and above all else, the different authorities have drawn up a very precise code of good conduct which deals with all the ethical problems posed by audiovisual communication.

The Code of Practice, drafted by the BSC, is principally focused on the representation of violence and sex on television and defines the rules of behaviour that must be followed by broadcasters. These rules vary according to the type of programme. For information and news programmes, special attention must be given to broadcasting times and the most shocking scenes must not be broadcast before 9 p.m. Broadcasters are also recommended not to linger over particularly violent scenes or events and to avoid giving a positive image of brutality and criminals. Privacy and the reputation of people involved in news items must also be respected, and any reconstruction must only be carried out with the co-operation of those concerned or the police. For entertainment programmes, the principles are generally the same and excessively violent or erotic scenes are to be proscribed on prime time. The same is true for erotic scenes which have no place whatsoever in television programming. As for children's programmes, broadcasters are invited to avoid violent programming with which the very young could identify. They are also required not to broadcast programmes which present acts of cruelty to animals or which imply that violence is without psychological consequences. Finally, and more generally, the use of swear words, especially those based on holy names, is prohibited.

The ITC, which is responsible for enforcing the BSC's Code of Practice, has significantly supplemented and interpreted this document and has in the process produced its own Programme Code. This fifty-page-long code of good conduct, obviously deals with violence, good taste and the representation of sex in programmes, but also tackles particular problems such as the representation of scenes of exorcism or hypnotism. Similarly, a whole chapter is devoted to the representation of crime, of terrorism or asocial behaviour, and numerous clauses specify the attitude to be adopted when dealing with the representation of religion or militarily sensitive subjects. Questions on the use of the English language and on slanderous remarks are also tackled. All the principles of the Code of Practice are evidently applicable to news programmes but particular care is expected from broadcasters when using hidden microphones or cameras. In addition, interviewing of children and telephone interviews are strictly regulated. The Programme Code of the ITC also devotes a chapter to impartiality, honesty and pluralism on television. Thus, all points of view on major political, economic and social events must be given expression. The editing of interviews must not alter their meaning and the broadcaster must never give his/her own opinion.

The vast majority of these particular provisions can also be found in the directives and decisions of the BBC, which is equally committed to enacting principles that will protect privacy and impartiality of information. The Board of Governors of the BBC has in fact instituted a code very close to that of the ITC, although its provisions are aimed primarily at producers.

The second key mission of the CSA concerns the monitoring of broadcasting and production obligations in the sphere of audiovisual and cinematographic works. These obligations are aimed at preserving national culture through the programming of French and European works, as well as maintaining the programme and cinema industry. These obligations, which have their source principally in the Law of 18 January 1992 and in two decrees of 17 January 1990 and 9 May 1995, find concrete expression in an extremely complex set of quotas, broadcasting time limits, and multiple contributions to audiovisual and cinematographic production. This particular type of obligation also exists in the U.K. but with the difference that much greater emphasis is given to the intervention of the different regulatory authorities, whilst the role of the law and the decree is secondary.

The third and final key mission of the CSA is to monitor the enforcement of regulations applying to advertising, sponsorship and teleshopping. Once again, the Law and the Decree clearly specify prohibited sectors (alcohol, tobacco, etc.), regulations on commercial breaks (breaks within audiovisual works broadcast on public channels are banned), the length of commercial breaks, and the rules for sponsorship and teleshopping. What is already a complex legal framework is further supplemented by the CSA which has in this domain greater regulatory powers, since it can lay down stricter rules (notably as far as teleshopping is concerned). Since 1991 it has exercised controlling power after advertising has been broadcast.

On this point the British system again offers numerous analogies. Indeed, with the exception of the BBC which is not involved since it does not broadcast advertising, the BSC and especially the ITC participate directly in the regulation of this type of programme. Moreover, the ITC has put into operation a 'Code of Advertising Standards and Practice', a 'Code of Programme Sponsorship' and rules on commercial breaks which define the obligations imposed upon broadcasters for advertising and sponsorship. The ITC also operates a posteriori monitoring but attempts above all to advise broadcasters and to compel them to adopt internal procedures to avoid sanctions.

Beyond these general powers allocated to the CSA, and in a more decentralised fashion than the various British authorities, other missions, more specifically linked to the French authority, need to be pointed out. Yet once again, the British system proves in fact to be very close to the French system. First of all, in the public sector, the CSA appoints among others, the Joint Chairman and Managing Director of France 2 and France 3. It offers advice on their statutory obligations, determines the rules concerning the production, programming and broadcasting of programmes arising from electoral campaigns, as well as the arrangements for the right of reply to government broadcasts. It is virtually the same for the Board of Governors, which designates the Chairman and Managing Director of the BBC, participates in the discussions on the renewal of the licence and draws up agreements with political parties and government which establish practical arrangements and broadcasting time.

For the private sector, the CSA allocates, after calling for bids, licences to broadcast on terrestrial, cable or satellite commercial channels. These licences are granted for ten years and can be renewed. The granting of these licences is subject to a convention drawn up between the CSA, on behalf of the State, and the applicant for a licence. This makes it possible to define both the obligations of the licence holder and the contractual prerogatives and sanctions which the CSA has at its disposal to enforce the agreement.

This system is relatively similar to the one set up by the ITC which draws up concessionary contracts with private companies and sets out their obligations. The content of the statutory obligations is adjusted in line with the type of service and particular circumstances, and it is the ITC's obligation to act as enforcement agency.

Moreover, the ITC must, as does the CSA, regularly account for the enforcement by the various operators of their obligations. The Board of Governors also acts in a similar fashion.

Relatively similar means

In order to ensure the effectiveness of their numerous missions, the French and British authorities hold on the one hand a prescriptive power and on the other a power of sanction. As far as the power to enact legal provisions is concerned, the constitution and French tradition being somewhat opposed on these matters (see above), this power finds concrete expression principally in the CSA's acknowledged ability to formulate opinions and recommendations. The situation is quite different in the U.K. where the majority of provisions is enacted by the regulatory authorities. Irrespective of this, the ability of the authorities in both countries to enact legal regulations either directly or indirectly constitutes their primary regulatory means.

Thus, the CSA has the power to enact rules on the technical conditions governing the use of frequencies for terrestrial broadcasting. Above all, it lays down the rules on the conditions for the production, scheduling and broadcasting of programmes arising from electoral campaigns, and sets out the arrangements for the right of reply to government broadcasts on public channels. The broadcasting arrangements for programmes which enable political groups and professional and trade union groups to express their own views on public channels are directly enacted by the CSA.

The legislator has also made provision to take note of the informed opinion of the CSA in various fields. The government must therefore refer to the opinion of the authority before adopting statutory orders relating to audiovisual communication or decrees enacting the statutory obligations of the public channels. The same situation holds for the definition of technical standards and for the allocation of frequencies to the different state services. Moreover, the CSA is consulted on the definition of the French position in international negotiations on radio and television broadcasting and radiotelephony. Finally, the government, the Presidents of the Assemblies, parliamentary commissions or the committee on competition policy can refer to the Authority for advice or information. It can consequently suggest legislative or regulatory modifications which it judges to be necessary. As a result, even though regulatory power is outside the jurisdiction of the CSA, this institution participates in a significant way in the drafting of texts.

Matters are even more self-evident in the U.K. where the regulatory authorities are regularly empowered by the law to supplement the legislative framework. However, the ITC has recently been divested of its power to monitor the internal operations of private companies and has been invited to set up regulation 'with a lighter touch'. Moreover, European law constitutes nowadays an increasingly significant obstacle to the prescriptive power of the British authorities.

Whatever the case, French and British authorities are also of one mind regarding sanctions that they can impose on television channels failing to respect obligations arising from legislative and regulatory texts or codes and licensing decisions specified by regulatory authorities. The CSA therefore can, after formal warning and depending on the seriousness of the breaches, adjudicate in a variety of ways.[1] The CSA can also refer matters to the Public Prosecutor in cases of criminal offences.

Since the Law of 1 February 1994, public channels are subject to the same sanctions, with the exception of the withdrawal of a licence or the reduction in the length of a licence. The legislative arsenal is therefore quite extensive and directly comparable to the ITC which also has at its disposal a wide range of sanctions.[2] As for the BSC and the BBC, they can, after hearing the accused broadcaster, issue a warning and force the channel to broadcast a summary of it in its programmes or in the press.

Conclusion

Although France has manifestly opted for unity and the U.K. for plurality of regulatory authorities, there remains none the less a certain homogeneity as far as their powers are concerned. Moreover, the construction of Europe and the arrival of digital television will almost certainly bring together in ever closer union these two systems that history and tradition seemed to have set apart.

Notes and References

1. The CSA can adjudicate as follows: suspension of the licence or of part of the programmes for one month maximum; reduction of the length of a licence for up to a year; financial sanctions; broadcasting of a press release, the content and the broadcasting arrangements being determined by the CSA; emergency ruling by an administrative judge enabling the CSA to oblige the licence holder (under threat of penalty) to conform to its obligations; withdrawal of the licence, without prior warning, in instances of significant changes in the operation of the licence allocated.
2. The ITC's sanctions are wide-ranging: – warning; obligation for a channel to broadcast an apology; fine; suspension of licence; reduction in the length of a licence; withdrawal of a licence (except for Channel 4).

Chapter 3

Two Conflicting Notions of Audiovisual Liberalisation

Serge Regourd

During the 1980s, European countries as a whole underwent a process of 'liberalisation', characterised by the abolition of state monopolies and the emergence of private operators. The structural characteristics of this general process of change, however, have significantly varied from country to country, national specificities resulting in highly contrasting situations. The U.K. on the one hand, and France on the other, appear to correspond in this respect to two markedly distinct models, to two conflicting notions of audiovisual liberalisation.

The main features of these two models appear paradoxical in themselves, given the respective identity traditionally linked to these two countries: the U.K., the archetype of a neo-liberal model in favour of the logic of privatisation; France, by contrast, more favourably disposed to state intervention. Yet, in the sphere of television, it would appear that a kind of reverse typology accounts for the reality of the situation: a number of state regulatory structures and arrangements have been for the most part perpetuated or safeguarded in the U.K., at a time when political choices regarding television broadcasting in France have by contrast been shaped by a conspicuous commitment to 'privatisation'.

Without giving way to an excessive Manicheism, it would not be an overstatement to maintain that the British system is more logical and balanced, is based on more stable principles that correspond more effectively to both the moral and social demands of television, and to the respective roles of state power and of market forces in the global regulation of the televisual system. It is almost as if the British were practising genuine audiovisual liberalism, necessitating in this field as elsewhere, real checks and balances, robust regulatory mechanisms guaranteeing pluralism and competition, whereas the French, with the zeal of the newly-converted, have conversely sinned through ignorance of the true mechanisms of the market, throwing themselves headlong into the processes of privatisation without setting up any adequate regulatory compensatory mechanisms. The result is that in France both the disadvantages of 'commercial excesses' and residually close links with political power remain prevalent.

Signs of divergence between the British and French systems became apparent initially in the very genesis of commercial television in each country: a gradual and planned process in the former, a total and violent transformation in the latter.

The U.K. was the first European country, after 1954, to make way for commercial operators within the framework of an institutional structure guaranteeing balance and pluralism. The regional organisation of the ITV network (Channel 3 since the 1990 reform) created a pluralism of commercial operators at an economic and editorial level, thereby preventing any hegemonic situation. This first commercial network was established over a period of time on the basis of a division of the British territory into regional zones, each one being allocated to a different company. This division was originally purely pragmatic, one company beginning its broadcasts in September 1955 in the London area, a second setting up a few months later in the Midlands, a third in May 1956 in the North-West of England. Later, however, it became a fundamental principle of the organisation of British commercial television.

Following the reform of 1968, there emerged a division into fourteen regional zones, corresponding to fifteen temporary broadcasting licences (to be renewed after ten years); the division of the London area, the most 'lucrative', was on a shared basis: one broadcasting licence for the week and one for the weekend. These fifteen independent regional companies were linked to one another through agreements to share overall programming and to exchange programmes. In addition, the ITV system included a sixteenth licence for the specialised production of morning programmes aimed at the entire network. The system was, moreover, supplemented when several bodies took on more specialist functions for various companies. At the outset were ITN, responsible for the production of news bulletins; ITP, a subsidiary company publishing the television programme magazine, and above all the IBA, the regulatory authority of all commercial companies (now the Independent Television Commission, ITC).

The creation in 1982 of the fourth channel, Channel 4, (alongside the state-owned channels BBC1 and BBC2 and the ITV network), a commercial channel with very specific organisational characteristics (see below), put the finishing touches to a British televisual system characterised by the virtues of balance, and with a capacity to forestall potential programming and operational excesses which would in following years characterise the audiovisual deregulation processes set in train in several countries in southern Europe.

In this respect, the French example assumes quite definitely the proportions of caricature. For it is in France that the emergence of commercial television produced the most far-reaching upheavals with consequences detrimental to the entire broadcasting system. The main reason for this can be found in the choice of solution that was adopted: unlike other deregulation situations (including the Italian scenario described by some specialists as 'Wild-West television'), the French process did not consist in simply allowing commercial operators to emerge either as a complement to state-owned channels, or else in competition with them, leaving to the market the task of creating the conditions for their development. In France, the emergence of private operators was essentially conceived in terms of the sale to the private sector of the principal state-owned channel. The objective of the Law of 30 September 1986 was therefore to facilitate the sale of TF1, the leading state channel with at the time 40 percent of the total audience and more than 55 percent of advertising revenues.

This remarkable way of proceeding – which has no equivalent in any other European country – bears witness to a quite distinctive and very French notion of the regulation of commercial television, which stands in marked contrast to the British system.

Two notions of the broadcasting market

The 1986 French Law envisaged the emergence of the private sector not as an addition but rather as an alternative to the public service sector. The relationship between public and private spheres appears to have been conceived in terms of the abolition of the former through the implementation of the law. Hence, the key component of the private sector, TF1, unlike the channels of the ITV network, cannot attribute its emergence and development to market potential but rather to a political decision of the state implementing what can be designated as 'regulatory deregulation'. This constitutes a quite remarkable contradiction on the part of those French liberals in power who had so little faith in the virtues of market self-regulation that they entrusted to the law the task of shaping the market. Implicitly assuming that the market would be incapable of generating a viable supply for commercial television, they substituted in its place the most typical legal instrument of the state: a privatisation law. Whichever way one looks at it, the supply of commercial television in France has character traits that stand in direct opposition to those which characterise the British system.

Whereas the latter has become progressively integrated within the framework of a structure based on a balance between the public and private sectors, and on the plurality of commercial operators, unified by complementary links, the French broadcasting system was brutally deregulated and thrown out of balance. From one day to the next, a commercial channel found itself in a hegemonic position in terms of audience share and the advertising market. Unlike the pluralism of the sixteen commercial operators of the ITV network, sharing between them the advertising revenues from the whole of the U.K., TF1 once privatised held an oligopolistic position over the entire domestic market.

This resulted in serious consequences for the remaining public channels as well as for the other competing commercial channels. Given its overall audience share of 40 percent, TF1 privatised was able to intervene in the French television market as the principal actor, since its advertising rates indirectly determined the advertising rates of its competitors. This situation even contributed directly to the disappearance of the other generalist commercial channel, La Cinq, which had none the less been managed jointly or successively by several large communication groups (Berlusconi, Hersant, Hachette). The latter attempted to compete directly with TF1 in the sphere of programming and star presenters, but it never succeeded in going beyond an audience share of 11 percent. Confronted by the 40 percent share of TF1, it was 'starved' of advertising revenues, since the costs of its commercial breaks could not be in excess of those charged by TF1 itself.

The balance of the British situation consequently stands in stark contrast to the imbalances in France. This opposition corresponds at the same time to two 'territorial' notions of television. The French model is almost exclusively national: the three terrestrial commercial channels (TF1, M6- the operator Métropole télévision 6 is la Compagnie Luxembourgeoise de télédiffusion-, and the encrypted channel Canal Plus) are organised on a strictly national basis which is both centralised and 'Parisian'. Local or regional commercial television remains a peripheral activity.

In 1985, when preparatory work was being carried out to set up commercial channels, an official report, the *Rapport Bredin,* had envisaged the possibility of eighty local television stations. Only three, however, ever came into being: Télé-Toulouse, Télé Lyon Métropole and Télé 8 Mont-Blanc. They are, moreover, experiencing considerable financial difficulties, and their continued existence is explained principally by the fact that the major shareholder is the subsidiary of a large urban service sector company, la Compagnie Générale des Eaux, which benefits in the urban areas concerned from particularly profitable delegated responsibilities in the sphere of public services, such as water distribution. Meanwhile the 'decentralisation' of television is moreover achieved in a very limited fashion through local opt-outs via M6 for six- minute news bulletins in a few cities.

The organisation of British commercial television constitutes in this respect a genuine counter-model. As already mentioned, the whole of the ITV network – nowadays Channel 3 – has been organised on a local basis. The entire system is, in fact, built upon a federation of regional channels, each of which holds a licence to operate in a specified region in which the companies themselves finance their activities by selling advertising space. In this context, national programmes appear simply as a series of programmes supplied by different regional companies, juxtaposed according to the allocation of broadcasting times and in proportion to the relative importance of those companies. The large companies – occasionally designated as the 'big five' (centred on London, Manchester, Birmingham and Yorkshire) – make the most substantial contribution to the production of national programmes from which all the companies in the network benefit.

It would consequently appear that the British commercial television system overall was undoubtedly conceived in terms of national broadcasting, but was also organised on the basis of regional divisions. What is at stake is not (as it is in Spain, for example) a regional notion of programming, but rather the very notion of the broadcasting market: although each company's principal objective is to be profitable, it is on the basis of a territorial division of advertising revenues. These regional links were retained when the licences were last reallocated even though candidates were able to apply for two regional zones (one large and one small next to one other). They also had to make provisions for weekly regional programmes of between two and a half and ten hours, the duration depending on local needs, and on the understanding that 80 percent of them were to be produced in the regions concerned.

Recent years have, however, been characterised by a marked attenuation of territorial fragmentation with, on the one hand, a loosening of anti-concentration mechanisms enabling the same groups to hold capital interests in several regional companies (see below) and, on the other, the creation of a fifth channel, Channel 5, licensed to broadcast nationally.

This fundamentally different notion of the broadcasting market in France and the U.K. is mirrored exactly in the legal conditions for allocating broadcasting licences to commercial channels in both countries. In the U.K., and consistent with a logic underpinned by liberal premises, the process of allocating licences is based on an auction organised by the regulatory authority of the commercial channels (the ITC succeeded the IBA, Independent Broadcasting Authority, in 1991). Licences are accordingly allocated to applicants with the highest financial bids.

This resolutely financial criterion is not exclusive, however: British law makes provision in the first instance that financial offers can only be considered after detailed verification that the applicants will respect given conditions relating to programming and to the quality of the envisaged programmes – 'the quality threshold'. The allocation authority can subsequently decide to allocate a channel to an applicant whose financial proposals were not the highest, but who had put forward a proposal for 'a television service of outstanding quality far outstripping that put forward by the highest bidder'.

The basis of such a system is quite straightforward. It consists in making deductions from the motives of the applicants: the British refer to it as 'printing money'. It consequently appears legitimate to impose upon them broadcasting standards that are in the 'public interest', consistent with a mass medium, and at the same time to enable the Treasury to benefit from part of the profits arising from the use by commercial interests of terrestrial channels in the public domain.

The French approach is diametrically opposed to such thinking: the allocation of television and radio frequencies are free. The successive allocation of licences to different commercial channels was carried out on an entirely free basis: Canal Plus at the end of 1984, La Cinq and TV6 in 1985 (then the reallocation of La Cinq and M6 in 1987), as well as the renewals of these licences and of that of TF1 in 1996. Only the sale of TF1 to the private sector involved at the outset financial commitments. But in this case it concerned the sale of the assets of the leading public service channel, not the cost of purchasing the broadcasting licence itself. Once again we encounter this rather strange notion of a broadcasting market held by French political decision-makers who seem to be of the view that resorting to such financial arrangements could be an obstacle to meeting programming standards (whereas the programme quality of French commercial channels appears to be very much lower than that of British commercial channels).

The implementation of the British procedure for allocating licences guarantees genuine competition untarnished by political manoeuvring, as well as changes in channel operators, which is consistent with the natural dynamism of a genuine market. Thus, when the licences were last renewed, following a decision of the ITC of 15 October 1991, four companies lost their licences to new beneficiaries. Among the 'victims' was Thames TV, the most important channel broadcasting over London, and TV AM, the most profitable morning channel. Two others, TVS and TSW, in the South and South-West of England respectively, had to a certain degree exploited the strict financial logic of the auction: their bid was considered to be too high and likely to put at risk programme quality even though TVS was supported by groups as powerful as Time-Warner, Canal Plus and la Compagnie générale des Eaux. Consequently, four new operators began broadcasting on 1 January 1993: Carlton TV, Sunrise TV, Meridian Broadcasting and West Country TV. The first of these, a capital shareholder in several other countries, was therefore able to establish itself as the new group leader of British commercial television.

The granting of a licence to the fifth terrestrial channel, Channel 5, also illustrated the successful combination of the logic of financial investment (required by the market) and the logic of programme quality (required by the public). An initial call for bids was declared unsuccessful in December 1992 and three years later, in November 1995, the ITC granted this licence to the 'Channel 5 Broadcasting' consortium (a partnership between CLT, the British groups MAI and Pearson, and the American risk capital company Warburg), even though it was not the highest bidder.[1] The quality threshold had therefore been decisive as it had been in 1991 for the renewal of the ITV network licences previously mentioned.

In this area as well, the French system appears as a counter-model. In contrast to the openness of the British solution which produced about forty bids when the ITV licences were last renewed, stands the very restricted, almost closed nature of the French allocation procedure. At the outset, in 1984 and 1985, within the framework of the Law of 29 July 1982, the first 'concessionary' licences were allocated on a strictly discretionary basis to the advantage of operators who were on friendly terms with the government of the day; there was no call for bids, no competition and a total lack of transparency. This way of proceeding, consistent with the legal regime for allocating contracts in the public service sector that was at that time in force, was not censored by the administrative courts.

The procedure for allocating licences established by the Law of 30 September 1986 was more open and more transparent, and was applied on the one hand to the sale of TF1 and on the other to the re-licensing of the fifth and sixth channels. In both cases, only two applicants came forward, significantly reducing any effective competition. In the absence of objective criteria linked to finance or programme regulations, the regulatory authority's choice of operators was likely to be based on highly dubious criteria (see below). Even the potential advantages of this system were negated by a new Law of 1 February 1994 which formulated the staggering principle whereby licences would be automatically renewed for two further periods of five years, in other words an allocation of ten further years for the channels originally licensed for ten years. On this basis, the three national channels concerned, TF1, M6 and Canal Plus, had their licences renewed without any new call for bids, nor the least competition. Their only constraint was the negotiation with the regulatory authority, the CSA (Conseil supérieur de l'audiovisuel) concerning their programming commitments.

One is entitled to ask whether these fortunate beneficiaries do not now have at their disposal a licence that is legally valid 'sine die', for it is difficult to imagine that a licence would be withdrawn at the end of twenty years when the very possibility of withdrawal after the ten years for which the licence had legally been awarded has been rejected.

The conclusion is inescapable: there clearly exist two conflicting notions of the broadcasting market, the British having opted for a notion based on 'venture capitalism' (risk of losing a licence if the bid is too low, risk of losing money if the bid is too high), whereas the French solution, such as it emerges from the Law of 1994, encapsulates a certain kind of 'land-owning capitalism', previously established groups being protected from the arrival of new competitors. Such a solution also illustrates the manner in which the logic of the politician – or political wheeler-dealer – infiltrates and disturbs the economic logic of the market. It would appear that the French system is incapable in this respect of breaking free from a degree of interdependence between commercial appetites and political calculations. These relations between television and political power are not, as has too often been alleged, a one-way process, television being subordinated to political power in an instrumentalist fashion. The interdependence that is at work in France also subordinates political power to television or to what some designate as 'media power'.

The first licences awarded to commercial operators were characterised by explicitly political choices. Symbolic of these 'dangerous liaisons' appears to have been the direct transfer of André Rousselet, Chief of Staff of the President of the Republic, François Mitterrand, to the post of Chairman and Managing Director of Canal Plus, the leading commercial pay television channel, set up in 1984 with statutory privileges and means wildly out of keeping with the normal logic of the market. When the first non-encoded commercial channels were given licences the following year, their setting up was part of a political calculation by the President of the Republic aimed at taking the wind out of the sails of the new right-wing majority that was predicted in the months that were to follow. More fundamentally, once the choice of operators had been made in this way, it was manifestly apparent that the whole process had absolutely nothing to do with programme quality and was motivated by political scheming. Thus Mitterrand chose Silvio Berlusconi, enthusiastically recommended by Bettino Craxi, First Secretary of the Italian Socialist party at that time, as operator for 'la Cinq', legally defined as a public service franchise, whereas Berlusconi himself had orchestrated Italian 'deregulation' to the detriment of public broadcasting.

When, in the following year (1986), the Parliamentary majority swung over to the right, the new Prime Minister, Jacques Chirac, had these licences revoked, and their reallocation enabled him once again to satisfy certain high-ranking political friends among whom was the owner of the press group Robert Hersant. The sale of TF1 was also conducted in the context of highly political considerations which have recently been analysed in several works with huge sales.[2] The Law of 1994 previously mentioned appeared to respond directly if not to the orders of the big business interests of the audiovisual sphere, at least to its expectations.

The British system does not appear to allow such confusions between political and economic interests, precisely because the self-regulatory market capabilities are not stifled. The bidding process and the cost of the licence, the regional division of the market and related plurality of operators comprise in themselves competitive tendencies which leave less scope for the misplaced intrusion of politics. There can be little doubt that the report that the British government at this time (1986) instructed Professor Peacock to produce on the future of the British audiovisual system was above all a consequence of political considerations on the manner in which the government had appreciated (that is to say, had little appreciated) the coverage by the BBC of the Falklands war and Northern Ireland. There had even been calls to privatise the BBC in this context. It needs to be noted, however, that the White Paper that emerged from the Peacock Commission specifically dismissed this possibility.[3]

These two conflicting notions of the broadcasting market find further expression in the field of regulatory methods.

Two notions of commercial television regulation

The territorial distribution of licences for commercial channels and the procedures for allocating them comprise a set of regulatory conditions in the U.K. stemming directly from a liberal notion of the broadcasting market. The French anxiety about the market, exacerbated by persistent political calculations, similarly finds expression in alternative regulatory methods.

The contrasting characteristics previously noted, postulating two very different ways of envisaging the broadcasting market, have in recent years been progressively played down in the context of a general deregulatory movement which has swept across all European countries. The British system has consequently lost some of the elements which constituted the purity or clarity of its regulatory model, but the contrast with the French system none the less retains its essential characteristics.

The example of Channel 4 is highly symbolic in this respect: a commercial channel that can be described as a 'cultural channel' or 'minority channel'. The very notion of such a channel would seem 'unthinkable' in France. In France the division between the public and private sectors consigns cultural or minority programming to the public sector alone, that is to say to certain elements of it. The private sector is envisaged solely in terms of commercial broadcasting, targeting the largest possible audience, the lowest common denominator. In essence, commercial television and cultural programmes are seen as mutually exclusive.

When TF1 was privatised, it was no doubt claimed that the method of sale included what the Minister of Culture referred to as the 'mieux-disant culturel', that is to say inviting applicants to put forward elements of cultural programming that would be to their advantage in their application. However, given the inadequacy of such elements, reference to this expression 'mieux-disant culturel' is now derisory. Soon after becoming the owner of TF1, Francis Bouygues offered his own thoughts on the matter, arguing that he was not taking over a commercial channel in order to subsidise culture which on the contrary was a natural component of the public service mission.

The organisation and mission of Channel 4 in the U.K. stand in marked opposition to such a notion. At its inception in 1982, the mission of Channel 4 was to develop a 'counter-programming' model by proposing broadcasts that did not appear in the schedules of ITV and even of the BBC ('a distinctive character of its own'). Its priorities were to target broadcasting for ethnic as well as diverse cultural minorities. Its legal and financial structure was organised to such an end: a 100 percent subsidiary of the regulatory authority (IBA, then ITC), it was financed from contributions made by the ITV companies of approximately 15 percent of their annual profits. The IBA levied these taxes and passed them on to Channel 4. They consequently appeared as a tax on the profits that the ITV companies were making from their activities as an advertising company for the benefit of the cultural channel. These companies benefited moreover from programme orders from Channel 4, which did not have its own production units, and acted essentially as programme planner – broadcaster (or 'editor') of programmes bought from ITV or from a multitude of independent producers benefiting from nearly half its programme budget.

In Wales the place and function of Channel 4 were devolved upon S4C, a regional channel with the same financing arrangements but under the control of a specific authority. Besides the programmes of Channel 4, its mission is to broadcast Welsh language programmes.

On the basis of the 1990 Broadcasting Act, Channel 4 assumed a different status from 1 January 1993. Separate from the ITC, it had now to become self-financing by selling its own advertising space, which has tended to bring it closer to the common law arrangements of a commercial channel. However, Channel 4 retains significant public service obligations, within the framework of the tripartite mission statement of the BBC ('to inform, to cultivate, to entertain'). This explains the establishment of mechanisms replacing the regulations that guarantee the continued existence of this mission: the law ensures that in future Channel 3 companies must provide financial contributions to Channel 4, in line with their income, when Channel 4's own revenues are lower than 14 percent of the total income of all the commercial channels. Alternatively, when Channel 4's income rises above this ceiling, it must hand over to the Channel 3 companies half of its excess revenue. This clause is currently being challenged by Channel 4 as a consequence of the payment that it has been forced to make to Channel 3.

Although the initial purity of the model has been called into question, these specific financial regulatory mechanisms and the continuing missions of Channel 4 remain as symbols of the differences between the U.K. and France when it comes to 'conceptualising commercial television'.

In France TF1 and M6 correspond to a strictly commercial notion of commercial television in which the sole objective is a maximum audience share that will generate maximum advertising revenues. The originality of French regulation is embodied more in Canal Plus based on encoding and subscription finance. But the programming of Canal Plus is centred on the most classical of commercial television products: sports broadcasts and films. Moreover, it levies advertising revenues for its non-encoded programmes, in addition to its subscriptions, without having to take on in return any 'public service' obligations. Conversely, its statutes have often been criticised as excessively privileged.[4]

The specific nature of British regulation, however, evidently goes far beyond the solitary example of Channel 4. The manner in which the Channel 3 network has itself been organised and regulated is in many respects poles apart from the notion that the French have of such matters. After an initial 'benevolent' period, which enabled the leading commercial companies to succeed in establishing themselves in a difficult environment, the first renewal of licences, following the Pilkington Report of 1962, established new obligations consistent with the genuine constraints of public service broadcasting. Until the reform of 1990 and the creation of the ITC, in place of the IBA, this regulatory authority was even, in a certain sense, included in the very structures of the ITV network: whereas the members of the IBA were appointed by the relevant Minister, which unquestionably confers on this authority the character of a public body, its revenues had their source in obligatory payments made by the network's companies. And this same authority would directly intervene in the key area of network programming.

In the sphere of broadcasting quotas, where French broadcasters tend to maintain that they are alone in Europe to be subject to them, the U.K. at one period even held the record. The quotas were originally fixed in the conventions drawn up between the ITV network companies and the regulatory authority, the IBA, responsible for guaranteeing that a 'fair proportion of programmes' were British productions. The enforcement of this directive resulted in an 86 percent quota of British works in the schedules of commercial channels. These conventions came to an end on 1 January 1993 when the new operators began broadcasting. But it is significant that beyond the undoubted easing of restrictions arising from the reform of 1990, one of the conditions imposed on all applicants for the new franchises consisted in a quota of suitable programmes set at 65 percent of broadcasting time (produced or ordered by the channel).

Among the other obligations imposed on applicants in the 'schedule of conditions', it is worth noting the specific commitments in the areas of information and weekly reporting, children's programmes, religious programmes (two and a half hours per week), and, even more extensively, the obligation to broadcast nine different kinds of programmes of 'high quality'.

The principal quantitative obligations on British commercial operators, however, relate more to economic clauses in the context of the arrangements made for the regional division of the Channel 3 network (see above). These anti-concentration arrangements have recently been significantly relaxed in two stages. In November 1993 the principle was accepted that the same operator could control the capital of two network channels (except for the two London channels which cannot be controlled by the same operator), and could have a 20 percent share in a third channel, and 5 percent in any other channel. However, the new Broadcasting Act of 1996 removed this limit on two general licences of Channel 3 and substituted in its place the criterion of 15 percent of the total television audience: no single operator can control more than 15 percent of the total audience.

The territorial division of the Channel 3 network has not been abolished, but its significance could be considerably reduced as a consequence of increased participation in capitalisation. This easing of the regulations has affinities with an idea that was quite prevalent in France a few years ago; fostering the emergence of large communication groups that could be competitive on an international scale. Even before the implementation of the 1996 reform, the relaxation of the regulations in 1993 had resulted in repurchases by several large operators: Carlton TV previously mentioned, Granada, Yorkshire TV and Meridian (the MAI group, a member moreover of the consortium, having already obtained the licence for Channel 5). These four groups alone, each one holding two licences, controlled more than 80 percent of ITV advertising revenues. Moreover, the majority of the operators were partners in joint companies selling their advertising space. Three companies consequently account for thirteen of the sixteen Channel 3 operators.

The limits of the challenge to regional organisation appear to reside in two principal elements: on the one hand, any modification to programmes broadcast after repurchasing must have the approval of the ITC, which has made it known that such instances would be rare. On the other hand, the 15 percent ceiling on audience share evidently constitutes a limiting factor on repurchases. Beyond the deregulation process enacted by these latest reforms, this 15 percent threshold highlights the distance which still separates the British system from the French system that for a long time has been characterised by a 40 percent audience share for the leading channel TF1.

The same deregulatory processes that are at work in most European countries have also resulted in French legislation on anti-concentration thresholds. Within the framework of the Law of 30 September 1986, no shareholder could hold more than 25 percent of the capital of a national commercial channel. Consequently, the repurchasing of TF1 by the Bouygues group did not prevent the enforcement of the 25 percent limit in the 'round table discussions' after the acquisition of the channel (40 percent of the capital, moreover, emanated from stock exchange transactions and 10 percent was reserved for the staff of the channel). In the same way, the CLT held 25 percent of the capital of M6, the second commercial channel, on an equal basis with the Société Lyonnaise des Eaux. But the previously mentioned Law of 1 February 1994 led to a rise in these thresholds to a level of 49 percent of the capital. This ceiling reduces, however, to 15 percent when the shareholder already holds more than 15 percent of the capital or voting rights of another company licensed as a national channel, and to 5 percent when he/she holds more than 5 percent in two companies similarly licensed.

In addition to these limits on capital involvement, there are also limits on the number of licences that can be held: the licence operator of a national terrestrial television channel cannot also hold another licence of the same nature even for a local television channel. To these so-called 'monomedia' restrictions can also be added in France multimedia restrictions dealing altogether with terrestrial television, radio, cable distribution services and the press: no operator can by law hold quantitatively more than two licences in these four specified areas. As far as the press is concerned, no terrestrial television operator can control more than 20 percent of the total circulation of all daily publications of general and political news. There is provision for similar restrictions in the U.K. Since the easing of restrictions in the 1996 reform, press groups controlling 20 percent or more of national circulation cannot hold more than 20 percent capital share in Channel 3 or Channel 5 licences.

There is little need to outline these economic arrangements in any greater detail, since it is apparent that the British system, despite the importance of the deregulatory measures that have recently taken effect, complies with measures which are frequently more constraining than those which confront the French operators. This was the case even when the Channel 5 licence was allocated in 1994 (after an adjournment in the process in 1992), the aforementioned financial constraints but also technical constraints (coverage restricted to 60 percent, then 75 percent of British territory, payment of the costs of transforming receivers) contrasting with the privileges granted at the same time to French operators by the Law of 1 February 1994.

Another specific feature of British regulation that is practically non-existent in France, concerns the detailed control by the authorities of the content of programmes based on an ethical approach formulated in 'codes'. Several regulatory authorities intervene in commercial television (see chapter 2): the ITC previously mentioned, but also the BSC (British Standards Council) created in 1990, functioning as the moral conscience of all operators, and the BCC (Broadcasting Complaints Commission) with powers in the specific field of privacy and the accuracy and impartiality of information. This plurality of organisations and the missions which are assigned to them (even though the latter two are to merge) are sufficient testimony to the prevalence of ethical questions and of meticulous regulations in the field of accepted standards which can only be described euphemistically as barely acclimatised to French regulatory conditions. Each of these authorities draws up specific codes of 'good conduct' that are regularly updated. The ITC and BSC have a particular interest in codes aimed at delimiting the representation of sex and violence and at protecting 'good taste and decency' in all programmes, as well as the protection of children and adolescents. These are regulatory criteria specific to the U.K. which are sustained and developed through regular consultation between the previously mentioned authorities, broadcasters and viewers' representatives.

The 'Code of Practice' of the BSC defines the different rules and ethical principles that broadcasters are subsequently under an obligation to integrate within their own internal codes. These rules are effective since they are the basis on which thousands of complaints are lodged by viewers or their associations to the BSC for failure to respect decency or good taste or the provisions relating to violence or sex. The ITC also deals in a detailed, indeed exhaustive manner, with questions such as crudeness, or coarse language or even criteria for humour, or on the contrary humour in bad taste. The BSC in its 'Code of Practice' and the ITC in its 'Programme Code' thus define a true 'Family Viewing Policy', finding expression in a very precise typology of programmes according to time slots.

Advertising also figures among those areas which are specifically regulated by the ITC. Its 'Code of Advertising Standards and Practices', modified in December 1995, regulates in a very detailed manner the diverse fields and forms of advertising on commercial channels, whether it be the National Lottery, financial advertising or medicines. A specific Code sets out more specifically the rules on advertising breaks. Equally strictly regulated is the field of sponsorship. The 'Code of Programme Sponsorship', the last version of which was revised by the ITC on 26 March 1997, is aimed at preventing 'commercial hijacking of programmes'. Each category of programme and each category of sponsor gives rise to prescriptive rulings and the code regulates precisely the forms of sponsorship itself.

This ethical regulation in the form of detailed codes is totally alien to the French system. French operators would in all likelihood see in this an unacceptable attack on their freedom in the sphere of programming. The French CSA has at its disposal a regulatory power only in very marginal areas (for example, electoral campaigns and government broadcasts) and over recent years, its 'doctrine' has consisted in distancing itself further and further from specifically legal matters, adopting instead an expert function in its annual regulatory reports or occasionally acting solely as 'mediator' opposed to the regulatory logic.

Programming principles give rise only to formulations of a very general nature in law, and these are progressed in agreements made in conventions drawn up between the CSA and commercial channels. These conventions were ratified on 31 July 1996 and replace the text of the licences issued in 1987. For the first time more specific commitments were included in these conventions as far as the protection of children and adolescents is concerned, and a certain number of ethical principles were made clear. But this is still very far from the 'pointillism' of the British tradition.

Given the serious downward slide in programme quality that had previously occurred, the CSA has formulated several recommendatory texts with no mandatory legal status in a number of particularly sensitive areas. Thus a 'directive' of 5 May 1989 on the protection of children and adolescents was sent to all channels. But these provisions remained declarations of intent requesting, for example, that channels do not broadcast programmes of an erotic nature or which might incite to violence between 6 a.m. and 10.30 p.m., or to warn the public in advance that certain broadcasts were likely to offend the sensibility of this young audience. Very recently, this question was the subject of a new regulation adopted by all broadcasters – public and private – under the aegis of the CSA. Operational since 18 November 1996, it establishes a sign system in five categories denoting the degree of violence or eroticism in films, television films, cartoon series and documentaries. The relevant signs (green circle, orange triangle, red square) were to be displayed at the bottom of the screen on the right at the beginning or throughout the broadcast.

'Recommendations' have also come forward regarding the principle of integrity of information in the use of archive film (24 March 1992) or morality in broadcasting 'reality shows'(24 April 1992). However, these different texts appear as circumstantial attempts to respond, a posteriori, to selective questioning by the public at large following serious attacks on fundamental ethical principles. They lack the general, systematic and a priori character of British regulation.

Conclusion

These final distinctive elements go beyond the mere question of commercial television broadcasting and point towards two general, historically and culturally quite distinct notions of television regulation in France and the U.K.. An analysis of the key aspects of this opposition demonstrates that in this sphere, perhaps even more so than in any other, the concepts of 'liberalism', 'market', 'deregulation' and 'freedom' correspond to polysemic notions that are extremely variable and that are liable to give rise to very different interpretations. From this perspective, the characteristics of the British system often appear poles apart from the fantasised notion that a number of French professionals have of it.

Notes and References

1. This group had bid on the basis of £22m per year, whereas one of the other three applicants, U.K.TV, had bid more than £36m.
2. See for example: M. E. Chamard and P. Kieffer, *La télé: dix ans d'histoires secrètes*, Paris, Flammarion, 1992; P. Péan and C. Nick, *TF1, un pouvoir*, Paris, Fayard, 1997.
3. In 1990 Professor Peacock had suggested that when the Charter of the BBC was renegotiated in 1996, a study should be carried out on the possibility of abolishing the licence fee in favour of financing from private sources which would benefit from tax exemptions.
4. See for example: J- P. Jézéquel, 'Canal Plus ... de privilèges', *Angle Droit*, no. 4, April-May 1991.

CHAPTER 4

THE FUTURE OF PUBLIC BROADCASTING

JEAN-CLAUDE SERGEANT

In a context of extensive programme supply provided by increasingly sophisticated technological devices – cable, satellite, digital multiplexes – the survival of public service broadcasting (PSB) looks uncertain in all European countries and particularly in Britain and France where state-controlled and publicly funded broadcasting systems have long been key players on the broadcasting scene.

While in Britain the BBC was confronted at an early stage with competition from commercial television (1955), it was not until 1982 that the French government agreed to waive its monopoly in the field of programme making. In five years (1982-7) the number of French television channels doubled, while public service channels were outnumbered by commercial channels following the launching of the subscription-based Canal Plus (1984), of La Cinq and TV6 (1985) and the privatisation of TF1, the most popular public television channel (see chapter 3). The withdrawal of La Cinq in 1992 as a result of financial difficulties and its replacement by a public consortium – La Sept-Arte – has hardly modified the respective market shares of public broadcasting and commercial channels, given the very low rating of the Franco-German Channel.[1] The main bulk of public service broadcasting in France is currently reduced to France 2 and France 3 operating since the 1989 law under a joint chairmanship and whose combined audience share in 1995 was no higher than 41 percent.

In Britain, the two BBC channels still commanded in 1996 43.7 percent of total audience share, to which can be added the 10.7 percent corresponding to Channel 4.[2] These figures illustrate the resilience of public support for PSB in both countries, FR3 having even gained over 6 percent of audience share between 1989 and 1995. Yet with the growth of cable and satellite television which account for 10 percent of viewing time in Britain, it is legitimate to wonder whether PSB will still be able to survive without substantial reforms, some of which have already been introduced notably in Britain.

Reflecting on the future of public television systems in Europe, Y. Achille and J.I. Bueno point out the difficulties with which these systems are currently confronted. Starting from the premise that public television channels have been destabilised by the aggressive dynamism of rival commercial channels, they suggest that public broadcasting organisations must overcome a threefold crisis. One, and perhaps the most fundamental of all, relates to the identity of public service broadcasting against a backdrop of competition with commercial channels. What is so special about PSB that justifies its preservation often through legally binding provisions? The second crisis identified by Achille and Bueno concerns the level of public funding required to keep PSB going at a time when national governments are endeavouring to cut public spending. Increasingly, they argue, public channels will have to tap the market for advertising and sponsorship revenues with inevitable consequences on the quality of their programmes. Finally, the last crisis they can see affecting PSB has to do with the necessary shake-up of the management of public channels which until recently had little incentive to operate cost-efficient policies.[3]

Somehow, it seems that maintaining PSB systems is best justified in terms of upholding the public interest, as Francis Williams argued as early as 1949 when defining the specificity of British broadcasting which in those days was mainly equated with radio: 'Broadcasting in Britain is we say...conducted as a public service. By this we mean that it is not governed by the making of private profit or run in the interests of advertisers, but solely in the public interest and without having to pay regard to purely commercial standards'.[4]

Public service broadcasting systems in France and Britain operated as monopolistic corporations within a legal framework defined by national parliaments, which are seen as custodians of the public interest. This included proper use of the radio spectrum defined as a national asset, as well as obligations of universality of access and editorial impartiality. In France where a government ordinance published in March 1945 gave the state the monopoly of the operation of broadcasting systems, the notion of impartiality was long used to keep the successive public broadcasting corporations – RTF and ORTF which succeeded it in 1964 – under the strict control of a specific government department. President Pompidou's historic pronouncement at one of his press conferences that ORTF was the 'voice of France' and should therefore reflect the government's views aptly epitomised the kind of relationship between the state and PSB broadcasters until 1982 when the state monopoly in the field of programme making was officially abolished.

The proliferation of television channels provided by cable or satellites, financed by subscription, was bound to raise questions about the legitimacy of the concept of public interest as defined by the state. This kind of paternalistic approach to what is suitable for viewers implies a suspicion about the ability of individuals to make their own choices. It is to some extent reminiscent of the attempts by British governments in the nineteenth century to prevent the development of a free press through the imposition of the so-called 'taxes on knowledge'. In that sense, public service broadcasting operating under the control of the state could be felt as excessively authoritarian and ill-adapted to an era where meeting the needs of the individual consumer has become the rule. There was no doubt that in the mind of most members of the Peacock Committee that such a system had outlived its useful purpose. Without rejecting the concept of public service broadcasting outright, the Committee advocated a consumer sovereignty model described as follows: 'A satisfactory broadcasting market requires full freedom of entry for programme makers, a transmission system capable of carrying an indefinitely large number of programmes, facilities for pay-per-programme or pay-per channel and differentiated charges for units of time. Such a system may be called the full broadcasting market akin to that which exists in publishing'.[5]

Such a model presented as a goal and ideal would do away with programme obligations imposed by the guardians of the public interest on current terrestrial television channels. A light-touch regulatory system would suffice to subject programme providers to legal principles concerning slander, obscenity, blasphemy, etc. In that perspective the viewing public is no longer considered as one homogeneous entity whose tastes and needs are supposed to be fulfilled by the blanket programmatic trilogy which has required the BBC 'to inform, to educate, to entertain'. Rather, the viewing masses are seen as an aggregation of mature and rational individuals able to make their own private choices among the wide range of programmes offered by innumerable suppliers.

This definition overlooks, however, the social and cultural dimensions of broadcasting which have traditionally underpinned the concept of public service in broadcasting. As Marc Raboy puts it: 'What social and cultural goals attributed to broadcasting require a specially mandated, non-commercially driven organization, publicly owned, publicly funded to the extent necessary, and publicly accountable?'[6] Furthermore, Peacock's model does not address the crucial question of the role of broadcasting in the healthy functioning of democratic societies. Gratifying consumers' choices would probably not be easily compatible with the provision of programmes needed for informed debates between enlightened citizens.

The sociopolitical argument seems to be the linchpin of all the attempts to justify the retention of the traditional PSB systems. In direct contrast to Peacock's advocacy of a free market in broadcasting, Janet Morgan, a former adviser to the Director General of the BBC, emphasised in the year that the Peacock Report was published the absolute necessity of operating broadcasting systems on the basis of collective purposes: 'the issue is not one of technology or economics but of politics, of how as a society we wish to use our joint resources and collectively manage our affairs'.[7] In other words, broadcasting does not boil down to a mere balance sheet or to the optimum use of available technologies. Neither can it be equated with an ordinary consumer market because television programmes, however profane or entertainment-led, are always predicated on values, whether social or moral. In that sense, broadcasting is perhaps too important socially to be left under the sole responsibility of broadcasters and too vulnerable to be abandoned to market forces.

Whereas PSB systems were until recently the dominant, if not natural, form of broadcasting in most European countries, they now seem to fight an uphill battle for survival and to be at pains to justify their preservation. A number of bodies and organisations have come to the rescue as they would in the case of defending a species threatened with extinction. In particular, the Council of Europe reiterated in 1994 the fundamental role of PSB systems in buttressing democratic institutions by providing a forum for broad public discussion as well as a common reference point for all members of the public.[8] The necessity of reflecting different ideas and beliefs in pluriethnic and multicultural societies was also high on the list of missions ascribed to PSB systems by the Council of Europe, which neatly summed up the near impossible brief public service broadcasting organisations have been saddled with. Indeed, requiring PSB systems to provide at the same time a kind of programming 'which is both of wide public interest and attentive to the needs of minorities', as the Council of Europe did, raises the problem of funding such systems.

This question was effectively addressed in the often quoted study by the now defunct Broadcasting Research Unit on the 'Public Service Idea in British Broadcasting' which, among the criteria of PSB systems, included the concept of universality of payment. Seen as the logical consequence of the 'universal access' principle which is invariably considered to be the main feature of PSB systems, the licence fee is often criticised as unfair because people tend to watch and listen to commercial broadcasting service more than they do public service channels and radio stations. Admittedly, it is more difficult to convince the public that there is no such thing as free television or radio. When they are not funded by subscription or pay-per-view charges, commercial channels are subsidised by advertisers who pass on to consumers – albeit surreptitiously – the cost of the commercials seen on the independent channels.

The point is to know whether in the current broadcasting context in Britain and France, whose consumer-led systems are bound to become increasingly visible, the idea of a licence fee has become irrelevant. It certainly makes economic sense to pay £91.50 or FF 700 (1997 figures) to have access to the 15,000 or so hours of TV programmes broadcast by the BBC or to the 17,000 hours provided by the three French public channels (including Arte). However, if added to the extra cost of buying a satellite television reception kit and subscribing to encrypted channels, the licence fee may appear as an unbearable burden.

The Peacock Committee had even described it as immoral, to the extent that it was imposed on consumers and therefore violated the Committee's preferred principle of consumers' sovereignty. In the 1988 White Paper entitled *Broadcasting in the 1990s: Competition, Choice and Quality,* the government had spelt out its wish to see the licence fee eventually replaced by subscription with a view to ending 'the insulation of the BBC from its customers and from market disciplines'. Although the BBC has always rejected alternative ways of funding on the basis that 'commercial funding methods such as subscription, sponsorship and advertising affect the types of programmes which are made and broadcast',[9] it would probably be better off if the licence fee were to be replaced by a funding system based on subscription. A market study carried out by the London Business School and published in 1990 suggested that there was general acceptance of the licence fee (£71 at the time) and that as many as 90 percent of television set owners would be willing to subscribe to both BBC channels provided the cost of subscription was similar to the level of the licence fee. As the researchers put it, the willingness to subscribe to BBC channels was 'price-inelastic', by which they meant that in the event of the subscription charge being substantially higher than the level of the licence fee there would still be a large proportion of television owners prepared to subscribe to one or both BBC channels. Typically their report revealed that 81 percent of their respondents would still subscribe to at least one channel for a subscription charge between £90 and £216.[10]

Obviously this loyalty to BBC TV would need to be tested again now that subscription and pay-per-view have actually made their way into the broadcasting scene. There is probably a limit to what households are prepared to pay to fulfil their needs in the field of audiovisual activities. Besides, even if the licence fee still represents the most visible expression of public willingness to organise and operate a public broadcasting system, it is not the only way of funding public service broadcasting organisations. In Spain, for instance, RTVE was entirely supported by advertising until 1993 when the government agreed to provide a grant to cover the cost of public service obligations. In France, the government allowed the introduction of advertising on the first channel as early as 1968. The attraction of this new source of revenue turned out to be addictive. Advertising and sponsorship revenues represented as much as 39 percent of the total budget of France 2 in 1992; this proportion was to rise to 43.8 percent in 1996. During the first six months of 1995, France 2 broadcast a daily average of ninety-seven minutes of commercials, a proportion similar to that of the independent sixth channel M6. During the 19-24 hours slot both France Télévision channels will often broadcast as much advertising as their main commercial competitor TF1. Although France 3 is less dependent on advertising revenue (about 20 percent of its total income in 1996), its growing popularity attracts more advertising than the channel can legally accommodate.

The share of advertising revenue in the income of France Television channels – its contribution to the budget of Arte/ La Cinquième being marginal – reflects the concern of successive governments to limit the progression of the licence fee, whose increase has been fairly erratic over the last ten years. As Prime Minister between 1986 and 1988, Jacques Chirac had even decided to bring it down by 6.50 percent. In the same vein a recent report presented to the Finance Commission of the National Assembly called for the end of the regular increase in the level of the licence fee, the *rapporteur* suggesting that given the current growth of statutory levies (taxes as well as national insurance and pension contributions), every step was to be taken to alleviate the burden of parafiscal charges.

A different opinion had been expressed by a commission set up in 1993 by Alain Carignon, then Minister for Communication, with a view to suggesting measures to ensure the preservation of public television in France. This commission made up of television professionals, politicians and academics, while recognising the necessary reliance on advertising revenues which was described as the desirable expression of the market's response to public channels programmes, called for a substantial rise in the amount of the licence fee on the grounds that its growth did not match that of inflation, at least during the 1982-92 decade. An additional argument pointed out that its level was markedly lower than similar fees in neighbouring European countries, notably Britain. The Commission went even as far as to suggest that the development of local programmes by France 3, as recommended by the members, should be financed by a special extra levy – not more than FF 15 (£1.60) according to the estimates of the Commission – which should be readily accepted by the public if it was clearly perceived to be linked to the supply of programmes with a local dimension.[11]

Not only does the French licence fee improperly relate to the true funding needs of national public channels but it also suffers from a poor collection system and socially inspired governmental measures which exempt 20 percent of television set owners, typically old age pensioners with limited income, from paying the licence fee. This deficit in the proceeds of the licence fee is partially made up by Parliament when appropriating the resources of public broadcasting as part of the national budget.

Deprived of the public funding they are entitled to expect, public broadcasters have inevitably tended to rely more heavily on advertising and sponsorship revenues which locked them into a relentless competition with commercial channels for increased audience shares. Such a drift can also be perceived in the more aggressive scheduling policy of Channel 4 since its establishment as a public corporation as a result of the Broadcasting Act of 1990.

The case of Channel 4 is original in more ways than one. Indeed as its Chairman wrote in the foreword to the 1995 Report: 'Channel 4 is the only public service broadcaster in the world to rely entirely on commercial revenues and without any public subsidy or licence fee'. At the same time, the remit of Channel 4, with its emphasis on innovative programming catering for minorities, seemed to preclude commercial viability which normally requires comfortable ratings. Yet Channel 4 managed to net nearly 21 percent of all TV advertising revenue in 1995, to increase its audience share among the ABC1 category and the 16-34 age group while ITV's share in the same categories was eroded. However provocative or controversial Channel 4 programmes are felt to be, particularly during the late Saturday evening slot, the channel launched in 1982 in the wake of the Annan Report has made a powerful contribution to the concept of public service broadcasting. More importantly, the current prosperity of Channel 4 demonstrates that public funding need not be the litmus test of genuine PSB systems. Recent rumours about the eventual privatisation of the channel which Michael Grade, its Director General at the time, tried to whip up in his dramatic intervention at the 1996 Edinburgh Festival simply confirm the good health of a channel that a number of observers had pronounced doomed a few months after its launch.

In France too, the public service broadcasting system seems to be threatened with partial privatisation. Since 1995 the hypothesis of the privatisation of France 2 has been floated by pro-market politicians. The resignation of Jean-Pierre Elkabbach, the Chairman of France Télévision, in June 1996 fuelled speculations to such an extent that Hervé Bourges, the current head of the Conseil Supérieur de l'Audiovisuel, the regulating body set up in 1989, described such privatisation as unreasonable. According to him, the transfer of public channels to the commercial sector would entail the risk of disrupting the broadcasting scene at a time when its operators are moving into digital television projects.[12] Obviously, given the shortage of public funding needed to keep the three public organisations properly endowed, a majority of RPR MPs would make no great fuss if the government decided to sell France 2. Yet, such a move would certainly be opposed by TF1 whose position as market leader has recently been eroded (1.9 percent of audience share in 1996). The most popular television channel would probably be concerned by the emergence of an aggressive competitor bound to siphon off a larger share of an already saturated advertising market. Newspaper publishing houses would be equally worried by the emergence of yet another rival competing for the same source of revenues. But above all, on the basis of the current financial performance of France 2, there is no prospect of seeing a host of applicants falling over each other to buy an unprofitable channel. The demise of La Cinq still lingers in the memory of media moguls and precludes the return of the gung-ho attitudes typical of the mid-1980s.

Yet, under the chairmanship of J.-P. Elkabbach, France 2 had become virtually indistinguishable from TF1. The management team embarked on a lavish programme policy designed to maximise audience shares. Expensive contracts were signed with popular programme hosts who at the same time produced the programmes, mostly talk shows and light entertainment, for which they charged extortionate fees. For instance, Jacques Martin and his production house pocketed nearly FF150 million (about £17 million) between September 1995 and June 1996 for a series of forty-two 'Dimanche Martin' programmes. By contrast, France 2 devoted only FF 58 million in 1994 to the production of 108 hours of children's programmes.[13] Jacques Martin was not the only host-producer to benefit from such golden contracts; five other programme hosts were also treated in a similar fashion, while the Board of Governors of the channel on which four representatives of the government sit was kept in the dark about the small print of those contracts.

It was this lax style of management which precipitated the downfall of J.-P. Elkabbach who had begun his term as Chairman of

France Télévision with the energising motto: 'Let's dare'. He had clearly intended from the start to give the public Corporation a high profile and to catch up with TF1 by outbidding the leading commercial channel to secure popular entertainment programmes. What is more intriguing in this case is the acquiescence of the Government whose members should have been aware, if only by some parliamentary reports, that the concept of public service broadcasting was seriously jeopardised by such critical drift from orthodoxy.

To survive, both British and French public broadcasting systems have had to adapt to a competitive market by cutting their costs in order to reflect shrinking budgets in relation to the actual increase in programme-making costs. The cost-cutting exercise has included the statutory obligations for both organisations to commission a certain proportion of specified programmes from independent producers. Mind-sets and attitudes have had to shed the smug complacency long associated with the secure status of a state-controlled organisation. In that sense, the BBC's current Director General, John Birt, has been more successful than his French counterpart in instilling a commercial ethos into the top layers of management. Clearly the introduction in 1993 of 'producer choice', the internal market strategy, has developed an unprecedented cost-consciousness in the organisation, even if the benefits of this policy are not obvious to all.

As a media consultant puts it: 'the internal market lacks safeguards to stop programme makers taking decisions which may make sense for their budgets, but cost the BBC as a whole more money.'[14] It remains to be seen whether the large scale reorganisation of the management and commissioning structure introduced in April 1997 will pay off eventually. Some critics argue that the six large components carved out by John Birt will lend themselves more easily to privatisation which some, like the former Chairman of the House of Commons National Heritage Committee, Gerald Kaufman, would contemplate with no displeasure.

France Télévision has not been so bold in its structural reorganisation; one would even suggest that the creation of a joint chairmanship without the setting up of a proper holding has compounded the organisational problems which have plagued France Télévision since 1989. Yet, Jean-Pierre Elkabbach had the same ambition for his organisation as John Birt. Both joined sides with commercial partners, particularly American, in order to keep their corporations in the race for global markets. France Télévision's deal with Time Warner in 1995 and the joint venture of more recent creation that the BBC got into with TCI's Flextech, testify to the dynamism of the public broadcasting sector in both countries, which will be further confirmed by current involvement in digital television projects.

Putting pressure on existing PSB systems to adapt to new rules and to survive financially with a shrinking dependence on public funding would, however, have little justification if public service channels became mere carbon copies of the commercial channels they would have emulated only too well. One may find some comfort in the thought that: 'PSB has proved durable because it regards broadcasting as a public, social goal'.[15] This is, after all, the proper raison d'être of public service broadcasting in general and particularly in the seasoned models that Britain and France have somehow managed to retain.

Indeed, one may even argue that public service broadcasting organisations, despite the inevitable tensions between their statutory commitments to universality and diversity, still manage to provide an effective articulation of the collective values that hold a country together. Although it is legitimate to wonder if 'the notion of a shared national culture is any longer meaningful',[16] particularly in Britain where multiculturalism achieves a higher visibility than in France, public television channels can be seen as the antidote to the social and cultural fragmentation brought about by the development of specialised, themed channels tapping the resources of niche audiences. This view, propounded in France by Dominique Wolton in particular,[17] emphasises the role of public television channels in exhibiting national specificities in a European context. Unlike commercial channels which tend to maximise their profits by applying well tested scheduling strategies practically identical from one country to another, public television channels, Wolton would argue, are, by virtue of their ethos, encouraged to reflect in their programmes the national culture in which they are rooted.

One such distinctive mission ascribed specifically to French public sector broadcasting organisations has been the defence of the French language and the spreading of French culture abroad, a mission spelt out, for example, in Article 5 of the 1982 Law on Audiovisual Communication. The fact that the defence of French has been enshrined in legislation could be interpreted as the typical obsession of French governments with the idea of national 'cultural exception'. Yet the contribution that public sector broadcasters can make to the development of a national language is now equally recognised in Britain where a recent report by the House of Commons National Heritage Committee accepted that 'the English language is increasingly the most used international language in the world, and that the BBC is a prime custodian. This custodianship is both an opportunity and an obligation, and we would wish that government will recognise the centrality of these issues to the future of this country'.[18]

Although the concept of public service broadcasting is now increasingly superseded by a lesser notion, hinging on 'general interest missions' which can be fulfilled equally by public as well as commercial broadcasters, it seems that public sector organisations are still relevant to the articulation of national values and cultures. Their generalist approach to the public, while attempting to reconcile universality and diversity, is arguably the proper way of providing the forum for discussion and transaction that democracy requires.

Notes and References

1. Arte which from 1994 has shared the fifth terrestrial channel with the educational channel – La Cinquième – was born in 1990 following a Franco-German treaty which provided for the creation of a joint cultural television channel. Arte operates as a joint investment group owned on a 50/50 basis by ARTE Deutschland and La Sept-Arte whose capital is provided by France 3, the French Government, Institut National de l'Audioviduel (INA) and Radio France. In 1995 Arte's audience share did not exceed 3 percent, which prompted criticism from a number of parliamentarians who felt that this public terrestrial channel could be put to better use.
2. Average figures for 1996, *Broadcast,* 21 March 1997.
3. Y. Achille and J. I. Bueno, *Les télévisions publiques en quête d'avenir,* Grenoble, Presses Universitaires, 1994, 13-14.
4. F. Williams, 'Public Service Broadcasting', *BBC Year Book 1949,* 10.
5. A. Peacock, *Report of the Committee on Financing the BBC,* Cmnd 9824, London, HMSO, July 1986, par.598.
6. M. Raboy (ed.), *Public Broadcasting for the 21st Century,* Academia Monograph, University of Luton Press, John Libbey, (n-d.), 2.
7. J. Morgan, 'The BBC and Public Service Broadcasting' in S. MacCabe and O. Stewart (eds.), *The BBC and Public Service Broadcasting,* Manchester, Manchester University Press, 1986, 31.
8. Draft resolution of the Council of Europe's Fourth European Ministerial Conference on Mass Media Policy, Prague, December 1994.
9. *Extending Choice: The BBC's role in the new broadcasting age,* BBC, November 1992, 86.
10. A. Ehrenberg and P. Mills, *Viewers' Willingness to Pay,* a Research Report published by *Broadcast,* 30 November 1990.
11. *L'Avenir de la télévision publique,* rapport de la Commission Campet, Paris, La Documentation française, 1993, 68-9.
12. Interview given to *Le Monde,* 21 janvier 1997.
13. Figures provided by P. Auberger's Report to the Finance Commission of the *Assemblée Nationale,* no. 2270, 12 October 1995.
14. Reported by *The Economist,* 23 December 1995.
15. P. Scannell, 'Britain: Public Service Broadcasting, from National Culture to Multiculturalism' in M. Raboy (ed.) *Public Broadcasting for the 21st Century,* 39.
16. Ibid., 36.
17. See for instance his article 'Pourquoi une télévision publique?' in *Medias Pouvoirs,* no.14, April-June 1989, 90-5.
18. House of Commons National Heritage Committee, *The BBC and the Future of Broadcasting,* vol. 1, London, The Stationery Office, March 1997, par.89.

PART II

PROGRAMMING STRUCTURES

CHAPTER 5

TWO PROGRAMMING MODELS

RÉGINE CHANIAC

Despite the unifying tendencies at work as a result of increasing competition and the internationalisation of programmes and broadcasting concepts, France and the U.K. still have two quite distinct programming models. The specific character of the programmes broadcast on the main generalist terrestrial channels in the two countries inevitably has its roots in strong traditions connected with the bases of the two television systems. The following comparative analysis of programming schedules in both countries clarifies the main aspects of the differences between them.[1]

1989: The fair-play model and the competitive model

In 1989, INA (the French National Institute for radio and television archives, research and training) conducted a survey of evening programmes broadcast on television in the leading European countries. Entitled *Le prime time en Europe*, it analysed the programmes published in television weeklies over a period of six weeks in order to determine the specific nature of programme schedules offered to television viewers evening after evening in different countries. The study highlighted different structural configurations of complementarity or competitivity, and identified two broad programming models.

At that time, the U.K., Germany and Spain represented what has been designated as the fair-play model ('modèle courtois'). These were countries where advertising space was still not an arena where any real competition existed, either because commercial television held monopoly control in a single group (ITV), or the largely dominant public sector was subject to strict advertising quotas (ARD and ZDF in Germany), or, oddly enough, the public sector wholly financed out of advertising was in a monopoly situation (Spain). The concern with audiences existed in these countries, but it was not necessarily the decisive parameter determining the structure of programme schedules. The big channels avoided confrontational competition, preferring instead a polite arrangement whereby they took turns to carry programmes with wide audience appeal and public-service broadcasts. The diversity of the broadcast genres, even at peak audience hours, was real and went hand in hand with a rather checkerboard programming pattern, that is, programmes which varied from one day to the next. Production activity took precedence over any other independent programming strategy, the schedule being the outlet for programmes conceived in production units. The creative people producing programmes had a central place in the broadcasting initiative.

In France and Italy, it was the competitive model that prevailed in television. Here public and commercial channels were already competing with each other for the largest share of television advertising. The privatisation of TF1 in 1987 abruptly ended the French public sector's supremacy and the scarcity of commercials caused by the limits set on the public service channels' advertising revenues. It suddenly became a situation where three commercial and two public service channels were competing for the advertising spoils and the supply of programmes offered by broadcasters exceeded the demand from advertisers. In this highly competitive situation, audience share (along with the projections they helped to make) became the principal regulatory instrument. The schedules now became quite regular from one day to the next or from one week to another. Every channel strove to become more easily recognised by its public and consequently offered viewers a regular and therefore easily remembered fare. Such regularity, conducive to establishing viewing habits, had the advantage of reducing the uncertainty of ratings and providing advertisers with the constant and 'smooth' audiences they preferred. The programmes proposed became standardised around a few genres appealing to a broad public, with less competitive programmes either dropping out altogether or being relegated to slots where the competition was weakest (morning and late fringe). Breaking free of production obligations, programming became a central and strategic function for the most part inspired by the American example: programmes were designed or purchased in keeping with goals determined by audience ratings.

1997: The liberalisation of British television

Eight years later, what are the major changes that have affected the television systems in France and the U.K.?

In France, the triumph of the commercial model was symbolised in 1992 by the collapse of La Cinq, precipitated by the constant erosion after 1990 of a market share that had originally been achieved with the help of American television drama. That same year, Arte, the Franco-German cultural channel conceived as an antidote to the excesses of the French television environment, took over La Cinq's frequency. In 1994 La Cinquième, the channel of 'knowledge, training and employment', came on air, moving into the daytime broadcast slot left vacant by Arte. But the fifth channel accounts for a mere 3 percent audience and relieves the general programming public service channels of the responsibility for taking on an ambitious cultural mission. The two commercial channels (TF1 and M6) and the public channels (France 2 and France 3) are quite happy with the 'neutralisation' of a channel which is one more drain on advertising revenue. A kind of implicit Yalta presides over the twists and turns of the geopolitical map of terrestrial television and the competitive model appears to have become stabilised. The only noteworthy development has been the steady erosion of TF1's audience share since 1992, which has profited France 3 most of all (see Table 5.1).

The foundations guaranteeing the permanence of the fair-play model in the U.K. have been seriously shaken. The equilibrium prevailing since the end of the 1950s was undermined in a matter of years by the Conservative government's determination to deregulate the market. The 1990 Broadcasting Act weakened the ITV network companies by opening the way to a new system of granting licences by auction, beginning in 1993, which considerably increased the government's tax take. At the same time, while the network's television advertising monopoly was already being threatened as a result of the expansion of satellite broadcasting, the same Act has-

Table 5.1. *Percentage audience share on French television*

	1991	1996
TF1	42.1	35.4
France 2	21.3	24.2
France 3	11.3	17.7
M6	8.0	11.9
Canal+	4.6	4.5
Canal 5*	10.9	3.0
Others	1.8	3.4

Source: Médiamétrie.
*La Cinq in 1991; Arte + La Cinquième in 1996

Table 5.2. *Percentage audience share on British television*

	1989	1996
BBC 1	39	32.4
BBC 2	10	11.6
ITV	42	34.1
Chann.4	9	10.7
Others	0	10.1

Source: BARB.

tened the transition to a competitive environment by granting Channel 4 the freedom to market its own advertising space and by setting up a new terrestrial channel, Channel 5, which began broadcasting only in the spring of 1997. Along with all this, linking the broadcast licence fee to the cost-of-living index resulted in a stagnation of the BBC's resources (see chapters 3 and 4).

In 1989, the year Sky Television went on air, the BBC's two channels and ITV/Channel 4 between them shared the British television audience in almost equal parts (see Table 5.2). By 1996, seven years later, the duopoly had lost control of 10 percent of that audience. In the universe of television homes receiving additional programmes via cable and satellite, the duopoly's audience share was only 63.5 percent (30.1 percent for BBC and 33.1 percent for ITV/Channel 4), with the satellite channels taking the lead (35.6 percent, half of which for the BSkyB channels). ITV was the terrestrial channel hardest hit by competition from satellite television: accounting for 43.3 percent of the market in 1990, it slid to 34.1 percent in 1996. Though still the leader, ITV can – unlike TF1 in France – find itself overhauled by BBC1 in some weeks. Finally, the newcomer Channel 5, with an audience share that seldom rose over 2 percent in the first few months of its existence, is not yet worrying its elders.

While British television has completed a smooth transition to the competitive environment,[2] an examination of recent programme schedules shows that the logic behind the programming is still very different from that of French television channels. The new competitive set-up has indeed resulted in changing British programme schedules, but this has come about only gradually without seriously affecting the structures that existed in 1989. The end of this cosy duopoly has not prevented the survival of a British model based on a strong historical tradition of quality, (see chapter 7), remarkably stable viewing patterns, a body of regulations which are both mild and quite severe (taste and decency requirements) (see chapters 2 and 3), and a particularly vigorous programmes production industry.

Programming schedules: similarities and idiosyncrasies

Without detailing all the contrasting elements that exist between British and French television schedules, some of the fundamentals of these differences in the more important parts of the day need to be highlighted.

Daytime

In the U.K. as in France, horizontal programming is the rule on weekdays from morning to early fringe, while the weekend schedule is quite specific. Departures from the repetitive nature of programmes from Monday to Friday are not of the same kind in the two countries.

In Britain, some time slots fall outside the daily regularity of programmes: this is particularly true in the afternoon. After the Australian soap *Neighbours*, BBC1 proposes a different menu every day from 14.00 to 15.00 with, in the winter season for example, a movie on Monday and a different drama series on each of the other days, followed by magazines also in checkerboard form. In the preceding season, the same series were programmed between 12.05 and 13.00, with the slot 'regularised' from January with the subsequent installation of a game show. On ITV, the genres even alternate between 13.50 and 15.30 with a drama (the Australian police series *Blue Heelers*) on Monday, a series (the New Zealand hospital series *Shortland Street*) on Friday, and the same mix of entertainment shows and magazines repeated on the other three days.

In France, the only departure from strip programming comes on Wednesday, when most school children have the day off. On this day the children's broadcasts are programmed in the morning slot (*Club Dorothée* on TF1 from 09.55 to 11.40, *La planète de Donkey King* from 09.25 to 10.40 on France 2 and *Les Minikeums* from 08.00 to 11.45 on France 3).

British children are far luckier than their French counterparts: not only do they finish school earlier in the afternoon, but BBC1 and ITV also programme two hours of broadcasts for them every day starting at 15.30. In France, after TF1 dropped its 16.50 children's broadcasts slot, children who finish school at 16.30 have to be satisfied with France 3's *Minikeums* at 16.40 on days when school is open and that runs for no more than an hour. Even at the risk of seeing the adult public switching to BBC2 and Channel 4, which are in a very good position in this slot, the big British channels decided to concentrate on the children's audience in an attempt to counter the influence of the specialised satellite channels (Cartoon Network, Nickelodeon, etc.) which have already cornered half the audience aged four to fifteen years. In France, on the other hand, the bigger French channels have gradually dropped their young public in the late afternoon slot, already considered a strategic one, to concentrate on broadcasts less likely to segment the audience (television drama, entertainment shows).

In general, the competition between the leading channels appears to be often more confrontational in France than in the U.K. For years, TF1 and France 2 have each been programming their respective daytime newscasts in the same time slot (13.00) hammocking them between a game show (*Le juste prix* on TF1 and *Pyramide* on France 2) and a television drama (*Les feux de l'amour* on TF1 and *Derrick* on France 2). ITV and BBC broadcast their national news at 12.30 and 13.00 respectively, with ITV programming regional information at 13.00. The direct competition starts with the Australian soaps which are strip programmed immediately afterwards, even though any overlapping is only quite partial (*Home and Away* at 13.25 on ITV and *Neighbours* at 13.40 on BBC1).

The regional ingredient is far more present in Britain's leading channels than in their French counterparts. Regional news has pride of place (13.00 to 13.30) on ITV given its situation as a network. But this is also true on BBC1 which slots such news between 13.30 and 13.40. In France, only France 3 accepts this mission by integrating a newscast and a regional magazine in a ninety-minute information slot from 12.00 to 13.30.

Just one observation about weekend television helps to illustrate everything that separates French and British conceptions of commercial television, (see chapter 3): *Morning Worship* on ITV on Sunday morning is part of the public-service remit accepted by the network. As soon as it was privatised, TF1 hastened to unload the religious broadcasts on to the public service channel France 2.

Prime-time access

The prime-time slot (early evening) helps to spotlight the differences between the two systems even more clearly than the daytime programmes. The 18.00-20.30 slot in France is a considerable stake in the competition between broadcasters. Very low before 18.00 (less than 10 percent of viewers), the audience here rises steeply and levels off around 20.45 (over 40 percent). Every quarter of an hour, between one and two million people turn on their sets. As the audience gathers volume, its character also undergoes a change. At the start of the prime-time access period, the audience is narrower and consists often of non-working persons living alone (pensioners, housewives), but subsequently broadens out to include more members of the family. During this gradual transition from an 'individual public' to a 'group public', it is essential for the channels to win over new viewers as and when they sit down before their sets, without however causing those already won over to switch to the competition. It is no less important to hold on to the audience from one day to the next.

It is this logic of building up audiences and retaining their loyalties that shapes the profile of French television programme schedules in this time slot: the programming is quite straightforwardly horizontal Monday through Friday; the broadcasts tend to be short format (twenty-six or fifty-five minutes) and are frequently divided up into several categories or levels (game shows) in such a way as to facilitate the accommodation of new waves of viewers and spreading the commercials around. Information apart, only the most lightweight genres are present. Drama, game show and entertainment form the dominant mix on both TF1 and France 2, while M6 almost exclusively depends on drama. As in mid-daytime, TF1 and France 2 also compete in the newscast slot at 20.00. All the channels adhere to this divide between the end of prime-time access and the rest of the evening.

France 3 successfully exploits counter-programming by scheduling its own news and current affairs programme *(19/20)* in the 19.00 to 20.00 slot. Competing with the game shows on TF1 and France 2 and the series on M6, its regional news programme (19.05-19.30) dominates the market, regularly taking an audience share of over 40 percent. The irony is that for many, many years, France's two leading public service channels were supposed to be providing regional news, as the France 3 network did not quite cover the entire nation. In 1985, TF1 (it was still government-owned) arranged to have itself relieved of the obligation to provide this service. Four years later, France 2 followed suit. Since then, with some help from *Questions pour un champion* which immediately precedes it, France 3's *19/20* has established itself as the leader in the slot.

Lastly, the continuing difficulty France is having in producing television drama (soaps and sitcoms) able to stay the course over the long haul for meeting its day-to-day requirements, is forcing the channels to programme generally U.S.-made drama in this slot as in daytime. Only TF1 has any significant sitcom production capacity (*Hélène et les garçons* or, more recently, *Jamais deux sans toit*). But these phoney, unimaginative and poorly cobbled together programmes are no match for American imports and are not kept on the schedule after 18.30.

By 18.00 it is already prime time (or peak time) in the U.K. Its mid-daytime audience is only half the size of the comparable audience in France, but by 15.30 it begins to increase slowly on weekdays, reaching a first stage with more than a third of viewers.

After that, there is only a slight increase between 19.00 and 19.30 and the total audience barely exceeds 40 percent during the evening. Over the weekend the audience increases steadily all through the day, the slight afternoon dip disappearing altogether. Peak viewing time extends over a much longer period than in France and quite simply contrasts with daytime. The disposition of the programmes buttresses this distribution of the audience throughout the evening: the formats and rhythms remain unmarked by differences; several newscasts of equal importance punctuate the evening without any polarisation of interest around the 20.00 news.

If the equivalent of France's prime-time access had to be found in the U.K., it would be between 17.10 and 18.00 when the number of people turning on their sets increases very rapidly on weekdays. The channels drop their children's programmes and start stripping in Australian soaps by mid-daytime, again with a slight overlapping of series (*Home and Away* at 17.10 on ITV, *Neighbours* at 17.30 on BBC1). With newscasts, which are first national then followed by regional reports still with a time-lag, the British schedules remain horizontal until 18.30 (ITV) or 19.00 (BBC1).

Evening

The evening on British television reaches a peak at 19.30. The half-hour which follows it has the largest audience. This is also the time when the two leading channels clearly dominate the market with their celebrated twenty-six-minute soaps, each regularly taking more than two-thirds of the viewers present. In typical British fashion, a head-on confrontation is avoided and, by the same token, stripping is confounded. BBC1 programmes *EastEnders* on Mondays, Tuesdays and Thursdays (and the omnibus edition on Sundays); ITV proposes *Coronation Street* on Mondays, Wednesdays, Fridays and Sundays. While one channel broadcasts a soap, the other schedules a magazine or a documentary series (*Tomorrow's World*, *Survival*, etc.) frequently on a weekly basis.

It should be noted that these soaps, initially designed to be broadcast at the rate of two episodes a week, have today expanded into three or four episodes a week. In 1989 *Coronation Street* acquired a third episode broadcast on Friday; in 1995, a third episode of *EastEnders* appeared on Monday, but at 20.00, as a matter of courtesy to avoid competition with the latter. ITV was less obliging when it added a third episode to *The Bill* on Friday at 20.00, thereby forcing Channel 4 to delay broadcasting the third episode of *Brookside* until 20.30. All the weekly drama broadcasts have been affected by this tendency which conveys well the temptation to regularise schedules so as maximise audiences. By programming *Emmerdale* three days running (at 19.00) and broadcasting a fourth episode of *Coronation Street* on Sundays, ITV comes closer to the French practice of stripping. Just how long will British television channels succeed in averting the danger of head-on competition brought about by a further extension of stripping?

After 20.30, British television programmes follow a strictly checkerboard pattern, the only regularity being afforded by the newscasts (at 21.00 on BBC1 and at 22.00 on ITV). Depending on the day of the week and the channel, the public has a choice of a succession of programmes lasting twenty-six, forty-five or sixty minutes. British-made drama is the leader in all its forms (police or medical series, sitcoms, mini series, serials). U.S.-made drama is not absent, but for most of the time is programmed after 21.30 (*X Files* on BBC1), if only because of the strict 'Taste and Decency' code which bans sex, violence and bad language so long as children are still watching television (see chapters 2 and 3). No other genre has succeeded in gaining public acceptance. There are a few magazines and special reports, some chat shows, reality shows and entertainment programmes. Formats of ninety minutes and longer are rare and are often kept for the weekend, a given slot accommodating a film, mini series or a television movie, depending on the week. ITV has still not been given permission to delay its *News At Ten*[3] by an hour or thirty minutes, and is therefore having to divide into two parts movies and television dramas that children should not watch.

On French television, the evening starts after the long 20.30 pause[4] and is characterised by the domination of a long format of at least ninety minutes, duration that is supposed to hold the viewer before the set until the end. Whereas in the U.K., a person can sit down before a television set at several moments during the evening and catch the news every hour or come in on a programme which is just starting, his/her counterpart in France is offered only a single 'show' starting more or less early depending on availability;[5] but which leads to the evening's main programme at exactly the same moment on all the channels. Specialist programme planner Pierre Wiehn considers that ninety minutes correspond better to the aspirations of the average person who sits down to watch television at 21.00. This is the moment when he/she has been freed from all the occupations that still require his/her attention in the preceding period (evening meal, household chores, small children) and is now available for a real show chosen on the basis of 'an expectation of maximum pleasure'.

The long format could be a full-length movie which is not present in daytime schedules. French regulations are very strict in this area: they limit each channel to two movies a week in prime time, while banning them on certain evenings (Wednesday, Friday and

Saturday), which accounts for the fierce competition on the other evenings, (see chapter 6). French television drama (television movies or ninety-minute series) are largely programmed in the prime-time slot – two evenings on TF1, three on France 2 and one on France 3. American television drama is, however, present, especially on M6 *(X Files)*, but also more sporadically on TF1 *(Columbo)* and France 2 *(ER)*. The other slots might be taken up by football (TF1), variety-show type entertainment or reality shows (TF1), game shows *(Fort Boyard* on France 2). Thursday evening, France 2 stands apart from its commercial competitor by programming *Envoyé spécial*, a magazine of special reports.

France 3 is alone in departing from the practice of scheduling a nationally made long-format programme: it broadcasts two hour-long magazines on Friday *(Thalassa* followed by *Faut pas rêver)*. When a channel purchases a series of hour-long programmes on the international market, it does not hesitate to broadcast two in a row, as *ER* on France 2, or even three, as *X-Files* on M6.

The persistence of two models

It is impossible in this brief chapter to go into greater detail concerning the differences between the two countries' programme schedules. Many other points would merit analysis – programming in the second part of the evening, the place of certain genres such as the documentary, cultural or sports programmes; the logic behind complementary and counter-programming and so on.

The specific issues raised in the preceding account should, however, suffice to highlight the broad principles which continue to play a part in determining the distinguishing characteristics of the television systems in the two countries.

Viewing habits and traditions

There are appreciable differences in the two countries' viewing curves. In France, the curve shows two rather short-lived rises in mid-daytime and in the evening, separated by a lengthy trough in the afternoon. In the U.K., the viewing curve reveals scarcely any movement at 13.00, but rises quite early in the afternoon and stays high all through a long evening. Viewing habits are linked to schooling and working rhythms and life styles (more or less ritualised mealtimes). Such habits are also shored up by a tradition which contributes to concentrating programme entries and exits around obligatory junctures and a major broadcast, as in France, or to proposing several entries which are all equally legitimate, as in the U.K.

Political bases, regulations

As Serge Regourd has demonstrated, coexistence between the public and the commercial sectors is not governed according to the same principles in the two countries, (see chapter 3). In Britain, equilibrium between the two sectors has been the rule for very many years, and this has helped to avert situations of head-on competition. This stability appears to be holding in spite of the entry of satellite television into the contest. Firmly abiding by its common law tradition, the U.K. simply lays down a few rules (they are often implied) defining the ideals of public service that the two sectors are expected to respect. The place of news and current affairs in the ITV schedule testifies to the power of the public service remit. The whole of television programming is characterised by the obligation to abide by standards of taste and decency which outlaw prime-time broadcasting of many foreign series deemed too violent, as well as a large number of movies. British programmers do not hesitate, when it is possible, to take their scissors to scenes of sex and violence. This puritanical tradition is continued in the television programmes magazine weekly, *Radio Times*, which in its weekly selection meticulously identifies the movies in which there is swearing.

Commercial television took a longer time coming to France and its advent was more violent, with a public sector partly financed by advertising being placed in a position of disadvantage; hence the ruthless competition. A complex and voluminous body of rules and regulations has not succeeded in preventing the transformation of programme schedules. Highly restrictive regulations governing the broadcasting of full-length movies, a programme form making the highest ratings on French television, have even had the effect of increasing the frequency of head-on competition, as when movies are concentrated in prime time on the four evenings on which they are authorised. It is the fall-off in movie audiences in recent years which has lately prompted the channels to give up their 'right' to broadcast two movies a week in prime time: for three months France 2 programmed *ER* on Sunday evening in place of its usual movie.

Share of national production and programming

The resourcefulness of the British television system has led to the rapid development of a fairly abundant programme production base which practically ensures the self-sufficiency of the public and commercial channels. As far back as the 1950s, BBC and ITV programmes (documentaries, drama and children's broadcasts) were known throughout the world, obtained many awards in international competitions and were being exported, particularly to France, where programme production was at an embryonic stage.

This production strength is reflected in the way schedules are devised. In drama, the programming rhythm is dictated by the logic of producing the most popular broadcasts. On the one hand, the programming frequency of the thirty-minute soaps and series broadcast all year round could be stepped up from two to three episodes a week, but then the broadcaster comes up against a limit beyond which quality and permanence would be threatened. On the other hand, the big successful longer-format series programmed once a week (*Casualty, Inspector Morse, A Touch of Frost, London's Burning,* etc.) are broadcast only during a single season in the year, that is, three months. This practice of limiting broadcasts to a single quarter in the year, which affects all the programmes serialised in prime time (magazines, documentary series, game shows, entertainment programmes), reduces even more the possibility of schedules becoming regular.

France's traditional weakness in producing dramas such as soaps and sitcoms has resulted in an overwhelming presence of American drama in horizontal programming slots both in daytime and in prime-time access. Nationally made drama reserved for prime-time broadcasting is therefore in the ninety-minute format. Series are turned out at a rather sluggish rate (six episodes a year at most) which cannot keep a weekly slot supplied. So they alternate in the same slot (*Navarro, Julie Lescaut,* etc., Thursdays on TF1) and succeed in being present in the programme throughout the year with the help of re-runs of old episodes. French schedules in fact show no seasonal variation, except in the depths of the summer doldrums.

Conclusion

Two differing programming conceptions still seem to set the two systems apart. In the U.K., programming continues to be determined by production activity, whether this is in-house or outsourced. ITV's very structure as a network of regional companies favours an interpretation of the schedule as the result of a compromise worked out between affiliates supplying programmes. On the other hand, in France, the 'technical' conception of programming, specific to public television, where the main concern was to fill time slots with products supplied by the programme units, has been replaced by a strategic conception, largely inspired by the American example. Schedules have become the expression of tactical choices where each programme is designed or purchased with the strict aim of meeting goals determined by audience ratings. The production imperative has given way to the necessity of securing audience loyalty.

Notes and References

This study is based on 1996-1997 programming schedules.
1. As far as France is concerned, the programming schedules studied are those valid from September 1996 to June 1997; for the U.K., they are those from the past winter season (January-March 1997).
2. The competitive system has also triumphed in Spain and Germany.
3. According to the Independent Television Authority (ITC), news and current affairs form part of the public service remit and must be broadcast at 'peak viewing times'.
4. Over the years, the divide has become a long tunnel in which commercials and trailers of forthcoming broadcasts frame tiny bits and pieces of the programme – weather report, racing results and so on – thereby delaying the evening's main programme almost to 21.00.
5. A French viewer unable to watch television before 20.45 does not have ready access to any other newscast. TF1 and France 2 have delayed their late evening news until after midnight. France 3 does have a newscast slightly before, but in time slots that vary wildly depending on the preceding programmes (between 22.30 and 23.45).

CHAPTER 6

CINEMA AND TELEVISION: FROM ENMITY TO INTERDEPENDENCE

Lucy Mazdon

To certain readers the very title of this chapter may seem to be a contradiction in terms. These readers would probably claim that the very act of transmitting a film produced for the cinema via the medium of television must inevitably undermine its status as cinematographic product; once shown on television a film becomes something other, diminished by the confines of the television screen and the distracted attention of the television audience. This type of reduction is exemplified by the practice of 'panning and scanning', whereby high definition wide-screen movies are reworked to fit the low definition images of the small screen. However, the attacks on the cinematic text do not end there. Films shown on television are also threatened by advertising breaks and, perhaps most notably in Britain, cuts in visual content and dialogue to avoid the transgression of television's censorship requirements (the infamous 'nine o'clock watershed' in Britain) or indeed the angry reactions of audience pressure groups so well embodied in the tirelessly outraged persona of Mary Whitehouse. This condemnation of the relationship between cinema and television is clearly located within those discourses which, in the very early days of television transmission, unequivocally described the new medium as the enemy of cinematic production.[1] When, in 1957, cinema box office figures fell dramatically as French television showed the visit of Elizabeth II to Paris, many commentators felt that the days of the cinema screen were numbered, a fear that seemed to be borne out in the ensuing years as cinema attendance figures continued to tumble. Significantly, in both Britain and France this perception of television as a threat to cinema was articulated as a threat to a specifically 'national' film culture and thus fed into, and reinforced, the long-standing debate about Hollywood and American 'cultural imperialism'.

Clearly there is some foundation to these fears. It is undeniable that television did have a nefarious impact upon cinema attendance in both Britain and France, and elsewhere. Moreover, many films have indeed suffered the indignities of 'panning and scanning' and ruthless cutting to please censors and advertisers alike. Nevertheless, such outright condemnation is overly reductive; by thus decrying the unquestionably close relationship between cinema and television these critics prohibit both close analysis of this interconnection and an understanding of the processes of exchange and transformation which occur as films move between the two media.

Cinematographic films shown on television do indeed become something 'other'. However this process of transformation need not be as malevolent as that described above. It is worth pointing out that Canal Plus, the French pay-television channel whose output is largely devoted to cinema films, systematically refuses poor quality prints, video prints or prints which do not respect the film's original format. This exigency, clearly a result of the channel's identity as both a pay channel and a cinema channel, has impacted upon other French television channels, obliging them to reject the ruthlessly 'remade' films shown in earlier years in favour of better quality prints. Moreover, the shifts from cinema to television can be far more subtle than the criticisms described above tend to suggest. Films shown on television attract different audiences, usually much broader (and certainly much bigger) than audiences for cinema screenings. The act of cinema and television spectatorship are manifestly very different. This difference is inscribed within the medium itself and within processes of reception. A much cited feature of contemporary television viewing is the phenomenon of 'zapping', a distracted spectatorship which lends the viewer a certain power over the image (not available to the cinema audience) and which breaks the continuity of narrative progression and hence the very identity of the film. Cinematic films shown on television become part of the flux of televisual programming. Their identity as complete works, entire unto themselves, is transformed by their location on particular channels and by their relationships to those programmes which precede and follow them. A striking example of this type of shift was provided by the attempted television transmission of Alain Cavalier's film *Thérèse* (1986). In 1989 Antenne 2, a co-producer of the film, had informed Cavalier of their intention to show *Thérèse* within the context of a discussion programme, *Les Dossiers de l'écran*, whose subject was religious faith. Cavalier refused to allow this screening, claiming that to show the film in this context would suggest it was about religion, an identity which he, as director, had always denied. In turn Antenne 2 refused to comply with his demands and so Cavalier took the channel to court, preventing transmission of this film through articles 6 and 47 of the *Loi du 11 mars 1957* which protects the rights of authors. Clearly this dispute reveals a clash between the discourses of *auteurism* and the requirements of television programming, yet it also illustrates the ways in which the identity of the cinematic text can be transformed by its transmission within the flux of television. Both the ways in which the film is shown (on the television screen, within the context of a particular channel and a particular type of programming) and the ways in which it is received (by new audiences, in radically altered viewing contexts, with very different viewing positions) redefine the film, transforming it into a new text, distinct from, and yet not necessarily inferior to, its cinematic manifestation.

Ultimately condemnations of the relationship between cinema and television repose upon an essentialism which claims clearly defined, unalienable identities for cinema films and television programmes. However, it is significant that these identities are usually based upon a particular conception of Hollywood films. In other words, television films are criticised for their 'smallness' in opposition to the epic aesthetic of Hollywood. It seems to me that such criticism sets up a false dichotomy. Hollywood may indeed be the dominant cinematic aesthetic but it is not the *only* aesthetic; the diversity of other cinematic forms and styles should not be denied. Moreover, Hollywood films cannot be defined solely in terms of this epic style. Many of the products of Hollywood have been far smaller in scale than this opposition would suggest, eschewing vast spectacle in favour of dialogue, well-developed characterisation and narrative structures, fluid editing and tight framing.[2] Indeed, as John Hill remarks: '...what is often noticeable about the conventional criticisms of British 'television films' (literariness and lack of visual intelligence, on the one hand, or subordination to a realist aesthetic, on the other) is that these are simply the same criticisms which have always been directed at a certain type of British filmmaking'.[3] This opposition tends to ignore the fact that neither France nor Britain is able to compete with Hollywood on its own terms. Neither cinema industry has the resources to produce the high-budget blockbusters central to contemporary Hollywood production. Indeed, it is precisely the kind of films financed by television companies and shown on French and British television (*intimiste* dramas, comedies, etc.) which, by locating themselves within specific constructions of a 'national' culture, are able to address 'national' audiences and thus provide some defence against the might of Hollywood. This obviously presents something of a paradox; as described above, television's influence upon cinema is condemned as a particular threat to the 'national' film industry and yet at the same time television can be seen to support these same 'national' products.

One thing which is certain is that the relationship between cinema and television, in France, Britain and indeed the United States, is now undeniable. Indeed, it is fair to say that in Britain and France cinematic production could no longer survive without the support of television companies. A close examination of these respective countries reveals the ways in which their cinematic and televisual industries coincide and interrelate.

Cinema and television in France

Films, both cinematic and televisual, have long been an important feature of television programming in France. In the early days of television the showing of a film would be lent the status of an 'event' by nature of its relative rarity (for example, in the week of 8-14 May 1967, the two French television channels showed six films, all at different times thanks to the absence of competition between the transmitters). However, in the same week in 1995, the free, terrestrial television channels (TF1, France 2, France 3, M6 and Arte/La Cinquième) screened twenty-four.[4] This explosion in the number of films on offer to the television viewer has been further extended by the decree of 1994 which allowed the free terrestrial channels and the non-specialist cable channels to show fifty-two cinematic works classified as '*art et essai*' on top of the quota fixed in 1987, and by the development of specialist cinema channels (Canal Plus and the cable channels Ciné-Cinémas and Ciné-Cinéfil). Indeed, the development of these channels is perhaps also behind a very slight drop in the number of cinematographic films shown on the terrestrial channels to figure in the lists of most popular television programmes in terms of audience. It is significant that since 1993 *téléfilms* (television fictions) have begun to win larger audiences for the free terrestrial channels than their cinematic counterparts. Indeed, in 1995, *téléfilms* and fictional series made up 41 percent of the list of the hundred most popular television programmes (this compares with 36 percent in 1994, 20 percent in 1993 and only 4 percent in 1992). These television fictions tend to borrow from an aesthetic more traditionally associated with cinema, notably a significant rise in production values. What this scenario seems to suggest is that the increasing presence of cinematic films on French television has led to a perceived need to produce television films able to compete with them. Clearly this in turn suggests an undermining of the distinctions between the two types of production.

Despite these seemingly high numbers, the programming of cinematographic films on French television is marked by strict regulation. Thus the Law of 30 September 1986, modified by the decrees of 26 January 1987 and 9 September 1988, fixes the following rules for the televisual transmission of cinematic films:

1. The number of feature-length cinematographic films shown on the free terrestrial channels is fixed at 192 per year. Of these only 104 can be shown during prime-time television (between half past eight and half past ten in the evening).
2. No cinema film can be shown on Wednesday and Friday evening (with the exception of *ciné-club* films which can be shown after half past ten) or on Saturday all day or Sunday before half past eight.
3. A waiting period of three years (two years for those films co-produced by the channel of transmission) between the according of the original *visa d'exploitation* allowing the film to be shown in cinemas and its screening on television must be respected. These periods can be reduced if, for example, a film proves unsuccessful at the box office, but this can only be through the agreement of the Ministry of Culture and Communication and can in no case be less than eighteen months.
4. 50 percent of films screened must be of French origin (either films produced solely in France or majority French co-productions) and 60 percent of films must be of EU origin.

The rules set for Canal Plus are rather different. This channel can show a total of 365 films per year of which 50 percent must be of French origin and 60 percent of EU origin. The waiting period between a cinema screening and television transmission on Canal Plus is set at twelve months for those films co-produced by the channel and two years for all other films.

These rules are not entirely inflexible; the differences in the status of the various channels (public and private, free and pay-television, etc.) mean that the CSA, (see chapter 2) can bend these rules at times in order to meet the general requirements of providing a forum for French and European works, respecting the film as a 'work of art' (and thus protecting it from overt alteration through advertising breaks, cutting and so on), and ensuring that television screenings do not prevent exhibition in cinemas. However, they do provide a clear framework for the transmission of cinematographic films on television. These films remain an important part of the French televisual landscape, gaining large audiences for the channels on which they are shown: for example, in 1995 a cinematic film screened at prime-time gained an average audience share of 37.5 percent for TF1, 28.1 percent for France 2 and 21.6 percent for France 3,[5] figures slightly lower than those gained by some other programmes (41.5 percent for a detective series on TF1 and 30.5 percent for an 'entertainment' programme on France 2) but nevertheless highly respectable. Through the rules set out in the *Cahiers des charges* of the different channels the temptation to show larger numbers of films (particularly successful American products), and hence threaten cinema box office figures, is tightly controlled.

The importance of cinematic films for television schedules is matched by certain obligations on the part of the television channels to invest in cinematic production. Clearly the possibility of showing films only two years after an initial cinema screening rather than the usual three led the television channels to greater investment in production. However, there was a tendency to invest very small amounts of money simply to get early access to the film. This was curtailed by rules set out in the Statutory Obligations in the late 1970s stipulating that in order to show films two years (or one year in the case of Canal Plus) after a cinematic release, the television companies must buy a part of the negative of not less than 10 percent of the film's overall budget and not more than 49.9 percent of the film's assets. In other words, the companies would not be able to use their dominant investment in order to control the production and turn the film's assets to their own profit and yet at the same time they would no longer be able to make symbolic investments simply to get quick access to the film. These rules were extended in the decrees agreed in 1984, 1985, 1987 and 1992, which set an overall minimum level of investment in the cinematic product for the television channels. This was fixed at 3 percent of the overall budget of TF1, France 2, France 3 and M6, and 20 percent of the budget of Canal Plus, of which 9 percent must be given to French production and 3 percent to European cinema.

Televisual investment in cinema can also take the form of pre-purchasing. All terrestrial channels are involved in the pre-purchasing of cinematic films, most notably Canal Plus which spent FF 678.45 million on pre-purchases in 1996 compared with FF 136.70 million spent by TF1, FF 67.08 million by France 2 and FF 54.25 million by France 3.[6] These two forms of investment combine to produce a large proportion of the money given to the French cinematic industry. Indeed by 1992, 40 percent of French cinematic production was financed by the television companies, a figure which has remained relatively stable ever since. The money spent on co-productions by the television channels has risen steadily since the early 1990s: in 1990 3.9 percent of total investment in French cinematic production came from the television companies and by 1996 this figure had risen to 10.3 percent. Television investment in pre-purchasing has shown a spectacular increase, rising from 15.9 percent of total film funding in 1990 to 31.7 percent in 1996.[7]

The dependence of French cinema upon the television industry is clearly undeniable. Particularly revealing is the central role of the televisual industries in the *compte de soutien*, the state's support for national film production. In 1986 Jack Lang, then Minister of Culture, imposed a *taxe audiovisuelle* upon the television companies, a tax on each channel's total annual turnover which was then fed into the *compte de soutien*. This tax became increasingly important as the *compte de soutien*'s other major source of finance, the *taxe spéciale additionelle* (TSA), a levy on box office takings, fell as cinema audiences declined. In 1986 television's contribution to the fund stood at just 8 percent but by 1995 over 70 percent of the fund's resources came from television. The contribution of the TSA on the other hand, had fallen to 25 percent. These figures are worth stressing as they underline the nature of the relationship between cinema and television in contemporary France. The *compte de soutien* has long been cited as the principal reason for the relative success of French cinema in the face of Hollywood. However the great majority of this fund now comes from the television industry, the very same television industry condemned for its threat to cinema and most particularly to the *national* cinema. It would seem that cinema and television in France can no longer be seen as entirely distinct.

Cinema and television in Britain

The relationship between cinema and television in Britain is certainly no less intimate than that described above. However, whereas this relationship in France is marked by strict laws determining quotas, transmission times and so on, in Britain these issues are more a matter of self-regulation on the part of the television channels.

1. In 1988 the British Screen Advisory Council, with the agreement of the British Film and Television Producers' Association and the Cinematograph Exhibitors Association, established a ruling whereby terrestrial channels respect a two-year waiting period between the original cinema exhibition of English-language films and their television screening. This period is reduced to eighteen months for those films whose budget is less than £4 million and

no delay is imposed upon foreign-language films (a ruling disputed by the EU's *Television without Frontiers* Directive). Cable channels are subject to a one-year waiting period before showing English-language films.
2. There are no government fixed quotas for the screening of cinematographic films on television in Britain. Instead the terrestrial television channels aim to show a 'fair proportion' of European films. This proportion, nowhere defined, tends to stand at about 86 percent of total film screenings on the BBC and 86 percent of total screenings on the independent channels between six o'clock a.m. and midnight, a figure which drops to 70 percent between midnight and six o'clock a.m.

Although there are clear differences in the ways in which the televisual screening of cinematographic films are regulated in Britain and France, there are nevertheless manifest similarities in the relationship between the two industries. Like its French counterpart, British cinema is now dependent upon funding from television. Just as cinema films feature significantly in the schedules of French broadcasters, so they are a central feature of the British televisual landscape. Indeed in some ways they can be seen to be more prevalent as Britain does not impose restrictions upon the day and times at which they can be shown.

At the beginning of the 1980s no British television company was directly involved in the production of cinematic films. However, in the ensuing years the number of films produced or co-produced by television showed a marked increase. Indeed by 1989, 49 percent of all British cinematic productions involved some televisual investment and television is now both the major financier and the major outlet for British films. It is worth noting that television is now a much more important industry in Britain than are cinema and video. At retail level, the combined cinema and video markets are worth about the same as the income the BBC earns from its licence fee. This in turn is equal to roughly 58 percent of the gross value of television advertising.[8] This disparity can largely be explained by the weakening of the British cinema industry throughout the 1980s. By the end of the 1970s it had become extremely difficult for domestic producers to find investment for British films. A change in tax law in 1979 which enabled financial institutions to claim tax relief against investment in films improved things slightly. However, this improvement did not last as in 1985 the government abolished both these tax incentives and the Eady Levy (a levy on box-office takings which was channelled back into film production) and closed down the National Film Finance Corporation, replacing it with

British Screen, a consortium which involved representatives of major film and television companies. Clearly these changes removed protection from the domestic industry and so, as Britain moved into recession, cinema production suffered accordingly.

This weakening of the British film industry clearly impacted upon television; as cinema audiences fell so television was able to provide a form of mass entertainment able to attract the wide audiences not present in the cinemas. However this sense of television as a threat to the cinema industry gradually began to be transformed into something more positive, notably after the establishment of Channel 4 in 1982. Indeed, as in France, the old enmity between television and cinema has been replaced by a rather more positive process of exchange. Channel 4's film production/ transmission arm, Film on Four, can be seen as a paradigm of this new relationship. Although a subsidiary of the Independent Broadcasting Authority, Channel 4 was from the outset given a public service mission described by the Broadcasting Act of 1980 as providing programmes not available on other channels and thus appealing to different audience groups. In contrast to the BBC and the ITV companies, Channel 4 did not produce its own programmes but instead bought in material from independent producers. John Hill suggests that 'it is this combination of a commissioning model of broadcasting and public service principles which also provided the context for the channel's support of films'.[9] The channel began producing films initially intended for television transmission only but gradually a number of these works began to be given cinema release, a fact which led in 1986 to the agreement to reduce waiting periods between cinema and television screenings for films whose budget was less than £1.25 million (this figure was increased to £4 million in 1988). The significance of Film on Four has increased as more and more of its products have received (often quite successful) cinema screenings and as its budget has risen, reaching about £12 million by the early 1990s. It is significant that this increased budget is now spent on a smaller number of films, suggesting that these films are very much produced with a cinematic release in mind; the larger budgets enable production values more in keeping with traditional cinematic aesthetics and are thus perhaps more likely to attract people into cinemas.

Like its French televisual counterparts, Channel 4 invests either through full funding, co-production or pre-purchasing and the amount invested in an individual film can vary quite dramatically. However, the total amount of money invested by the channel is certainly striking; according to Channel 4's own records, between 1982 and 1992 it invested £91 million in 264 cinematic works.[10]

These films display a great diversity, ranging from popular comedies and 'heritage' dramas to more experimental works (notably those produced by the non-profit making workshops financed by Channel 4) and regional films supported by the Scottish Film Production Fund (part financed by Channel 4) and S4C (Channel 4's Welsh-language television channel). Despite this clear diversity it is significant that many of those films seen as being in some way representative of contemporary British cinema were financed by the channel. Films such as *My Beautiful Launderette* (1985), *A Room With A View* (1985) and *Shallow Grave* (1994) can be seen to exemplify different strands of British cinematic production of the 1980s and 1990s as well as being amongst the more successful British films of recent years both in terms of audience figures and critical reception. Thus in some ways British cinema has become coterminous with Film on Four, once again underlining the inextricable nature of the relationship between television and cinema.

Channel 4 is not the only British television channel to invest in cinematic production. Both the independent television companies and the BBC (and to a lesser extent the satellite channels of BSkyB) have film production arms and invest through co-production and pre-purchasing. Like Channel 4, the BBC has shifted from its earlier policy of producing films for television transmission alone to investing in films destined for a cinematic release. These forms of funding are now the main source of income for the British cinematic industry; as in France, a 'national' cinematic product would no longer be possible without the support of the television companies. It is perhaps somewhat ironic that threats to television, so long depicted as the enemy of film, must now also be a threat to the cinema. Thus the system of competitive bidding used to decide the allocation of independent television franchises in 1991 meant a drop in the amount of money available to spend on programme making. Evidently this threat to television production can no longer be a source of glee for the defenders of the cinema, for any such reduction impacts directly upon this industry.

Conclusions

What this overview of cinema and television in Britain and France reveals is the impossibility of defining entirely distinct identities for each medium and for the filmic texts they produce. Cinema is now dependent upon the television companies for financial support but equally television turns to the cinema for a significant proportion of its programming. Television may indeed transform cinematic aesthetics but by the same gesture cinematic films work upon the products of television, a process revealed by the television fictions described above and by the numerous television programmes devoted to the cinema. Television is not, and perhaps never has been, a straightforward threat to the cinema. Current media debate in Britain about the rejuvenation of the domestic film industry is certainly not without truth. However it should be remembered that part of this rejuvenation can be attributed to the television companies which have not only financed film-making but by transmitting films have also established new audiences for the cinematic product. Indeed by showing films on television it may be that they have created a new 'invitation to cinema' articulated through the status and/or the popularity made possible for films by their particular moment of television transmission and reception. To say that television *only* prevents people from going to the cinema is clearly false. The weekly discussion of new cinematic releases on the main French evening news is manifestly an attempt to persuade television spectators to attend cinema screenings. Moreover, as cinema in Britain and France increasingly means a visit to a multiplex or leisure centre, the two experiences can be seen to diverge once again. Audiences may indeed watch films on television but this need not preclude a cinema visit which is now often part of a whole network of leisure/entertainment practices.

This new diversification in terms of reception suggests the need to retain a notion of the difference between cinema and television. Television is implicated in our daily lives in a way that cinema has never been. The negotiation of public and private spaces and identities and the direct transmission of everyday life are central structuring features of this medium; think again of that trip to Paris by Elizabeth II which seemed to so threaten the existence of cinema.[11] Indeed, as I write this chapter and the media come to terms with the death of Diana, Princess of Wales, what appears to be emerging is a very strong sense of the role of television in constructing out daily experience, our public and private identities. The ubiquitousness of television, along with a whole host of other features linked to both production and reception, clearly means that it will never be identical to cinema. However as the relationships described above demonstrate, it is now surely erroneous to posit distinct identities for each medium or to describe the relationship between them in the rather Oedipal terms of threat and ultimate death so often articulated over the last decades. As television companies continue to support the cinema industry and as films are increasingly viewed on the television screen (both through television transmission and video) it becomes imperative to rethink our understanding of filmic texts and of the industries which produce and exhibit them.

Notes and References

1. An example of this type of discourse is provided by the establishment of the Film Industry Defence Organisation (FIDO) in 1958. FIDO set out to protect the cinema industry by extracting a levy on exhibition venues in order to create a film purchasing fund which would prevent the sale of British films to television, and by imposing restrictions on television sales and scheduling. Its impact was limited and it failed to halt the growing relationship between the two industries.
2. Martin McLoone provides an interesting example of this type of dichotomy in his discussion of Alan Parker's film of 1986, *A Turnip-head's Guide to the British Cinema*, in J. Hill and M. McLoone (eds.),*Big Picture Small Screen: The Relation Between Film and Television*, The University of Luton Press, 1997, 76-106.
3. Ibid., 166.
4. 'Le cinéma à la télévision', *Dossiers de l'audiovisuel*, Paris, INA/ La Documentation française, No. 62, July-August 1995.
5. Indicateurs statistiques de l'audiovisuel: données 1995, Paris, La Documentation française, 1996.
6. CNC info, 1997.
7. Ibid.
8. BFI, *Film and Television Handbook*, London, BFI, 1995.
9. J. Hill, M. McLoone, *Big Picture Small Screen*, 1997, 156.
10. Ibid., 158.
11. It is also worth pointing out that early television drama was always transmitted live again suggesting a direct experience, part of 'real time', very different from that provided by the cinema film.

CHAPTER 7

QUALITY, CULTURE AND EDUCATION

SUSAN EMANUEL

> How to marry television and school, how to create a channel that will embrace knowledge, curiosity, continuing education; how to avoid the fatal danger of scholastic programmes; how to include teachers in a venture that can only be managed by media professionals; how to develop interaction between the small screen and its surroundings? These are the major questions posed on the eve of the indispensable creation of a new network. Educational television has finally left the field of abstractions to enter that of concrete experimentation.[1]

The French were wrestling in 1994 with abstract issues that British broadcasting had turned into 'concrete experiments' decades previously. This lag can be ascribed in part to fixed French ideas about the three missions of television (to inform, educate, entertain) and their inherent incompatibility, as well as to their more rigid notion of 'quality' – revolving around high cultural ideas of authorship, artistic expression and distinction. So the French were uncertain how even to start developing educational television for a popular audience. La Cinquième went on air in 1995, occupying the daytime hours of the network belonging in the evening to Arte, itself the troubled cultural channel operating in an uneasy partnership with the Germans, which in turn is the heir of La Sept, the purely French cultural channel the Socialist government had created to compensate for the depredations that followed on the heels of audiovisual deregulation back in 1982. Quality would find a haven in an audiovisual landscape that had been 'polluted' by commercial broadcasting, or rather, by the 'dictatorship' of the ratings. Yet in 1996 the quality bedfellows were not pleased: Culture (Arte) was horrified at having to share a channel with Education (La Cinquième), let alone merge with it, as the latest in a never-ending flurry of legislation in the audiovisual field would have them do.

'Education' and 'Culture': these two stalwart areas of public service broadcasting have fared very differently in the two countries: enshrined in the BBC charter and in U.K. commercial television licences, educational programmes are produced by long-standing specialised production departments. At the BBC for decades now, 'Childrens', 'Schools', and 'Further Education' departments had developed tight links with outside educational and other institutions (often issuing joint support materials and courses), as did Channel 4 even since it was established in 1982. They have cultivated a pluralistic approach to their mission. In France, by contrast, despite efforts at *formation* by ORTF, the media have only recently been conceived as a partner of education – which is still a monolithic national establishment. As programmes with a general pedagogic purpose have been squeezed off the deregulated landscape, the new compensatory channel (this one launched by a conservative government) – a 'meeting between television and school that was missed in the 1960s', according to Francis Balle (a media scholar who has been both on the media regulatory body and in the Education Ministry) – was finally created, overcoming a long-standing lack of political will to make the match. La Cinquième, chiming in with the vogue for *éducation permanente*, ironically occupies the daytime airwaves of the defunct commercial channel created by Silvio Berlusconi. It promises, in the words of its chief, Jean-Marie Cavada (a former current affairs producer who was head of Antenne 2 but failed to get the top job in state television), to 'link knowledge to pleasure', to 'arouse curiosity without being boring'.

But the separation of cultural and educational programmes from the television mainstream (on a channel received by just 83 percent of its citizens, and in competition with the two remaining cash-strapped public channels) risks further fragmenting the national audience. Moreover, the French and German branches of Arte have for several years been trading accusations of 'pedagogic' and 'didactic' about each other's programmes. There is no perceived symmetry between 'quality' and 'popular education' in France – in fact for decades the terms 'culture' and 'television' were thought to be antithetical. Britain, by contrast, has long enjoyed a national and vibrant *television culture*, in which viewers can be enlightened and entertained at the same time, where what is good for you is not hived off from what you want to watch.

History

The vocation of public service television in Europe is no longer taken for granted, as it was before deregulation, (see chapter 4). France has witnessed the most dramatic shift, from three state-run channels to a situation in which the most popular channel (TF1) and the most prestigious (the pay channel Canal Plus) leave dwindling audience shares and advertising revenues for the remaining state ones, France 2 and France 3, who must also contend with a host of cable and satellite channels. Following the Television without Frontiers initiative (TWF), voluntary quotas of works of European origin and French expression were dropped by commercial competitors or shunted to off-peak hours. In this highly competitive atmosphere of deregulation and struggle for audience share, quality television programming was in a particularly vulnerable position. La Sept was created in 1987 to redress some of these trends: the choice was made for an explicitly cultural and educational, rather than a generalist, channel – despite widespread fears that this would exacerbate the drift toward 'ghettoisation'. Originally intended partly as an industrial gamble in new communications technologies (enabling Europe to rival America and Japan in hardware), it soon dropped its initial satellite platform and then its D2Mac format, (see chapter 14). It struggled to find an identity that could not be accused of being metropolitan, intellectual and élitist, as well as to secure a measurable audience before legislative patience ran out. La Sept was truly an orphan: after a period 'squatting' on FR3, it was awarded La Cinq's old frequency, to the fury of conservatives; then it became the unwilling bride of Germany, as Mitterrand held the diplomatic shotgun as part of his Maastricht strategy. Paris is now the French co-production wing of Arte's headquarters in Strasbourg; the German branch in Baden Baden draws on the output of the federal networks and satellite channels, which already have a cultural thrust.

Somewhere along the way, Sept's only explicitly educational department, '*Jeunesse*', which had specialised in media and cultural literacy series (as pioneered in the 1970s by INA, the Institut National de l'Audiovisuel) and then switched to magazines about '*insertion*', finally disappeared altogether. Budgetary constraints inflected Arte's schedules toward documentary, studio discussions and 'theme evenings'; nationalist resistance to reading subtitles spelled two further departures from the 'purity' of the image: the introduction of dubbing and the use of on-camera (bilingual) presenters. Still enjoying the high profile backing of cultural élites, Arte claims to have raised its ratings share from 2 percent to 3 percent.

While Arte does not really monopolise 'quality' programming in France – other channels have made imaginative imports from abroad and/or explored popular genres like serials and the 'reality show' – it *thinks* it does, and it is *perceived* as doing so, and therefore merits extended scrutiny.

Arte

According to its English-language press release at its launch coinciding with the Maastricht treaty, Arte 'is not a proposition for impatient 'zappers' who are whimsically drawn to some programme only to linger there a few seconds. It wants to attract enquiring minds.' Synthesising the high cultural mentality of La Sept and the more generalist German approach that stressed social and political issues, Arte promised it would offer a selection that 'transcends the 'official' concept of culture...a menu served up fresh, not from tin cans' – a culinary metaphor that obliquely takes a swipe at the common adversary – the U.S. mass media. Its defensive stance was apparent:

> The European Cultural Channel might be open to two kinds of misconception. The word 'European' is equated with the administrative machinery in Brussels, while 'Culture' is perceived as a mixture of extravagance and boredom. The viewer should feel quite free to dismiss these prejudices. Arte takes culture beyond the concepts of theatre, music and literature. And no contribution is ripped apart [sic] by publicity.

For the German and French partners, then, the bipartisan approach is a negative one, defined less in respect to national-popular broadcasting traditions than in opposition to what is perceived as the American broadcasting model: entertainment and its pernicious effects on European television. The ghosts at the Strasbourg banquet belong to the Frankfurt School.

The low take-up of cultural programmes on television is something that had worried French state channels in the 1970s as a by-product of the 'cultural democratisation' movement. There is still a kind of nostalgia for the Buttes-Chaumont studio plays, when the whole nation sat down to watch an adaptation of Aeschylus. France saw a slow shift from the use of television to disseminate high culture relayed from other media, to an incorporation of 'creative television' on the *auteur* basis of the cinematic aesthetic (the name Jean-Christophe Averty heads the list of *télé-auteurs*). Television, it was felt, might indeed become the '8th art' if directors were left alone by the ratings-obsessed executives. But *auteur cinema* was still the aesthetic model, (see chapter 6). Arte markets its programmes on the basis of authorship, usually the directorial signature.

The best television in the world?

The advantages held by Britain – from the legacy of wartime radio, to 'arm's length' regulatory oversight, to its world-wide Anglophone market – in developing and sustaining a popular television culture are well known enough to permit me to skip over them. The label of quality was long synonymous with the BBC copyright, no matter what the genre, from dramas to sit-coms to series on generalist subjects (astronomy, cooking, dog-training), invariably presented by quirky figures who became household names. The experience of explicitly cultural programmes is paradigmatic. In the 1960s, when the Music and Arts Department led viewers on the 'involuntary ascent of the cultural pyramid' (as one Director General put it), the paternalist motive of developing the audience was paramount. The 'relay' approach was succeeded by the profile and then by a more creative interpretation of the arts, involving some elements of emotionalism and narrative. This form was pioneered by *Monitor* in the 1960s and still appears on *The South Bank Show*, the flagship of commercial television's arts coverage (and imported by an American cultural cable channel). In parallel ran the tradition of illustrated lectures: Lord Clark's *Civilisation* (1969) was the forerunner of a long line of blockbuster (and lucratively exported) arts series that did not fall into disrepute until the late 1980s – although Sister Wendy's art history series seems to have revived it! Then there was a strand of creative (or self-indulgent) biographies, typified by the work of Ken Russell. As John Wyver concluded:

> This trilogy of the profile, the lecture, and dramatised biography retains its dominance today, as do the organising principles which each element utilises: narrative, individuals, feeling rather than analysis, and a positivist concept of knowledge. These principles are complemented by a series of assumptions about the value and worth of the 'arts', assumptions which also issue from a specific history.[2]

But, importantly, 'quality' has not been identified with high culture, but rather found to reside across the spectrum of broadcasting: in sketch and situation comedy, in serials, made-for-television movies, even game shows (*Mastermind*). Nor has British television been averse to drawing lessons from American television, or from importing what are perceived as the best the United States has to offer.

A hunger for knowledge?

Together, Children's, Schools and Continuing Education, and The Open University transmitted over 2000 hours in 1995-6, or about one-seventh of the total airtime of BBC1 and BBC2. These departments consumed about 11 percent of the total television budget, with costs per hour roughly midway along the spectrum between expensive drama and cheap parliament. Occasionally one of their programmes emerges into the mainstream, as happened with the stylised adaptation of Dickens's *Hard Times*. They are busy exploiting new technologies like the Internet and CD-ROMs. Meanwhile, at Channel 4 power is held by commissioning editors: with a mandate of diversity, heads of units such as Minorities have pioneered topics, presenters and formats that occasionally achieve popularity and/or critical acclaim, in turn stimulating the BBC and commercial broadcasters. Significantly, the television institutions in Britain privilege the *producer* not the writer or director (except in drama).

France's specific history is quite different from Britain's: a relatively monolithic hierarchy of taste, centrally maintained by a pyramid of funding institutions and arbiters. As dependent as the British on the notion that 'art is good for you,' the French are more analytical and less positivist than the British. A comparison of the web sites of the British and French channels reveals the extent to which French television still markets authorship and seeks validation among film juries, as well as the narrower and more traditional subject demarcations for school-targeted series and the amount of unstructured 'general interest' material for everyone else. Creativity is held to be the purview of the *réalisateur*, not the producer or departmental unit from which the programme arises. There is no strong documentary tradition (except as an adjunct of 1960s *auteurism*) nor a commitment to production in series, and the approach to television, despite disclaimers, is resolutely intellectual, condescending and oriented to spoken discourse. The widespread view is that the written word is subverted by the image, that audiovisual communication is an obstacle to thought. The notion that television could serve education has scarcely gained a foothold in France. As Balle, one of the promoters of an education channel, put it in 1994:

> I am agitating these days for a reconciliation of the image with thought, as well as for the use in school of images that in the future their users will mix with sounds and texts, which will similarly serve both entertainment and education. Technical progress shows us what is at stake: to put audiovisual or computing educational tools at the disposition of teachers of whatever discipline.[3]

Significantly, Balle's plea ends with the statement, echoing countless others, that seizing this opportunity is one sure way of escaping the deluge of American images. In the same media journal, Jean-Claude Carrière, scriptwriter and head of the French film school, maintained that there was indeed a great hunger for knowledge – and not just among students – but that entertainment should not be neglected; the governing spirit of the new channel should be

Rabelaisian. Jean-Marie Cavada was quoted by *Le Monde* as drawing a distinction between two types of viewers, the *'citoyens exigeants'* who are looking for generalist fare, and the *'consommateurs plus fluides'* who stumble onto a programme via zapping. Though La Cinquième clearly prefers the former, it soon altered its continuity style toward short segments.

Media scholars often remark on a convergence between serious and popular television. But the quintessential American educational series, *Sesame Street*, is regarded by hostile French critics on the left as a symbolic matrix of the fusion of compensatory education, media technology and mass culture. It is an industrially produced commodity, as Michèle Mattelart observed in 1985:

> The series is poles apart from that 'inspired' improvisation, that form of creativity associated with the solitary genius of an author, of a scriptwriter of a director, of an entertainer. [It is] the work of an interdisciplinary team to co-ordinate areas of knowledge and to map the educational initiative with all the instruments of science and techniques of management.

Sesame Street is prototypical of the seepage of the advertising aesthetic into television as a whole, she says. If educational television in France took as its aim, as Carrière urged, a media literacy that encouraged viewers to watch other channels, it would fall victim to the same syndrome. Therefore educational television should be opposed on principle, as a threat to reading, argue its opponents in the educational establishment. Moreover, with twelve hours a day of programming to fill, on a budget of FF 775 million (half what Arte has for its five prime-time hours), it remains to be seen whether La Cinquième could *afford* to package its education entertainingly enough to attract a significant audience. (And Arte does not relish having to build up its audience from an educational platform – much as BBC2 tried to get the Open University off its late afternoon and early evening schedules – and instead has often started off the evening with British comedies like 'Monty Python', very weirdly sub-titled, as you may imagine). Public television that is free of advertising is not thereby immune from ratings pressure.

Quality

Whatever the combination of financing by licence fee and by advertising, television institutions in Europe strive for quality by balancing what is particularly national with what is internationally marketable, what is critically acclaimed (the aesthetic values espoused by forums such as the Prix Italia) with what wins a good sized audience. For many years, co-production with foreign countries was seen as a panacea for the panic caused by escalating programme costs; this trend was aided – and inflected in the direction of international art cinema, I believe – by various European subsidy schemes, (see chapter 13).

While there is a tendency in both countries to equate quality with big budgets that feature star actors and recognisable production values, 'quality' is a term that has become problematised on both sides of the English Channel. Whereas it used to connote national prestige and the production values and ethos of the public service, by the 1990s it was carrying negative connotations: over-budgeted, stuffy, beholden to literary or high culture values. As Anthony Smith noted in his introduction to the BFI monograph, *The Question of Quality*, it would be the keyword of the 1990s, as 'monopoly' had been in the 1920s. The Broadcasting White Paper of 1988 made it one of three themes (after the more Thatcherite 'Competition' and 'Choice'), and marked a shift away from paternalism and toward consumerism. In Britain, quality had moved from being synonymous with specialist and minority and toward synonymy with commercial success. In fact, it had become 'television's Holy Grail'; pursuing the subject beyond the ritual invocation of *Brideshead Revisited* and *The Jewel in the Crown,* but amidst a general academic reticence on the matter, the commentators on the issue in 1990 delineated seven clusters of meaning around Quality that may help us in comparing British and French discourses on the subject.

1. **Professional definitions** (by broadcasters and critics) value craftsmanship and 'creative freedom' and sovereignty in general. In the BBC milieu, for example, 'features' producers value the well-crafted literary adaptation above all but will appreciate a 'quirky' documentary if it got on the air against opposition from 'upstairs'.
2. **Traditional aesthetics** attempts to derive value from specific characteristics of the medium itself – its ephemerality, for example. This approach has both conservative variants (Neil Postman) and liberal ones (Umberto Eco).
3. **Realist paradigms** are common to popular taste and have been particularly important in British cultural studies, where texts are often valued on the basis of their authentic depiction of actual social conditions.
4. **Market** definitions shift the centre of gravity from producer to consumer; the simplest makes quality a function of ratings. More sophisticated neo-classical economics takes into account different rewards offered to different audiences by different programme

types, and may even argue for zones of protection for some that are not commercially viable.
5. **Moral paradigms** ascribe quality to those forms of television that convey information and inspire action, whether by addressing the viewer as a citizen or as an expressive person. The debate about children and exposure to violence falls into this category.
6. **Ritual and communion** paradigms value television for the social link and democratic levelling it may promote.
7. **Diversity** would measure the quality of television by its pluralism; one of the underlying rationales for the creation of Channel 4.

Observing Britain in 1990, Charlotte Brunsdon concluded that official British discourse about quality was a combination of 3 and 5, the realist and moral paradigms. Realism pertains to both commonsense aesthetics and to professional codes, deriving from the film documentary movement of the 1930s and its subsequent influence on the style and content of feature and television films (Ken Loach, Mike Leigh). Moral purpose was the sine qua non of Quality in critical discourses about film from the Second World War onward. Protection of the population from vulgarity and violence has been a preoccupation of all Broadcasting Standards Councils. Brunsdon finds nothing wrong with these two discourses in themselves; the problem 'lies in conceiving of cultural texts solely or primarily in moral or realist terms which remove the possibility of what we might call the 'aesthetic defense'.[4] For her and other critics on the left, the most important principle to be advanced in thinking about quality was diversity (7).

By contrast, as I have argued, the aesthetic defence predominates in France. Until recently, quality was seldom discussed in relation to television at all; hence professional definitions (1) have had the field to themselves, though some sociologists of the media (e.g., Wolton) have put stress on ritual functions (6). In any case, there is remarkable divergence between British and French discourses of quality.

The internationalisation of the television market, however, is shifting the definition of quality: in France, the term is no longer confined to European and cinematically oriented products, and is even being newly applied to imported American drama series in a realist tradition (one summer France 2 had a critical and ratings hit with *Urgences/ER*) which have long been part of the British landscape. There is a reaction to the fingerprints of Jacobin production styles in France, I believe, to the extent that *'de haute qualité'* can assume negative overtones there, too. Insofar as Arte claims to stand for 'quality' in traditional terms, it marks it as marginal to mainstream broadcasting. It seems likely to me that La Cinquième, despite its use of independent production companies, will be similarly constrained by this cultural ideology, especially if it tries to combat the accusation of being 'too generalist' (filling its hours with films such as *The Wizard of Oz*). This split between high and low would be inconceivable in a television culture like Britain's, which has cultivated (and exported) outstanding work in all genres and which maintains no dichotomy between 'popular' and 'quality.'

In conclusion, the internationalisation of the television market will both mitigate the fear of American media imperialism (and make it possible to adapt formats like the 'reality show') and also increase the circulation of quality and educational series and one-offs, ranging from scientific and historical documentaries to European magazine programmes like *Continentales* and *Confetti*, (see chapter 12), not forgetting adaptations of literary works – all tailored to pre-sale if not co-produced. Whether or not popularisation in the sense of what the French call '*médiatisation*' can be achieved without a concomitant loss of what *they* would consider quality, remains an open question as long as culture is separated from everyday life, education from pluralism, and quality is measured by the standards of official culture.

Notes and References

I would like to express my thanks to Professor Shoggy Waryn of Ohio State for commenting on a draft of this paper.
1. J. Chancel (ed.), *Les écrits de l'image*, no. 2, Spring 1994.
2. J. Wyver, 'Representing Art or Reproducing Culture? – Tradition and Innovation in British Television's coverage of the Arts (1959-87)', in P. Hayward (ed.) *Picture This*, London, John Libbey, 1988.
3. F. Balle in J. Chancel (ed.), *Les écrits de l'image*.
4. C. Brunsdon, 'Problems with Quality', *Screen 31:1*, Spring 1990, 67-90.

PART III

THE NEW MEDIA

CHAPTER 8

SATELLITE TELEVISION

PETER GOODWIN

In early 1996, just before the launch of digital satellite services in France, some 5.3 percent of French households had a satellite dish. This was, noted *La Lettre du CSA*, a spectacular eightfold increase over the previous four years. But, the CSA analysts immediately added, that figure looked distinctly limited when compared with an estimated 15.9 percent of British households having a satellite dish in March 1996.[1] One can quibble about the exact figures,[2] but the quibbles do not get us away from the basic fact that in the middle of the 1990s, roughly three times as many British households as French, had bought themselves into 'satellite television'.

In this chapter, I want to explore answers to two questions. The first is straightforward. Why has there been such a striking difference in take-up of satellite between the two countries? The second is more complex. What is the more general significance of this difference for the future of television in the two countries? The two questions are clearly related, but, as I shall argue, they are, both logically and substantially, distinct.

What is 'satellite television'?

The term 'satellite television' is a sloppy one. And, in Britain in particular, it has often been burdened with a baggage of quite contingent associations.[3] So it is wise to start with a reminder of what exactly it is. In essence, satellite is no more and no less than one of three main current technologies for the distribution of television programmes. The other two are terrestrial and cable.

Satellite can, and is, widely used to transmit pictures and sound to a broadcaster. The broadcaster can then redistribute those pictures and sound to the homes of its viewers by one or more of either terrestrial, cable or satellite means. So, to give any precise sense to the term 'satellite television' we have to narrow it down to a potentially misleading shorthand for Direct-to-Home (or DTH) television distribution via satellite.

That definition carries with it one terminological caveat, and three important reminders. The caveat is that satellite distribution to the home does not necessarily mean a dish on that home. It may mean a dish on that apartment block or group of apartment blocks. This is known as Single Master Antenna Television or SMATV. In practice, for the purposes of this chapter, we can more or less forget about SMATV. It has been of little importance in U.K. satellite television developments. In France, relative to 'pure' DTH, SMATV may have been more important. But it has not been sufficiently important to alter the basic fact of very marked differences in home satellite take-up between the two countries.

The reminders are much more important. They need emphasising, because the term 'satellite television' has so often conjured up much more than a mere technology of distribution. The first reminder is that the means of distribution of television programming to the home in itself carries no inherent implications as to what that programming will be, who will provide it, how it will be packaged, nor how it will be paid for. Any one of terrestrial, cable or satellite distribution could in principle carry anything from pornography to business news, could package it in any way from the completely generalist to the most esoteric niche, and could pay for it by public funds, advertising or direct charge to the viewer. So, for example, although subscription is commonly associated with cable or satellite distribution, in France it has happily been employed to fund a significant terrestrial channel, Canal Plus.

The second reminder is that the distribution of programming by one means, is no barrier to it being distributed by another. In principle any channel can be distributed to the home by any combination of cable, terrestrial or satellite, or by all three. In Germany, for example, a dozen channels, including most of the main ones, are each distributed by all three means.

The last reminder is that consumers are likely to choose channels not simply, or even primarily, because of how they are distributed, but because of what is on them and how it compares with what they already have. Of course, consumers are not indifferent to how much the differences in distribution may cost them. And they clearly cannot be indifferent as to whether one particular technology of distribution actually reaches them while another does not. But, those important qualifications aside, it is programming, and the marketing of that programming, that counts most with the viewer, not the technology of distribution.

These three reminders should add up to one big warning against the sort of technological determinism that has underpinned so much debate on television broadcasting in so many countries for so much of the last twenty years. But they should not be taken to imply that there are no differences between the technologies, nor that these differences can, under certain circumstances, have more far-reaching implications.

Traditionally, in most countries, television has been distributed to most households terrestrially. So terrestrial distribution is very widely established and the reception of extra channels (or, at least, extra analogue channels) requires little or no extra purchase of equipment by the viewer, or investment in distribution by the broadcaster. Terrestrial distribution suffers from the disadvantage that (using analogue technology) it can only deliver about half a dozen channels. However, it is important to note that the precise number of terrestrial channels available is a question both of technological development within the terrestrial field and of regulatory decision. In Britain, for example, the fourth and fifth terrestrial channels started broadcasting many years after they were first technologically available (see chapter 3).

Cable distribution is as old as television and has always offered the technical potential of extra channels, but technological developments and regulatory requirements have increased the number of channels potentially available on 'standard' cable systems over the last thirty years. The great disadvantage of cable is that to reach homes by it requires the substantial sunk cost of laying the cable system. Moreover, that cable system is laid area by area. So more widespread distribution involves proportionately greater sunk costs (see chapter 8).

Direct-to-Home satellite distribution offers the same possibility as cable of extra channels (although, whether more or less than cable, varies). However, DTH has the advantage over cable, that its services are immediately available to national audiences, if they buy (or rent) a dish, once the initial investment in a transponder is made by the broadcaster. Like cable, the number of extra channels potentially offered by satellite has increased over time, from the couple offered by early analogue DBS (Direct Broadcasting Satellite) systems to the hundreds offered by digital broadcasting on current medium-powered satellites. DTH broadcasting by satellite has the additional technological feature, which neither cable nor terrestrial has, of being able to cross international frontiers freer (but not absolutely free) of national regulatory constraints.

Lastly, we need to add that digital technology increases the number of channels potentially deliverable by all distribution systems.

With digital, rather than analogue, broadcasting, terrestrial distribution can deliver, not half a dozen, but twenty channels; satellite and cable can deliver, not dozens, but hundreds.

We should not underestimate the importance of such technological developments within each of the distribution systems. In the early 1980s the early DTH (or DBS) satellites offered as few as two channels in addition to the handful potentially available via terrestrial television. Together this was considerably less than can be offered by purely digital terrestrial television distribution in the 1990s. So, we cannot just limit ourselves to the general observation that satellite or cable offer extra channels. We also need to ask, in the given circumstances, how many extra channels? Just two satellite channels may offer no more 'extra' television, than full and skilful allocation of the half dozen terrestrial channels potentially available. Two hundred satellite channels offer the possibility of new forms of programming, like near-video-on-demand (using perhaps ten channels for a single movie) which would simply be impossible with only two.

We can now turn to examining how these general observations bear on concrete developments in Britain and France. The comparative progress of satellite television in the two countries can best be understood, by dividing developments into three distinct periods. The first runs from the beginning of serious practical consideration of satellite television in the late 1970s and early 1980s through to the end of the eighties. It is the period of plans for 'official' national high-powered DBS. The second runs through from roughly the end of the 1980s until the middle of the 1990s. It is the period of medium-powered analogue DTH. The third begins in mid-1990. It is the period of digital broadcasting, and also of more established cable systems in the two countries. We are still in its early stages.

Phase One: failed dreams for DBS

The practical possibilities of DTH satellite broadcasting hit both Britain and France at almost exactly the same time. In 1977 the World Radio Administrative Conference awarded each country a handful of television channels on high powered satellites (often referred to as DBS) for direct broadcasting to the home. By the early 1980s both French and British had governments embarked on ambitious plans for these.[4]

There were important differences in the approaches of the two governments. The French government was earlier in formulating its initial plans than the British; it envisaged a greater role for state support; it paid more attention to some of the specifics of possible programming; and unlike the British, its plans involved both an element of collaboration with another country (Germany) [5] and the parallel national development of medium-powered satellites alongside the high-powered DBS ones.

Most of these differences could be easily interpreted as exemplifying some of the more general stereotypes of French and British approaches to communications policy: the French more dirigiste, cultural and European; the British more laissez-faire, less cultural and less European (see chapter 14). Had either project succeeded, no doubt much would be made of this. But these apparently important differences in government approach to DBS were eventually to prove much less important than the similarities between the two strategies. Both strategies were based primarily, not on broadcasting considerations, but on industrial ones. Early plans for satellite development in both countries were motivated far more by what they could do for the French and British aerospace and electronics industries, than what they might do for the respective country's broadcasting ecology.

Both projects were also delayed and transformed by the difficulties in motivating the appropriate parties to come together to deliver them. And by the time that both projects actually got their satellites into space in the late 1980s, events had overtaken them. Both French and British high-powered DBS satellite systems, each delivering only a handful of extra channels, effectively became white elephants soon after they were launched.

Phase Two: Murdoch in Britain. Why no Murdoch in France?

In Britain the event that overtook the plans for national high-powered satellites, was the development in the technology of medium-powered satellites, which by the late 1980s enabled them too to deliver direct to the home with a modestly sized dish. High-powered, nationally controlled DBS satellites were no longer the only potential players in the DTH market. This opened the real possibility of using satellite distribution to cross national frontiers, thereby by-passing national regulators. In the British market, Rupert Murdoch rapidly took full advantage of that possibility by announcing in 1988 the launch of a British-oriented multichannel Sky package, broadcast via Astra, the Luxembourg licensed private medium-powered satellite. The British-directed Sky package of channels launched on time in March 1989, fourteen months before the launch of BSB, the 'official' (i.e., DBS) U.K. satellite television.

Those fourteen months proved decisive. In the few months of its independent existence BSB never even approached clawing back the advantage Sky had gained from its earlier start.

The burden of launching the British-directed Sky was a considerable drain on the then debt-ridden News Corporation. So, instead of BSB simply being ground into oblivion by its upstart rival, the demise of BSB took a slightly different form – a merger with Sky, and the creation, largely on Murdoch's terms, of BSkyB, at the end of 1990. The result was that Britain had, from that date, an effectively monopoly provider of 'extra' television services, with an effective monopoly of feature film and sports rights, and of subscription management. Excluded from terrestrial distribution, and with cable networks still covering only a fraction of U.K. television households, BSkyB grew largely by satellite distribution. By the end of 1990, according to one estimate,[6] 5 percent of British households had a dish, by the end of 1995 16 percent had one – virtually all of them for only one reason, to receive BSkyB's programming package plus the channels that clustered around it. In practical terms, if you wanted extra television in the U.K. in this period, there was no alternative to BSkyB. BSkyB had the movies, it had the sport and it had the subscription management service.

In France, the 'official' DBS service turned out just as dismally as in Britain, although for rather different reasons. When it eventually arrived it broadcast only one channel – and that, a not widely attractive, 'cultural' one – which was not available via terrestrial distribution. And even that channel was soon to be distributed terrestrially (after the demise of La Cinq). The result was that satellite television in France in the early 1990s lacked the single-minded drive that BSkyB offered in the U.K. It grew, but far more slowly than in the U.K. And what growth there was, was split. There were those who got a dish because of inadequate terrestrial distribution, and there were not insignificant numbers of North African immigrants who got a dish to receive Arabic programming.[7] The more conventional 'extra' multichannel package was only provided (by Canalsatellite) in 1992 – three years after Sky's U.K. launch. By the end of 1995 it had gained only 305,00[8] subscribers (less than 2 percent of French households).

The crucial difference in satellite take-up between France and the U.K., is, therefore, primarily a phenomenon of the first half of the 1990s. In both countries 'official' DBS was late in starting, and when it did start rapidly fizzled out. But in Britain BSkyB successfully filled the gap; in France there was no equivalent.

Why? We might seek for explanations on the demand side. Two immediately offer themselves. The French have in general been slower than the British at taking up new communications technologies. French households, for example, spend less on videos and have fewer home computers than their British equivalents. But these general differences do not seem enough to explain the three-to-one difference in satellite take-up. Secondly, there is the question of the existing offer of 'free' terrestrially distributed television in the two countries. The stronger that existing offer, the weaker we would expect the demand for additional television services to be. Before satellite actually got started there were five 'free' terrestrial television channels reaching most of the French population, compared with only four in the U.K. But the U.K. channels were better funded, and because of their history and regulatory framework, more diversely programmed, than the French (see chapters 2, 3 and 5). Differences in the strength of the 'free' terrestrial offer, therefore, also do not seem sufficient to explain the striking difference in satellite take-up between the two countries.

What may be more important on the demand side (and as I shall argue is certainly important on the supply side) is the successful establishment in France in 1984 of a fourth terrestrial channel, financed primarily by subscription, Canal Plus. By the time Sky launched in the U.K., Canal Plus already had over 2 million subscribers in France. Two important programming strengths of Canal Plus were first-run movies and premium sports events. In the U.K., BSkyB's provision of these two programme strands were widely seen as the main reason for dish take-up. So it may be that multi-channel satellite television grew in Britain, from 1989 onwards, because it provided the same premium and subscription-funded services that had already been (at least in part) provided for five years by a single terrestrial channel in France.

So the early establishment of Canal Plus would appear to be the main explanation for the relative performance of satellite in France and the U.K. And that speculation is reinforced when we look at one other alternative explanation. Perhaps demand for 'extra' television services was satisfied by cable in France more than in Britain. But the progress of cable build was little greater in France than in Britain during most of the relevant period.[9] The thesis that the comparatively slow growth of satellite in France is to be mainly explained by the fact that Canal Plus already delivered terrestrially the centrepiece of what BSkyB delivered in the U.K. would only have been fully tested had an equivalent of Rupert Murdoch launched a French-directed DTH service around 1990. No such equivalent appeared. Why?

Three possible explanations present themselves – one regulatory, the other two concerned with business strategies. The French government positively discouraged an 'extra-national' DTH player. In particular it used its influence to discourage CLT (Compagnie Luxembourgeoise de télédiffusion) from playing such a role. The British government, in contrast, was friendly to Murdoch and, at the very least, turned a blind eye to his infringements of regulation. Secondly, the potential candidates for a French-oriented DTH service, again most particularly CLT, were, during the relevant period preoccupied with the birth of commercial television elsewhere, for instance in Germany and the Netherlands. Thirdly, any potential DTH player in the French market faced the problem that the rights to much of the programming most attractive to subscription customers were already held in France by Canal Plus.

Canal Plus therefore figures on both the demand and supply sides of the basic explanation for the difference in satellite take-up in France and Britain in the first half of the 1990s. In the U.K. satellite television has in practice been about subscription,[10] largely for films and sport. In France Canal Plus already provided that, thus largely meeting latent programming demand without the need for satellite. The established position of Canal Plus also added to the other factors in France which discouraged possible satellite supply.

Phase Three: digital prospects

Reviewing the position of satellite in France in 1992, Raymond Kuhn concluded, 'in comparison with Germany and Britain ... France is well behind in the satellite television race and there seems little prospect of it ever making up the lost ground'.[11] That might seem a reasonable enough prognosis if we view developments solely through the distorting lens of something called 'satellite television'. It looks distinctly less reasonable if we look at recent television developments from a wider perspective. Here, one other race stands out, the pay-television race. And in that race, by 1992, France was not a laggard, but the co-leader in Europe, alongside the U.K. British-directed BSkyB and French-directed Canal Plus were the two pay-television kings of Europe. In that pay-television race it mattered little that Canal Plus was distributed primarily terrestrially, while BSkyB was distributed primarily by satellite. Both companies had within their respective national markets a dominant position in respect of subscriber management, major film and sports rights and the packaging of 'extra' television services.

Direct payment by the viewer has not only been a major development in the television marketplace, it has also seemed to carry with it a desire for more. Viewers who become used to paying for one extra bit of television soon seem to become willing to pay for further bits. That provides openings for new pay-television players, but the people best placed to provide and market those further bits are the already dominant players in the pay-television market. So, in Britain, BSkyB has continually added to its own and associated channels, while in France, Canal Plus took a share in new cable channels and, in 1992, launched them via satellite as Canal satellite. As we have seen, the results of the analogue Canal satellite initiative were not impressive. But perhaps Canal Plus was not yet really trying on the satellite front. It had, after all, a still growing terrestrially distributed pay television business to protect. By the mid-1990s that business was reaching its limits. There was also the prospect of powerful consortia (including both multinational commercial broadcasters and other French terrestrial operators) challenging Canal Plus's dominance of the French pay-television market by using digital satellite technology. So Canal Plus tried harder by launching its own digital satellite service, Canalsatellite Numérique in April 1996. Only a year later that digital satellite service had more than 300,000 subscribers (as many in a year as its analogue satellite service had gained in more than three) of whom perhaps a third were conversions from Canal Plus's old analogue satellite service, while two-thirds were new. The anticipated digital satellite competition arrived in December 1996 with the start-up of Télévision Par Satellite (TPS), a consortium including the commercial television multinational, CLT-UFA and French terrestrial broadcasters, TF1, France Télévision and M6. By April 1997 TPS had received 116,000 orders.[12] So, from 1996, France had, in one sense, leapt ahead in the 'satellite race' – it already had digital satellite up and running, with a consequent mushrooming of channels, and the reality of new services like pay-per-view.[13]

In the U.K. BSkyB was still hedging its digital bets. Perhaps wisely. As cable infrastructures are eventually laid down, and as the digital revolution increases the capacity of cable, terrestrial and satellite, potential pay-television players have a variety of distribution systems to choose between or combine together. By the mid-1990s, BSkyB was adding new subscribers almost as rapidly via cable distribution, as via DTH.[14] But, so far as programme packaging was concerned, the U.K.'s cable companies remained effectively dependent on BSkyB. Even within cable households BSkyB and its associated channels remained predominant in the viewing of 'extra' television. The cable companies remained unable to establish an effective alternative 'cable-only' package.

At the same time BSkyB looked likely to take advantage of the U.K. government's determination to take a lead in digital terrestrial television by being a major programme supplier to the consortium which has been awarded the British digital terrestrial multiplexes.[15] So digital terrestrial television will provide BSkyB with an additional platform to market its most successful pay channels to homes it has not yet reached via cable or satellite. Finally, by 1997, BSkyB was poised to take advantage of the hundreds of extra channels offered by digital satellite broadcasting (which enabled new programming possibilities like near-video-on-demand, NVOD) by launching a U.K.-directed digital DTH service.

In other words, the already dominant U.K. pay-television player was set to use all the technologies of distribution to extend its pay-television market. And because it was the already dominant pay-television player in the U.K. market, BSkyB is in pole position to exploit all new distribution developments in that market.

The same goes for Canal Plus in the French market. There are, of course, important differences. Canal Plus had built up its dominant pay position via terrestrial distribution, BSkyB via satellite. Canal Plus was earlier in the field with digital satellite, BSkyB looked like being earlier in the field with digital terrestrial. But these historical differences in use of distribution systems look set to fade into insignificance in the late 1990s, as in each case a single dominant national pay-television player exploits its established market advantages to extend pay-television using a combination of all distribution technologies.

Conclusion

There are four crucial lessons to be drawn from a comparison of British and French satellite developments. The first confirms our initial general propositions about the nature of 'satellite television'. Satellite is only one among several systems of television distribution to the home. What can be done via satellite can be done (wholly or partly) via other distribution systems, and what is done via satellite is inextricably bound up with what is being done via cable and terrestrial distribution.

Secondly, the key television development in both Britain and France over the past decade and a half has been neither 'satellite television' nor 'cable television' nor even 'multichannel television' – rather it has been pay-television. It is only by grasping that central development that we can begin to understand how the growing distribution possibilities have and will be used.

Thirdly, France and Britain provide two key examples of the enormous advantages that accrue to those who establish themselves early in a national pay-television market. They tend to be near-monopoly players in their respective national markets and that dominance tends to persist. It is a dominance based on rights, programme packaging, marketing and subscriber management – not on the monopoly of a particular technology of distribution.

Lastly, how much have different national government policies influenced these pay-television developments? A comparison between France and Britain suggests both the possibilities and the limitations of national government policy in this field. In both countries early government DBS policies failed miserably, largely because they were industrially and technologically driven rather than programme driven (the same might also be said of early cable policies in both countries). In Britain Rupert Murdoch's successful launch of Sky/BSkyB was, on the face of it, proof of satellite's supposed technological ability to completely circumvent national regulation. Comparison with France, however, suggests that national governments are by no means rendered completely powerless by a single new distribution technology. In France, as we have seen, there was no equivalent of Murdoch largely because of the prior existence of Canal Plus. And the prior existence of Canal Plus was most definitely the result of a national government decision. Also, as pay-television operators become as dependent on cable and digital terrestrial distribution as on satellite, then even pay-television's satellite operations have to take note of national regulation. For example, if the U.K. government was policing its cable systems in the same way as the French government is, then by the mid-1990s even BSkyB would be forced to take at least some note – because a significant proportion of its business is now via cable. At the same time, as it extends its operations into satellite, Canal Plus eases itself away from previously tight domestic regulation.

If BSkyB is now apparently unsusceptible to national regulation, that is more because of its size and dominance in the pay-television market, not because of its original main technology of distribution. What goes for BSkyB also increasingly goes for Canal Plus, as it spreads out from its terrestrial origins. Increasingly, how much each of the nationally dominant pay-television players is nationally regulated will be a question of the political will of its respective government, and of its own market power, rather than a product of its technology of distribution.

Five years from now the satellite origins of BSkyB and the terrestrial origins of Canal Plus are likely to seem matters of history. Instead of comparing the progress of the by-then archaic category of 'satellite television' in Britain and France, we will be examining how much each of Europe's two early pay-television giants – using a variety of means of distribution to the home – has held on to and developed its national dominance into the digital age.

Notes and References

1. *La Lettre du CSA*, no. 87, December 1996, 2.
2. Counting dishes, even in a single country, is not an exact science. It can be based on household surveys or it can be based on broadcasters' figures for subscriptions (thus excluding dish-owners who only receive free-to-air services or have pirate decoders). It can include or exclude SMATV. So when comparisons are made between different countries one may not be comparing like with like.
3. For example with both subscription and 'multichannel' television. In many other countries, most notably the U.S.A., these two developments have historically been far more closely associated with cable.
4. Useful short accounts of the evolution of French DBS policy can be found in R. Kuhn, *The Media in France*, London, Routledge, 1995, 220-8, and of U.K. DBS policy in T. O'Malley, *Closedown? The BBC and Government Broadcasting Policy, 1979-92*, London, Pluto, 1994, 141-5.
5. Franco-German collaboration on satellite television had two distinct elements. One concerned satellite hardware – as early as 1979 the two governments announced technical collaboration on developing DBS satellites. The other, coming to fruition more than a decade later, concerned satellite programming – the Franco-German cultural channel, Arte. Because high-powered 'national' DBS satellites were effectively sidelined by the rise of medium-powered DTH satellites in the late 1980s and early 1990s, the first initiative has left little long-term result. The second initiative leaves a more substantial legacy. Arte has built a one or two percentage point audience share in France. However, whether that modest success can be considered a success for satellite, is doubtful. Since 1992, Arte's audience has been gained primarily through terrestrial distribution (on the frequencies previously occupied by the failed commercial channel, La Cinq). There must also be a question mark over how much Arte's audience is a result of its bi-national format, and how much it is simply a result of it being a public cultural channel. Would a specifically French public cultural channel have fared better or worse than a Franco-German one?
6. *Screen Digest*, March 1997, 59.
7. In 1995 an estimated 100,000 Arabic-speaking homes in France received Algerian, Moroccan and Tunisian programmes via dishes directed at Eutelsat II F3. These channels were not available on cable. *Cable and Satellite Europe*, 23 November, 1995, 10.
8. *La Lettre du CSA*, No 81, June 1996, 3.
9. Between 1990 and 1995 cable connections in France grew from 422,000 to 1,821,000, in the U.K. from 149,000 to 1,327,000, *Screen Digest*, March 1997, 63.
10. In the year to June 1995 BSkyB had a revenue of £657 million from satellite and cable subscriptions, but only £92 million from advertising. *Cable and Satellite Europe*, October 1996, 46.
11. R. Kuhn, *The Media in France*, 226.
12. A third French digital satellite service, AB Sat lagged way behind with only 4,300 subscribers by March 1997. Canalsatellite Numérique clearly had the advantage over TPS of an earlier start. In the few months after TPS's launch the two main French digital satellite services put on subscribers at roughly the same rate, but by May there were signs that Canalsatellite Numérique might be pulling further away from its rival. In that month and early June, it put on 37,000 new subscribers, compared with only 11,000 for TPS. *Screen Digest*, May 1997, 113, and July 1997, 161.

13. According to Canalsatellite Managing Director, Bruno Delacour, Canalsatellite Numérique added two extra services per month during its first year and intended to go on adding one a month thereafter. After a year, it was already gaining 15 percent of its revenue from pay-per-view, with an average buy rate per subscriber of one event a month. Meanwhile, in the U.K., BSkyB was still only offering pay-per-view on an occasional experimental basis. *Cable and Satellite Europe*, June 1997, 16.
14. In the year mid-1995 to mid-1996, the number of cable households in the U.K. grew by 348,000, the number of DTH households by 428,000. *Cable and Satellite Europe*, October 1996, 50.
15. BSkyB was originally a shareholder (along with ITV companies Carlton and Granada) in British Digital Broadcasting (BDB), one of the two main applicants for the U.K. digital terrestrial multiplexes. But, when the ITC awarded the multiplexes to BDB in June 1997, it did so on the condition that BSkyB withdraw from any equity stake in the consortium. However BSkyB remains a major programme supplier to BDB.

CHAPTER 9

CABLE TELEVISION

JEAN-CLAUDE SERGEANT

Cable television started about the same time in both countries. In Britain, the report by the Information Technology Advisory Panel set up by the Prime Minister in 1981 was published in February 1982. It was in November of the same year that the French government released its Plan Câble which appointed the Direction Générale des Télécommunications, later to become France Télécom, as the single organiser of an ambitious scheme to be implemented with the co-operation of local authorities who would manage the commercial exploitation of the cable networks set up by the DGT.

The British IT Panel made its case in no uncertain terms: 'We are convinced that there are powerful economic and industrial arguments for encouraging cable systems in the United Kingdom. Further, we believe that given the right conditions, these could be entirely financed from private sources.'[1] Besides, the seven-member panel tried to impress on the government a sense of urgency which was translated into a sober warning: 'A delayed decision will be the same as a negative decision'.[2] If the wiring of Britain was felt to be necessary for industrial purposes, the IT Panel was fully aware that business data transmission could only ride on the back of enlarged entertainment supply. The 1982 Report frankly accepted that: 'cable systems will go through an initial phase when their attraction will be based on 'entertainment' considerations'.[3]

The response to the proposals of the IT Panel were on the whole positive. If the *Guardian* in a leader dated 23 March 1982 warned against 'the serious pitfalls which lie along the way', *The Economist* expressed an unqualified approval of the project which it compared to the laying of the railway network in the nineteenth century, its only caveat being inspired by the protectionist undertone detected in the document. With some foresight, the weekly suggested that 'it [would] be right to award several cable contracts to the American and Canadian giants.'[4]

The British government lost no time in implementing the recommendations of the IT Panel. The Hunt Committee's Report (October 1982) paved the way for the Cable and Broadcasting Act passed in 1984 which dealt with the provision of cable television services as well as with DBS and the role of the IBA in the supervision of the projected satellite services. The Act provided, in particular, for the creation of a separate Cable Authority whose members were to be appointed by the Home Secretary.

The prospect of cable television was not endorsed with unanimous enthusiasm in Britain. If the BBC and ITV could legitimately be expected to object to a development which was to bring down their respective share of the market, the left-wing critics were no less vocal in denouncing the dangers of increased commercialisation of British television. Typically, the *New Statesman* in an editorial devoted to the Hunt report, wrote: 'Lord Hunt's report would have had greater intellectual integrity if it had admitted that it had not really considered the social and political consequences of the proposals being made'.[5] Admittedly, this criticism was largely irrelevant to the extent that the terms of reference of the Hunt Committee only mentioned the consideration of the expansion of cable systems 'in a way consistent with the wider public interest, in particular the safeguarding of public service broadcasting'.[6]

More fundamentally, the government's approach was criticised for its insistence that cable was the way to provide an enlarged choice for television viewers who could be better served by satellite television. The case for cable, according to the same critics, could have been argued more convincingly had it included a clear commitment to fibre optics which alone could provide interactive services to customers and thereby justify the cost of cabling up large parts of the country. As it was, the Hunt Report remained technology-neutral and restricted itself to defining the roles of the different industrial contributors to cabling operations as well as the degree of regulation to be applied to the new services.

In France, the ambitious Plan Câble adopted in 1982 anticipated at least 6 million connected homes by 1992 and no fewer that 1.4 million connections during the first year of the programme, based on fibre optics technology, in which the DGT (the telecommunications arm of the French Post and Telecoms Department) was to lay the necessary infrastructure. French local authorities were supposed to act as operators as a result of a Decentralisation Act which had been voted the same year. But they could equally decide to contract out their operating responsibilities to a private company, which a majority of them did. The objective of the government of the time was to demonstrate in the field of cable technology the expertise of the DGT, which had been convincingly illustrated in catching up with its European competitors in terms of telephone services during the 1974-81 period. This technological white elephant was imposed by the government on the DGT which, understandably, failed to meet the prescribed target for a number of reasons.[7]

The most obvious reason for the sluggish growth of cable television has to do with the contradictory attitude of the government which, while launching its costly cabling policy, affected the potential market of cable television by allowing the creation of two terrestrial channels (La Cinq and TV 6) as well as granting a franchise to the encrypted Canal Plus (1984). The rather extraordinary concession made to Canal Plus, allegedly for political reasons, if one recalls the close relationship which existed between President Mitterrand and the then Chairman of the new channel, André Rousselet, lay in the authorisation to use a terrestrial channel for broadcasting an encrypted television service. Canal Plus, with attractive programmes combining a large proportion of newly released feature films and sports events, could then be made immediately available to prospective subscribers without the channel having to build the costly infrastructure that cable operators would have to finance. To some extent, Canal Plus managed to steal a march on cable television operators who were to find that the public's notional wish for complementary television programmes was more than fulfilled by Canal Plus, not to mention the programmes provided by the existing five non-encrypted terrestrial channels. In other words, French cable television operators had the daunting task of tapping an already saturated market. This they tried to do with inadequate tools in terms of programme supply. Every channel available on cable must get a licence from the broadcasting authority (currently the *Conseil Supérieur de l'Audiovisuel,* the CSA*)*, the terms under which the licence is granted reflecting the broad provisions of the TWF Directive of the European Commission. In addition, cable television channels aimed at foreign communities living in France have to comply with the requirements relating to quotas of programmes of French and/or European origin. By that standard, Turner's channels – TNT and the Cartoon channel – have not been allowed on cable, nor channels in Arabic and Turkish, in particular, for which there is a substantial demand in France. The needs of those categories of public have until now been met by the satellite aerial which has become a typical fixture sprouting on the balconies of local council flats in urban areas.

With limited commercial prospects, cable television has seen its development further handicapped by the growing unwillingness of

French local authorities to act as operators of the *Plan Câble* in partnership with the DGT as technical provider of the network. Although by 1984 about 150 local authorities had applied to the DGT for starting a cable television service , most of these decided later to opt out of the management operation of the service whose responsibility was transferred after 1986 to commercial operators, notably water distribution companies such as la Compagnie Générale des Eaux and la Lyonnaise des Eaux. The reason for this withdrawal was above all the financial burden entailed which, added to the size of the debts already incurred by municipal authorities, seemed unreasonable.

Finally, the promise of interactive services which might have helped to sell cable television to an indifferent public seemed largely irrelevant in a country where MINITEL consoles, many thousands of them supplied free, were providing cheap access to data banks and information services. By the end of 1994 MINITEL was in use in over 6.5 million households. Although this piece of IT equipment, based on ordinary telephone lines, was mostly used as an electronic directory in its first years of existence, MINITEL was soon to develop as a major provider of consumer services (teleshopping, telebanking, rail and air tickets reservation, etc.). By 1994, nearly two billion queries were processed through MINITEL.

In this context, it is hardly surprising that cable television should be rated as one of the resounding industrial failures of the 1980s. With FF 25bn of public money invested by the DGT, there were only 2.7 million homes passed in 1990 out of which 514.800 were actually connected. This penetration rate of 18.5 percent included the 158,000-odd SMATV connections which normally provide access to the six terrestrial channels, as well as to local channels and foreign channels in areas where their signals could be picked up.[8]

Given the reluctance of municipal authorities to be involved in the operation of cable systems and the understandable reluctance of the DGT to squander profits made in telephony on building sophisticated networks which were left largely underexploited, the 1986 broadcasting law (*Loi sur la liberté de la communication*) relaxed the rules whereby the Post and Telecommunications Administration was supposed to be the sole provider of cable systems. As from 1986, municipal authorities have been allowed to contract out the physical building of a cable system to a private provider who could also be chosen as operator of the system. Besides, the original technological standards which has imposed fibre optics as the exclusive component of cable systems were eased so that trunk cables using fibre optics technology could be complemented by coaxial links to individual subscribers.

It turned out that the private providers-cum-operators managed to achieve a higher penetration rate than the former operators, presumably because they had a more powerful incentive to sign up new subscribers than their predecessors. Even if, compared with other countries, Germany in particular (where 60 percent of all homes were connected to cable TV in 1996), the French record in terms of cable penetration still looks unimpressive, recent data suggest that cable television has finally got into a stride of some sort. In 1995, out of 21.4 million television homes, 5.8 million had been passed and 1.6 million homes had actually signed up for a basic cable television package (about fifteen channels including the five terrestrial channels), as shown in Table 9.1.

What characterises the current situation of cable television in France fifteen years after the launching of the Plan Câble is the extreme heterogeneity of the local arrangements made in terms of infrastructure and system operation. Including five broad-band cable systems which preexisted the implementation of the Plan Câble, cable television in France is made up of 304 sites covering nearly 800 *communes*.[9] Most of these sites have been developed by cable providers who as a result of the 1986 law have also been allowed to act as operators. These so-called 'new deal' operators have filled in the gaps left by the original Plan Câble which concerned large urban areas. Resorting to a coarser technology and to a more aggressive marketing policy, this new category of operators, some of whom decided to promote their joint interests by setting up an association in 1992 (Association des nouveaux opérateurs constructeurs de réseaux câblés – ANOC), have been awarded nearly all the licences granted by the CSA since that date.

As usual, Paris was to single itself out from the rest of the country. As early as 1983, the Mayor of Paris decided to make his city

Table 9.1. *Growth of cable television in France*

	1990	1991	1992	1993	1994
Total homes passed (in thousands)	2,776	3,744	4,662	5,283	5,802
Number of homes passed each year (in thousands)	848	968	918	620	518
Homes connected (in thousands)	514	762	1,048	1,286	1,607
Of which SMATV (in thousands)	158	226	339	416	469

Source: Agence Câble, AVICA.

the shop window of French technology. Although the original fibre-optics system to be installed by France Télécom was scaled down to include coaxial components, the original target has not been met by the operator Paris TV Câble, in which the Paris local Council has a 25 percent stake. By May 1995 only 174,000 homes had become subscribers to cable television out of the million homes passed. Here again the alternative offered by Canal Plus seems to constitute the main obstacle to the spreading of cable television whose prospects could be improved by a more realistic pricing policy.

Born out of a political decision based on a technological gambit, French cable television has evolved by fits and starts. The former all fibre optics systems to be laid by a single State-owned operator for the benefit of local authorities have given way to a variety of situations. The distinction between provider and operator has been blurred while the technological requirements have been relaxed. Even if local authorities are still considered as the natural overseers of cable systems, local council tenements can also apply for a licence to operate such systems.

The disappointing performance of cable television has furthermore resulted in a reduction in the number of operators. While, at the end of the 1980s, Communication Dévelopement, the cable TV arm of the Caisse des Dépôts specialising in loans to local authorities, was one of the key players in cable television alongside the two major water companies, it has by now completely withdrawn from the sector after transferring in 1995 its systems to the Compagnie Générale des Eaux (CGV/Région Câble), Lyonnaise Communications and France Télécom Câble. These three companies now account for 77 percent of all connected homes and 84 percent of homes passed. Under the current licences, 6.7 million homes remain to be wired by the cable providers, three-quarters of this total being found in the areas covered by the three major providers/operators.

Yet the French cable market is likely to go through a number additional upheavals following the recent increase of the share of Compagnie Générale des Eaux (CGE) in the capital of Havas, the sixth largest media group in the world. In February 1997, J.-M. Messier, Chairman and Director General of CGE, revealed the terms of the agreement with Havas whereby CGE was to become the main partner of Havas with 30 percent of the shares, after buying over most of the stake Alcatel Alsthom held in the capital of the leading French media group which is also the dominant financial backer of Canal Plus. The cost of the operation, estimated at FF3.4 bn, implies the sale by CGE of some of its assets, among which is CGV, its cable TV subsidiary. With 335,000 subscribers in its thirty-three operating systems, CGV, in which CGE holds a 72 percent stake, the remaining capital being shared between Canal Plus (20 percent) and the banking group Société Générale (8 percent), reported a FF 300 million loss at the end of 1996. For a number of years CGV has been known to talk to potential partners, notably Time Warner and the American Baby Bell SBC which is already associated with CGE in the operation of a couple of systems. However, the first French cable operator – Lyonnaise Communications – which by the end of 1996 claimed 417,000 subscribers, would certainly consider an extension of its current leading position in the sector by buying over the systems that CGV might eventually decide to put up for sale.

A slow maturing market, cable television seems now poised for a new start with the arrival of three digital channels bouquets and the forthcoming ending of France Télécom's monopoly in the field of telephony. Besides, the drop in the cost of cable installation (25 percent compared with 1992) and the relaxation of programme constraints decided by the CSA in January 1995, notably the exemption of the prescribed quota of 40 percent of French programmes for pan-European channels broadcast in at least three different languages, are paving the way for an increased dynamism of the sector which, according to a recent study by the CSA, could achieve profitability with a penetration rate of 30 percent.[10]

As Hervé Bourges, the current Chairman of the CSA, put it recently: 'Cable TV is at the crossroads...It is confronted with technological innovation which is progressing at a very rapid pace and with the potential competition of increasingly efficient communication carriers'.[11] Only a bold adaptation of the existing regulation would allow cable television to compete with satellite on a level playing field and to take full advantage of the new prospects emerging in the telephony sector.

Cable television in Britain has developed along markedly different lines in a fairly original context, characterised by the efficient competition of satellite television. This competition started to materialise in April 1990 when British Satellite Broadcasting (BSB) first went on air, adding its five channels to the four Sky television channels which had been beamed off an Astra satellite for the preceding fourteen months to 600,000 British homes or so. At the time, only 87,000 homes had been connected to broadband cable systems out of a potential half a million homes passed. This unimpressive record five years after the Cable Authority had awarded the first licences was mostly accounted for by the sheer size of the investments required. The decision by the government in March 1984 to end the 100 percent capital writedown tax allowance for cable operators had understandably put off potential investors who were expecting a quick return on their capital. As the Cable Television Association

(CTA) remarked in 1987: 'It takes some five years to construct a system serving 100,000 homes and until the system is complete there is, of necessity, an outflow of cash'.[12] The £200 million which had been invested by 1987 had not proved sufficient to allow cable providers to reach their targets and the cable industry could but support the view of the Cable Authority's Chairman expressed in the 1986-7 Report that 'the removal of the restrictive requirement in the Cable and Broadcasting Act [1984] that no-one outside the EC may control operations would increase foreign interest and investment'. In other words, the CTA was calling for the intervention of American companies which for some years had expressed an interest in the British cable market, their home market being saturated. Besides, national U.S. regulations prevented cable companies from providing telephone services and the Baby Bell companies resulting from the break-up of AT & T from moving into cable television.

The removal in 1988 of the ban on the ownership of cable systems by non-EC operators triggered off an influx of American cable and telephone companies who rapidly acquired a dominant position in the U.K.'s cable market, 80 percent of which was controlled by U.S.-owned operators in 1995. This is in marked contrast to the French cable market which, because of its heavily regulated nature, has failed to attract US investors except in a limited way (Time Warner runs a small number of systems in the Rhône 'département' and in Limoges, while TCI has a stake in Vidéopole which by 1997 included 70,000 subscribers scattered over seven different systems).

The prospects offered by the British market proved even more irresistible after the government decided to open up the telecommunications sector to cable operators. The market had been deregulated in 1984 when Mercury was set up to compete with the newly privatised BT for the provision of telephone services. Until 1990 the cable operators who wished to offer such services to their subscribers had to negotiate switching operations with either of the two companies. Only four operators had chosen to do so. A White Paper published in November 1990 entitled *Telecommunications Policy in the 1990s* led to a review of the telephone duopoly and an Act which as from January 1991 allowed cable operators to switch their own traffic and to connect to BT or Mercury for long-distance calls. Additionally, cable operators running adjoining franchises were permitted to interconnect. At the same time, British Telecom was banned from providing television services on its network until 2001 in order to give the fledgling cable market enough time to gather strength.

These developments removed whatever hesitations U.S. companies might have had to invest in the British market. In 1991, the

Vice-Chairman of United Artists Entertainment Company listed the reasons why he felt 'the United Kingdom [was] a great business':

> The franchises are large and federally controlled; system density enables us to achieve profitability at lower penetrations; customer satisfaction is high; we are allowed to grow basically unfettered by regulation; we can provide telephone service while the British telcos are prohibited from providing cable; our closest competitor, direct to home service, is actually our best supplier.[13]

Telephony has certainly proved to be the main incentive which has boosted both the activity of cable operators as well as the attraction of cable to potential subscribers. For instance, Telewest, the largest U.K. cable operator, reported in January 1997 an increase of 33.8 percent in the number of its customers compared with 1996, half of whom were taking both television and telephone services. As a matter of fact, Telewest has more telephone customers (627,000) than cable subscribers (528,142). In general terms, the number of telephone lines operated by cable providers roughly doubled every year between 1994 and 1996 while the rate of penetration of cable remained stagnant at slightly over 20 percent, as shown in table 9.2.

Reflecting on the way cable television had developed in Britain, Jon Davey, former head of the Cable Authority and Director of Cable and Satellite at the ITC, rightly diagnosed the original misconception which had hampered the growth of cable: 'The lesson of the supposedly 'entertainment led' growth of cable is still with us: it did not work, and in practice cable growth leapt only when it became telecommunications led.'[14]

Table 9.2. *U.K. cable performance, 1991-6*

	Homes Passed (in thousands)	Homes Connected (in thousands)	Penetration (percent)	Total Telephone Exchange Lines (in thousands)
1991	828	148	17.9	2.2
1992	1,300	267	20	21
1993	1,900	434	22.4	109
1994	2,700	610	21.9	312
1995	4,100	915	22.2	741
1996	6,000	1,300	21.9	1,400

Source: *Independent Television Commission*

Although the general public does not seem to be prepared to admit that cheaper telephone services may be the main attraction of cable,[15] there is some evidence that cable companies are making inroads into the traditional preserve of the two public telephone operators. Industry sources suggest, for example, that in 1996 BT was losing between 30,000 and 50,000 customers a month to the cable operators. After all, most American companies which have progressively dominated the cable market are telephone companies. The recent shake-up which took place in the sector in October 1996 following the merger of Mercury – Cable and Wireless telecoms arm in Britain – with Nynex Cablecomms and Bell Cablemedia, further demonstrated the undiminished appetite of telecoms operators for cable. The market, which is expected to yield a total of £5bn revenues a year by the turn of the century, is preparing for a major confrontation between Cable and Wireless, which is locked into an expansive alliance with current cable operators; and BT which has agreed with BSkyB, the leading Astra-based satellite company in Britain, to set up British Interactive Broadcasting. This joint venture which is meant to develop interactive services to be included in BSkyB's forthcoming digital package, will also feed BT's customers in the Milton Keynes area, the only cable franchise that BT operates through its subsidiary New Towns Cable television, due to be upgraded to broadband standards. This will serve as a training ground for BT, which might be allowed to offer interactive services to broadband system operators following a review in 1998 of the ban under which BT has been precluded from using its telephone network to provide television services.

The setting up of Cable and Wireless Communications not only highlighted the increasingly valuable stake represented by cable for telecoms companies but also heightened the degree of concentration in the ownership structure of the market. While by 1990 eighty-eight cable systems were operated by thirty-five distinct companies, ten leading players now share most of the franchises covering 10 million homes awarded by the ITC. Put together, the three cable operators – Nynex, Bell Cablemedia and Videotron – incorporated into the new company account for one third of all cable television subscribers and of the total of homes passed as Table 9.3 indicates.

This trend towards increased concentration is likely to bring about further reductions in the current number of operators. Ultimately three or four large players are expected to remain in the market. With larger areas under their management, these strengthened companies could benefit from economies of scale and the integration of commercial operations that such extensions could allow. A more aggressive and efficient marketing policy could also

Table 9.3. *Major cable operators in 1996*

	Home passed (in thousands)	Homes connected (in thousands)
Telewest	2,274	485
Nynex	1,156	226
Cablecomms*	819	166
Bell Cablemedia*	552	123
General Cable	444	115
Comcast	417	89
Telecential	318	80
Cable Tel U.K.	353	72
Videotron*	190	44

Sources: Cable Communications Association, ITC
* Part of Cable and Wireless Communications.

boost the penetration rate of cable and cut the crippling 'churn' rate which, in the case of Nynex for example, was as high as 30 percent at the end of 1996.

If telephony has arguably been the driving force of cable since 1991, revenues from telephone services often exceeding those from television subscription for most operators, it remains that cable is above all seen as a provider of innumerable television channels. In that sense, cable television is dependent on BSkyB for a supply of popular channels that keeps growing. The addition of seven new channels in October 1995, among which are Play Boy and the Disney Channel, has increased the attraction of BSkyB packages to viewers, who in some areas have seen their subscription rate cut as a result of the deal made in 1995 by BSkyB and the two leading operators Telewest and Nynex.

As it is, very few channels are available on cable only except on a very limited, local scale. Attempts to set up cable-only channels with a larger market power have so far been rather timid or have failed altogether. For instance, CPP1, a consortium made up of the seven largest cable operators, agreed in early 1995 to launch a sports channel – Sports Wire – with a view to offering an alternative to Sky sports channels. The agreement petered out when BSkyB required Nynex and Telewest to abstain from entering into competitive programme deals in exchange for reduced subscription fees for the reception of Sky channels. There may be, nevertheless, a reasonable market share for a small number of cable-only channels, as the examples of Channel One and Live TV, both backed financially by newspaper groups, seem to suggest.

There is no denying, however, that the most popular channels watched by cable television subscribers are those supplied by an

Astra satellite and above all some of the Sky channels, including premium channels. In all satellite/cable TV homes, BSkyB channels accounted for 18.3 percent of total viewing time in 1996[16] out of a total share of 33.1 percent for all Astra channels. The non-terrestrial supply was dominated by Sky 1 (4.7 percent of viewing time), Sky Sports *1* (5.8 percent), Sky Movies (3.2 percent), the Movie Channel (3 percent) and the two Turner channels, TNT and the Cartoon Network, with a combined share of 2.8 percent.

In France where all cable television channels can also be accessed through satellite (Telecom 2 A and 2 B as well as the Astra Satellite for foreign channels) RTL9, Monte-Carlo TMC, Planète and the all news channels LCI launched by TF1 in 1994 draw the largest audience in satellite/cable TV homes where non-terrestrial channels account for 23.8 percent of the total viewing time (1996 figures). With 47.1 percent of the audience share, RTL9, a generalist channel owned by the Luxembourg-based company CLT, confirmed in 1996, its well-established leadership on the non-terrestrial television market. More interesting, perhaps, is the fairly unexpected good standing of the French music channel MCM which has displaced MTV as the most popular music channel, while Paris Première, a cultural channel with an interest for current artistic events, got a fairly high appreciation rating by viewers. More predictable thematic channels such as Eurosport and Canal J, the French equivalent of the Children's Channel, also feature among the most watched channels.

More importantly, cable television systems are now poised to become the natural carriers of the new digital bouquets that satellites are already beaming off. In France, three bouquets of digital channels launched in 1996 are competing for the market of the 1.5 million satellite owners who, for the price of a new decoder, can choose between the eighteen channels offered by CanalSatellite mounted on Astra, the twenty-five channels of TPS broadcast from two Eutelsat satellites and the twenty-or-so channel bouquet assembled by AB Sat which are also supplied by a Eutelsat satellite. This abundance of channels poses a dilemma to the viewer who would need to rent two different decoders to receive the CanalSatellite as well the TPS bouquets. Lyonnaise Câble has innovated in making both bouquets available to its 425,000 subscribers, a difficult commercial decision to make given that Lyonnaise Câble has a 10 percent stake in the capital of TPS which is predominantly controlled by TF1, M6, CLT, France Télévision and France Télécom. Moreover, cable is the obvious vehicle for TPS which offers a wide range of interactive services and pay-per-view formulas. The full complementarity between satellite and cable has thus been fully demonstrated, as it will be in Britain when BSkyB starts broadcasting its planned 200 digital channels by the end of 1998, at a time when the first batches of multiplexed digital channels promised by the government have started to operate.

Clearly cable is no longer a pipe dream. Conceived as the prime conveyor of a technological revolution which was supposed to need the extra boost of entertainment, it was eventually rescued by technology – telephony and digital compression. Although not yet profitable, the cable market will no doubt receive the extra fillip it still needs when every cable subscriber can access the Internet system and become a citizen of the new information age.

Notes and References

1. Cabinet Office. Information Technology Advisory Panel, *Report on Cable Systems*, HMSO, February 1982, 3.
2. Ibid.
3. Ibid., 48.
4. *The Economist*, 6 March 1982.
5. The *New Statesman*, 15 October 1982.
6. *Report of the Inquiry into Cable Expansion and Broadcasting Policy*, Cmnd 8679, London: HMSO, October 1982, 1.
7. For a challenging overview of the situation, see J.-P. Chamoux, `Cinquante ans de télécommunications, *Médias Pouvoirs*, nos. 39-40, 1995, 210-28.
8. Data supplied by the yearly report compiled by CNC, CSA, INA and SJTI, *Indicateurs statistisques de l'audiovisuel*, Paris, La Documentation française, 1994.
9. Mid-1995 data.
10. 'Le câble français: vers de meilleures perspectives de rentabilité?, *La Lettre du CSA*, no. 81, juin 1996.
11. Opening speech to the 1995 Médiaville Conference, Montpellier, 6 September 1995.
12. The Cable Television Association, 'Proposals to Government by the Cable Television Industry', October 1987.
13. S. D. Blair, 'Investment in U.K. Cable – A US View; Financial Times Cable Television and Satellite Broadcasting, London, 26 and 27 February 1991, Speakers' Papers, 15.4.
14. J. Davey, 'Growing Underground' , *Spectrum*, Summer 1996, 5.
15. In a 1995 ITC survey only 31 percent of the respondents accepted that they had been 'attracted to cable more by the possibility of a cheap telephone service than by the different television channels on offer'. *The Public's View 1995*, ITC Research Publication, Table 3.6.
16. *Broadcast*, February 1997.

CHAPTER 10

BEYOND DIGITAL TELEVISION

PATRICK VITTET-PHILIPPE

Situated at the crossroads of digital convergence 'beyond the telephone, the television and the PC' (Oftel), New Digital Services (NDS) cover a wide spectrum of applications at different stages of development, some already fully operational, some still in their testing stage, some yet to be developed. These range from connectivity-enriched digital video services – such as video-on-demand and near-video-on-demand; to video-enhanced computer on-line services – such as the emerging applications built on high-speed access technologies; to the future commercial and entertainment uses of the Internet, a free-form network of networks of ever increasing bandwidth, intelligence and connectivity – such as 'WebTV' and 'Netcasting' applications which are quickly closing the gap with interactive television in terms of visual contents, aesthetics and production values.

The *primum mobile* and main engine of the Information Society in Europe, NDS have been the focus of urgent attention among European Institutions and Member States which are suddenly confronted with the arduous task of transitioning regulations conceived in a very different analogue environment. Pushing some governments into 'knee jerk' pre-emptive regulation, NDS have sparked acrimonious controversies between broadcasting and telecoms regulators (ITC v. Oftel in the U.K., CSA v. DGT in France, Bund v. Länder in Germany), each of them equally determined to bring new services within their jurisdiction. Similarly, the issue of convergence – technological, economic and regulatory – has fuelled passionate debates between cultural traditionalists for whom '*la convergence ne passera pas*', and techno-determinists for whom convergence is an irresistible 'tidal wave', sweeping away geographical frontiers, industry boundaries and existing models of regulation. At the focal point of digital convergence, New Digital Services pose, therefore, the central question of the future regulatory framework for electronic media in Europe and raise crucial implications for future Community policies.

The factors of convergence

Convergence: technological factors

Not unlike the *Tyrannosaurus rex* in Steven Spielberg's movies, convergence is the product of the digital revolution and of the combined powers of formerly separate industries and creative communities; both have escaped from the reaches of research laboratories to irrupt centre stage in the market; both have elicited highly emotional responses, fear in some quarters, enthusiasm in others, as well as a great deal of 'hype' and cynicism; and both appear unstoppable. Unlike the *T.rex*, however, 'deep convergence' seems much better fitted to the logic of evolution and has undoubtedly a bright future.

In many ways, technological convergence is a *fait accompli*. The convergence of technologies has been happening for over a decade, as digitisation blurred the boundaries between different means of storage and distribution of information. Driven as well as enabled by technology, convergence can be defined as the simultaneous collapse of traditional boundaries between industries and of existing borders between regions. It is therefore a truly global phenomenon, marked by the emergence of new types of highly decentralised networks such as the Internet – itself the symbol and main driver of convergence – as well as of new, essentially transnational, applications such as electronic commerce – another force of convergence, and, like the Internet, 'born global'.

The irresistible rise of software and the exponential growth in computing power represent, undoubtedly, the most powerful factors underpinning digital convergence. Compared with majestic past evolutions of broadcasting (with its cycles of thirty years between each new technology), and with the linear growth of telecommunication infrastructures (whose deployment has historically remained limited by costs and physical constraints), software and processing power have been growing exponentially over the past twenty years. Measured by 'Moore's Law', the doubling of processing power every eighteen months, this inexorable rise in raw processing power means that digital devices are becoming faster and more convergent with each product release, and that, conversely, the price of a given level of computing power is decreasing at the same dramatic rate. This phenomenon is reinforced by a sharp drop in the price of memory – from $60 to $0.17 per megabyte between 1985 and 1995 – generating, in ever faster cycles, constantly more powerful, flexible and convergent digital platforms and products (computers, digital set-top boxes, hybrid PC/TVs, etc.) This growth in performance, which shows no sign of abating for at least the next ten to fifteen years, is likely to be the single most critical factor in the 'deep convergence' of the traditionally separate sectors of broadcasting, telecommunications and computing.

At the same time, as a direct consequence of this software revolution, advances in data transmission technology are bringing rapid increases in connectivity and capacity to all networks, allowing for seamless delivery of ever richer and ever more interactive content over a variety of networks. As networks grow, the utility of being connected grows. Thus, as prices for a given level of bandwidth continue to drop, the value of a connection to the Internet increases exponentially, generating more usage, more revenue and, in turn, more and more complex and convergent multimedia applications.

Networks themselves, whose capacities are enhanced by lightening progress in compression technologies, are undergoing a similar revolution, reinforcing convergence. In the Internet environment, in particular, the nimbleness of Internet Protocols (IP) allows seamless routing of different types of data (text, sound, video files) across a wide variety of delivery mechanisms (dedicated networks, telephone, cable, satellite). The flexibility of these protocols – the Internet is, indeed, less a network than a set of protocols – allows innovative technologies (such as video streaming, which adapts the flow of data to available bandwidth, or distributed caching, which maximises resources of each link in the transmission process) to bridge gaps between heterogeneous networks. Rather than a *'tout ou rien* situation', advances in software compression provide for pragmatic substitutes to fully fledged integrated broadband infrastructure. Thus, compression makes it possible to approximate connectivity in existing broadband cable or broadcast networks (as in the digital multiplexing of television channels, or in the combining of digital broadcasting with Internet return path). Conversely, it makes it possible to emulate bandwidth for existing narrowband switched networks (as in the ADSL [Asymetric Digital Subscriber Line] video-on-demand trials by a number of telecom operators). Unlike in the traditional telecoms or broadcasting environment, where all parameters have to be in place up front before service can start, computer networks are fundamentally scalable. Scalability allows new applications and new markets to start and to expand gradually as more bandwidth becomes available – a crucial factor in the convergence process.

Rather than the classic vision of a single integrated broadband infrastructure which held sway in Japan and in Europe in the 1980s, the Global Information Infrastructure in the 1990s can be seen as a portfolio of interconnected and converging networks (telecoms, broadcasting, cable, satellite, wired and wireless, public and private-corporate, Internet, etc.), each growing in bandwidth and connectivity, according to its own technological and market logic, towards full Information Superhighway status. Stressing scalability, seamlessness and connectivity, this new convergent model is particularly well adapted to network structures and corporate practices in the U.S. market, where 'capacity resale' already thrives, but may represent a particular challenge in the traditionally more static European environment.

The Internet, the best example of a portfolio of networks, has established itself as the main building block of this new order. The model and prime driver of convergence between telecommunications and IT industries, the Internet is gradually extending its reach to encompass and often replace pre-existing networks, as private corporate networks become Intranets and robust IP protocols take over from proprietary networking software. Thus, the Internet is seen as a mix of threats and opportunities by players and regulators alike. Full of promise for some economic actors (as it enables new forms of electronic commerce, giving small companies essentially the same access to global markets as that of large corporations), the Internet is perceived by others as a menace to their core business (as Internet telephony overturns hallowed economic models of long-distance telecommunications). For traditional telecommunication or broadcasting regulators, the Internet is no less a threat, challenging as it does such fundamental concepts as national jurisdiction and classic enforcement mechanisms.

Unlike other traditional networks, such as broadcasting and telecoms, the Internet is essentially user-driven, with users themselves, rather than established broadcasters and publishers, generating a substantial part of the content. It is also highly decentralised. No one 'owns' the Internet and, effectively, no one can 'regulate' the Internet. This decentralised nature and 'bottom-up governance' is seen by many as the single main reason for the Internet's success. A unique characteristic of the Internet is that it functions simultaneously as a medium for publishing and communication – a key factor of convergence. Unlike traditional media, the Internet simultaneously supports a variety of communication modes: one-to-one, one-to-many, many-to-many. An Internet user may 'speak' or 'listen' interchangeably, weaving public communication (whose content is traditionally regulated) with private communication (traditionally unregulated) at the click of a key. The Web, therefore, differs radically from broadcasting. It also fundamentally diverges from telecommunications. This constant shift from publishing mode to private communication mode, regulated through very different principles and legal instruments, undoubtedly constitutes the main challenge of Internet regulation.

Convergence: economic and market factors

While technology is an enabler of convergence, convergence is ultimately driven by the marketplace, as operators multiply and industry boundaries rapidly shift. In this environment, converging new services have been the focus of considerable attention and substantial investments by a number of European industries – telecom operators, broadcasters, cable companies, publishers, databank and on-line service providers. Functioning traditionally on separate markets, these players are now increasingly encroaching on each other's turf. In all cases, these new services are considered a strategic extension of core competence and a crucial source of revenues in the years to come.

For incumbent telephone operators, shifting from POTS ('Plain Old Telephone Services') to PANS ('Pretty Amazing New Services') is seen as a way to compensate for the stagnation of revenues caused by price caps on voice telephony (annual decrease of 7.5 percentage points in relation to the RPI [Retail Price Index] imposed by OFTEL in the U.K.) and by growing pressure from new entrants on newly liberalised sectors. Added-value multimedia services are seen as a means to maximise the use of the existing copper plant (in the case of ADSL) and to offset the cost of installing new infrastructure (as with ATM [Asynchronous Transfer Mode]). Bringing in fresh, unregulated revenues, NDS are perceived by many former monopolies as 'the very future of the telecommunications industry' (Deutsche Telekom).

Similarly, for new entrants in the telecommunication business (cable operators, alternative carriers, service providers), long prevented in most Member States from expanding into voice telephony, new services such as near-video-on-demand and electronic commerce represent a crucial component of 'mixed communication services' packages and a powerful marketing tool to enlarge their subscriber base. As in the case of Veba in Germany, added-value multimedia services justify the huge infrastructure investments.

Coming from the other end of the convergence spectrum, commercial broadcasters are also aggressively expanding into a variety of terrestrial and satellite-delivered NDS, with pay-television and new services currently the only expanding sectors in the television business. Confronted with stagnation of traditional revenues (flat television 'adspend'), commercial broadcasters face competition from alternative forms of screen-based entertainment. A growing phenomenon in Internet-friendly countries in Europe (Holland,

U.K., Finland), competition for viewers' attention and advertisers' money in multiscreen multiplatform homes is reaching dramatic proportions in the more advanced US market, where computer use has already overtaken television viewing in several key demographics ('screenagers'; affluent young males). According to a 1997 Nielsen survey, U.S. Web users consume 59 percent less television than average viewers. As an answer, commercial broadcasters, such as Canal Plus/C: in Europe or Direct TV/Direct PC in the U.S., are pushing 'digital multimedia broadcasting' as a cheap, powerful and ubiquitous means of broadband distribution of video and high-speed data.

For public broadcasters, the ability to operate new services is considered a matter of survival in the new multichannel, transaction-based broadcasting environment. Simultaneously threatened by shrinking advertising revenues, like their commercial counterparts, and by growing attacks on their public funding, public broadcasters consider commercial forays (specialised subscription services) or abroad (European digital bouquets) as a legitimate extension of their traditional public service remit. For European regulators, such an expansion raises potential issues of cross-subsidies and distortions of competition. In response to these concerns, some public broadcasters have balanced their demands for guaranteed access to converging markets with a commitment to financial transparency and to 'fair and open competition'.[1]

For content providers such as publishers, databank operators and information services, NDS constitute a natural extension of their traditional know-how, the structuring and packaging of information, and an ideal means to 'repurpose' rich stores of data. For the press, in particular, NDS promise to compensate for shrinking advertising share and escalating costs of newsprint. The electronic distribution of press titles, like the Electronic Telegraph, also allows publishers to broaden their audience base and tap into younger and more affluent demographics than their hard copy parent. Simultaneously, a growing number of electronic publications ('Infozines' such as Slate.com) now completely bypass the written stage, fostering a new publishing model which takes full advantage of new technologies such as intelligent agents and 'push programming', and builds on customers' new relations to the medium ('Web users are accustomed to interactive features, and will not accept plain text'). It is undoubtedly for content providers that digital technologies are currently having the most significant impact.

Even more than publishers, information technology companies are wielding crucial influence in shaping the new services market in Europe and are the prime movers of convergence in Europe and in the U.S. This is confirmed by the computer industry's aggressive expansion into the on-line, advanced television, and content businesses (MSNBC [Microsoft Network and National Broadcasting Corporation]); by the general move towards the on-line distribution of multimedia content and software, already the leading application of e-commerce; and by the involvement of computer companies as the necessary architects and integrators of all advanced television projects. Underpinned by the irresistible push of software, kept nimble by rapid product cycles, historically unfettered by regulation, steeled by years of cut-throat competition (for the Chief Executive Officer of Intel, there are only two types of IT companies, 'the quick and the dead'), the computer industry is resolutely taking the lead in the convergence of technologies, businesses and, more importantly, of content. The emergence of powerful and well-funded players (Microsoft invested more to launch MSNBC than News International did for Fox Network), with no tradition of regulation except through competition law, and no intention of letting themselves be assimilated to broadcasters or telecoms operators, will have, no doubt, important consequences on the future regulatory landscape in Europe.

Forms of convergence: from market to content convergence
Coming from both ends of the digital spectrum, two basic models for convergence are emerging: the intelligent television model – i.e., connectivity-enriched digital video applications such as data-enhanced television which adds content and interactivity to television broadcasts, and the video-enabled Internet model – i.e. fast-emerging applications which add audio and video content, without losing the flexibility of access and robust interactivity of the on-line environment. Despite current limitations, a number of applications are thus quickly closing the gap between smart television and video Internet. The area where these two converge currently constitutes the most fertile ground for innovation and entrepreneurial activity – as well as for the creation of entirely new types of content. Pushing the boundaries of 'content convergence', innovative forms of video-rich 'Internet channels' are dynamically building on the creativity of previously separate *métiers* of video production, computer graphics, and information management. Of all the facets of convergence, content convergence is the least recognised, yet without any doubt the most significant phenomenon.

In the general move towards convergence, British and French operators are among Europe's leaders. Canal Plus, in particular, is currently extending the reach of digital television, pioneering exciting new services such as downloading of software and outline networked games, while devoting a substantial amount of its programming to 'cybermedia'. Similarly, on the British side, new ventures such as DBI, joining a digital satellite broadcaster, (BSkyB) and a telecoms operator (BT) are pushing the limits of multimedia data broadcasting.

Obstacles to convergence

Technological and market convergence do not, of course, automatically entail regulatory convergence. In fact, regulation and regulators themselves often constitute the main obstacles to convergence. In terms of authority to operate, for example, regulation often represents a barrier to the entry of new operators. In some Member States it is difficult or impossible to obtain the authority to operate in a particular sector, due to policy decisions to limit the number of licences (e.g., a single operator per cable franchise in the U.K.), or to grant exclusive rights to particular operators (e.g., preserved public broadcasting monopoly in Austria). Often, procedures to grant licences are non-transparent, and rely on discretionary decisions or subjective factors (such as the controversial 'quality threshold'). The length of a licence can also be an obstacle: too short a licence (four years for a commercial television licence in Greece) may deter investment; too long a licence (eighteen years for some cable franchises) may restrain competition. A major barrier to convergence, the ability of third parties to have access to cable networks remains severely limited in Europe.

Beyond licensing structures, the multiplicity of regulators, the complexity of regulation, and the lack of independent regulators, all contribute to the rigidity of the system and hinder convergence. In the U.K., no less than twenty-five regulators are involved in the regulation of broadcasting. In nine Member States out of fifteen, broadcasting licences are still delivered by a Government Ministry rather than by independent regulators. Across Europe, content regulation varies substantially between media, while the fields of competence of regulators vary widely, leading to turf wars between regulators and, generally, to damaging legal uncertainties for operators. Similarly, in the area of business activities, ownership restrictions (hampering cross-industry investments), and line of business restrictions (preventing in particular cable and telecommunication operators from providing entertainment services), are a major stumbling block in the path towards convergence. In the area of content regulation, the contrast between regulatory regimes for publishing and broadcasting, the complexity of positive and negative rules imposed on broadcasters, the regulatory discrepancies between terrestrial and satellite broadcasters, conjure up a regulatory maze which traps operators and hampers investments. If one considers that convergence is a positive factor, increasing choice and convenience for users and bringing overall growth to the convergent industries, regulatory reform may be therefore a crucial step to enable pan-European provision of New Digital Services.

Regulatory challenges in the converging environment

Compared with past evolutions in broadcasting and telecommunications, the present technological acceleration – measured by the relentless growth in computing power rather than the stately progress of infrastructure – constitutes an unprecedented challenge for regulators. Indeed, some experts claim that, with the lightening change of technologies, traditional regulation has become all but impossible. In an environment where rules often become obsolete even before they are enacted, new, flexible and technology-neutral forms of regulation may be required. As convergence forges ahead, the industry itself may have to take a leading role through self-regulation, while governments 'keep the fire under the industry' to make sure that commitments are respected.

Same services, different regulations: distortions of competition in the digital melting pot

It is generally acknowledged that the aim of regulation is not to treat all sectors on a strictly equal footing. Indeed, there is no such thing as a totally level playing field. However, the emergence of similar services offered by different industries (operating traditionally under different regulatory regimes but now competing head-on in the same markets) may be creating substantial risks of asymmetric regulation and of distortion of competition.

An example of asymmetric regulation is the present difference in legal regime between near-video-on-demand (NVOD) and video-on-demand (VOD), two closely related, yet differently regulated, new services. NVOD, defined in the Television Without Frontiers Directive as the distribution 'point to multipoint' of digital multiplexed film channels by a broadcaster, falls at present under that Directive. Although distributed also 'point to multipoint' by a telecoms or cable operator via a media server, delivering simultaneously thousands of video streams, VOD is not covered by the Directive. Similarly, virtually similar types of NVOD may be regulated differently according to whether they are delivered off the air by satellite or on-line by server. Another de facto regulatory asymmetry, and potential distortion of competition, exists between the NVOD and videocassette markets, two very similar economic sectors which nevertheless fall under very different regulatory regimes.

Another example of regulatory gymnastics in a converging environment, the setting up of an electronic commerce Web site constitutes, according to French law, an act of public communication, similar to operating a television teleshopping programme. However, the act of selling goods from the same site (the exchange of digital signatures, payment and acknowledgement) becomes, like giving one's card number on the phone, an act of private communication – two activities falling, once again, under very different regimes.

Reassessing regulatory criteria

The above examples stress the need to reassess regulatory criteria in a converging environment, and in particular to test the validity of maintaining the classic line of demarcation between broadcasting and new services. This is a fundamental question, at a time when some are attempting to export broadcasting regulation to new forms of communication, denying that the concept of new services has any validity under the law, while others, conversely, try to project Internet regulatory paradigms back onto broadcasting activities.

Traditionally, technology-based criteria have been widely used to draw 'lines in the sand' between different communication media to justify sector-specific regulation. Of all the technology-based criteria, the screen-based criterion ('same screen–same regulation'), whereby desktop video becomes an 'audiovisual' service regulated as broadcasting, is undoubtedly the least pertinent. The general trend towards hybrid PC/TV platforms and seamless networks makes it hazardous to use the screen as benchmark for regulation. Indeed, there would be considerable risk in regulating as broadcasting all screen-based digital information services with video content.

Platform-based criteria are no less absurd. Imposing different regulations to different sides of the same equipment – i.e., regulating the 'left side' of a digital integrated receiver decoder (broadcasting functionalities) differently from its 'right side' (telecoms functionalities) – would prove impossible. Similarly, differentiating between 'quota-bearing' revenue streams, and 'quota-free' revenue streams for a given operator in a diversified transactional video environment might represent no less of a challenge for regulators.

Widely used in the 1980s in the field of satellite regulation, the classic difference between 'point-to-point' telecoms services (low-power satellites, requiring a reception licence) and 'point-to-multipoint' broadcasting services (high-power DBS, assimilated to over-the-air reception) has resisted neither technological evolutions (emergence of medium-power satellites like Astra) nor market demands for direct-to-home reception. In a convergent digital environment which provides seamless 'multipoint-to-multipoint' connectivity, this purely legal construct becomes meaningless.

The concept of scarcity of resources which, for more than seventy years, has traditionally justified broadcasting regulation might also need serious reconsideration. The key question is: when does scarcity stop? Does scarcity vanish with fifty cable channels, with 200 digitally compressed satellite multiplexes, with the unlimited offer of 'Internet in the Sky', or with one single dedicated channel for each user-the model 'market of one'? While it is generally agreed that scarcity of delivery will disappear in the new digital environment, thanks to better spectrum management, other forms of scarcity may, however, persist – scarcity of available content, scarcity of financial resources – and continue to require the attention of regulators.

Confronted with an environment in technological and economic flux, a number of regulators and lawmakers have refused to be blinded by technology and concentrated, instead, on content criteria. In this technology-neutral approach, it is content, not technology, which differentiates among various types of NDS.

Defending the 'primacy of content over delivery', proponents of an *oeuvre*-based' approach are thus calling for similar regulation of content across all technological delivery means. In their view, content regulations, as defined in the TWF Directive, should apply across the board to all services – broadcast television, satellite PPV, cable NVOD, server-delivered VOD, and WebTV. Actually going further than the Directive, such an 'oeuvre-based' approach raises many questions. The concept of *oeuvre*, with its heterogeneous mix of economic and aesthetic aspects, might not be the most effective yardstick for regulation. Similarly, *oeuvre*-based regulation (and, in particular, content quotas) which is only enforceable with difficulty in a classic five-channel television environment, becomes impossible to police in a multichannel transnational market, and becomes a nonsense in an open on-line environment like the Internet. Casting the net even wider, proponents of the concept of 'audiovisual' new services have attempted to encompass as audiovisual 'any animated image sequence, with or without sound'. Critics of that approach have noted that, by the interplay of definitions, audiovisual new services would effectively include anything that moves on any screen, and would include not only VOD movies (not covered by the TWF Directive) but also networked computer games, Java-enabled sites on the Internet, and even telemedicine and video conferencing.

Of all the criteria proposed to discriminate between broadcasting and new services, that of scheduled versus non-scheduled may be the most effective. In this perspective, the crucial difference may be between, on the one hand, broadcasting services (which involve the broadcaster in an editorial role, with the constitution of a programme schedule) and, on the other, on-demand services such as VOD, NVOD, PPV (which effectively constitute an electronic database or video library). At a later stage of convergence, the difference between scheduled and non-scheduled may itself become academic. As navigation tools from the Internet world (browsers, push technologies) and from the digital television world (EPGs or electronic programme guides) gradually coalesce, intelligent agents will automatically determine viewer preferences and deliver a tailor-made and seamless mix of content selected from a variety of on-line, off-line and off-the-air resources.

Linearity, like scheduling, is also a useful benchmark. The difference here is between 'linear' services (such as traditional television, NVOD, and most types of VOD, where the user views a programme without any possibility of manipulating it) and 'non-linear' services where the user can influence the sequence of delivery, manipulate the content or reinject data into the network. The linearity criterion has been used recently in the landmark Information Technology Agreement (ITA) recently negotiated in the framework of the World Trade Organisation, to separate between 'non-interactive' products such as films on DVD (Digital Video/Versatile Disk), which will still face tariffs, and 'interactive' products such as multimedia CD-ROMs which will be tariff-free.

Beyond technology and content, there is a strong case for making economic criteria the basis for regulation. Indeed, transactional versus non-transactional services represents a true watershed, separating traditional television (advertising-supported, or subscription-based) from on-demand electronic library services like PPV, NVOD and VOD (transaction-based and on individual demand). While the multiplexing of existing television channels into digital bouquets is clearly an extension of advertising-supported or subscription broadcasting, all on-demand transaction-based new services imply radically different consumption patterns and economic relationships between service providers and customers. There is, therefore, a strong argument in favour of considering digital PPV, NVOD and VOD in the same category as advanced on-line services – 'pay-per-use', 'pay-per-band', 'pay-per-hit' or 'pay-per-megabyte' services – and being regulated in the same way as the on-line industry rather than as broadcasting.

Economic efficiency, public interest objectives: clarifying regulation principles

Beyond a reassessment of regulatory criteria, convergence demands a clarification of the rationale of regulation. Traditionally, regulation has been concerned with ensuring that two types of objectives were met: economic efficiency and wider, sometimes more diffuse, public interest. Economic efficiency and public interest objectives form two complementary sets of objectives under which specific regulatory criteria can be developed.

Telecommunication regulation has traditionally stressed economic efficiency. The drive towards full liberalisation and full competition in telecommunication, in Europe and in the wider international environment, has demonstrated that competitive markets lead to optimum pricing. The rebalancing of tariffs (so that prices paid by users reflect as closely as possible the real costs to the operators), and interconnection rules (so that new operators are not forced to dig up roads before they start doing business) are classic examples of regulation for economic efficiency. On the contrary, broadcasting regulation has traditionally focused on public interest objectives, such as protection of children and cultural policy, rather than on economic efficiency. While economic efficiency regulation rests on straightforward principles, public interest objectives may vary considerably from country to country (e.g., the very British, but unexportable, concept of 'taste and decency' (see chapters 3 and 4).

Often amalgamated in the past, these two principles need to be clearly distinguished. The main regulatory challenge in the converging environment of convergence is to achieve a new balance between regulation for economic efficiency and regulation for wider public interest objectives. Generally, economic efficiency is considered a priority, and competition policy, rather than a priori regulation, the tool of choice. The crucial question is whether competitive markets can provide for all public interest requirements – for example, if competition in new markets will guarantee pluralism, diversity and cultural objectives. If, as is probable, they cannot, safeguards must be put in place, and highly targeted regulatory action may be needed to guarantee public policy objectives, especially in the transitional phase leading eventually to a fully converged environment.

Which role for Community policies?

The development of New Digital Services will rely primarily on 'private initiative and market forces'.[2] However, the Community will wield powerful influence in defining the regulatory framework which will accompany the emergence of this new industry. The question of the choice of regulatory regime is therefore of paramount importance. Four basic models exist. Should NDS be governed as broadcasting – using traditional content-based regulatory criteria?

Should they be ruled as telecommunication services – focusing on telecommunication issues such as access, interconnectivity and universal service? Should they be regulated as the print media, or even the IT industry, primarily through self-regulation and, when necessary, competition law? Or should they be primarily considered in an internal market and competition policy logic – though with a 'horizontal', rather than a sector-specific or technology-specific approach?

NDS and broadcasting regulation

The extension of broadcasting regulation to new services has been the subject of considerable debate among European institutions, in Member States, and among industry players (public broadcasters versus electronic publishers). This debate has pitched cultural absolutists for whom 'Information highways are highways for creative works', against the techno-fundamentalists for whom 'video-on-demand means shifting 6 MB files from a server'. Heated confrontations about the relative merits of broadcasting and telecoms regulation have opposed public broadcasters calling for 'the subordination of telecommunication regulation to broadcasting regulation' (EBU) with publishers adamantly refusing 'the extension of broadcasting regulation to all screen-based information services' (European Publishers Council).

In this context, repeated attempts were made to include new services in the field of application of the TWF Directive. Doubts, however, were expressed in the industry (publishers, computer software, etc.) as to whether an instrument originally conceived nearly ten years ago to regulate television in a very different five-channel analogue environment was the best regulatory model for a fast-converging digital information environment. It was repeatedly pointed out that the scarcity of frequencies, which had historically justified broadcasting regulation and concepts of 'internal pluralism', no longer applied in a digitally compressed, content-rich, and network-neutral digital environment.

Considering the global continuum of new services, it appeared obvious that broadcasting regulations could not be exported wholesale to converging applications such as high-end video games networked over digital television decoders (Canal Plus), video-based transactional databases (Reuters TV), video-enriched Websites (cnn.com), and tomorrow's video-enabled Internet (WebTV). High-end on-line multimedia services more and more closely resemble audiovisual services, yet remain essentially different.

Similarly, it was generally felt that exporting sector-specific broadcasting regulation on an issue such as protection of minors from analogue television to new services would go against the principles of economy and efficiency of regulation. Rather than through a vertical, sector-specific approach, such important issues should be dealt with 'horizontally' across different media – an approach successfully adopted by the Green Paper on the Protection of Minors and Human Dignity in Audiovisual and Information Services published in November 1996. More generally, as regards content regulation, it is evident that traditional broadcasting tools employing numerical content quotas and restrictions on the amount and frequency of advertising, designed for a channelised, one way-medium, are simply unworkable in the Internet environment.

NDS and telecommunication regulation

The main thrust of the telecommunication policy has traditionally been to empower service providers and operators to develop the market as economically appropriate; to remove asymmetrical regulation favouring one mode of communication against another (for example, wired services against mobile services); to abolish exclusive rights and dismantle monopolies. Calling for full liberalisation and full competition on all telecommunication sectors, the new telecommunication framework in Europe serves as a constructive point of reference for regulating the converging environment. Similarly, telecom regulators, steeled by years of curbing powerful former monopolies, may be uniquely suited to apply competition policy in key areas like conditional access services, as OFTEL is currently demonstrating in the U.K. There is a strong argument, therefore, that NDS should be primarily regulated using telecommunication criteria, such as access and interconnectivity, rather than traditional content-based broadcasting criteria.

As regards the Internet, however, it is obvious. that the 'network of networks' cannot be regarded as a 'telecommunication service' in the conventional sense. Rules aimed at universal access to services, price controls, and controlling the allocation of scarce resources make little sense in the Internet environment where physical resources for service delivery are increasingly varied and abundant. At the same time, rules relating to liberalisation and ensuring competition through interconnection requirements and other safeguards offer important guidance for the formulation of the new framework. The ONP (Open Network Provision) directives are going in this direction, illustrating a flexible, future-proof and service-led approach to regulation; likewise the Directive on Licensing, which streamlines the procedures for new operators in a converging environment, eliminating artificial limits to the number of operators and replacing cumbersome authorisations by class licences, or by simple declarations. For, even in a competitive environment, government has a central role to play in ensuring competition and preventing abuse by dominant players.

Towards a primacy of competition law: lessons from the publishing and IT industries

The regulation of the publishing and Information Technology industries, both essential players in the new order, also holds useful lessons. Both industries have thrived in a flexible, yet predictable regulatory environment, dominated by self-regulation and strong enforcement of competition policy. The regulation of the IT sector has been particularly light – a fact that is considered by many experts a key to its commercial success and to the rapid pace of technological innovation. In addition to generally applicable rules of law, the regulation of the sector has focused principally on the protection of intellectual property rights and on the application of competition law. Based on the principle that innovation is stimulated by the preservation of private incentives and economic reward, this regulatory model offers a useful lesson.

This model illustrates the key importance of competition law applied to industrial players *ex ante* (for issues of structure) or *ex post* (for issues of behaviour). There is, indeed, a strong body of evidence that, rather than traditional a priori sector-specific regulation, it is competition law applied by competition authorities with ever more specialised sector-specific expertise, that will become the main tool for regulating the converging environment.

NDS and internal market policies

While competition law deals with companies, traditionally, Internal Market policies apply to Member States. Internal Market instruments therefore complement telecommunication and competition policies and add a crucial dimension to the overall regulatory framework.

One of the aims of Internal Market regulation is to assess the extra risks (real or perceived) to the free circulation of goods and services in the new environment. In terms of pluralism, controlling a 'journal télévisé' (a mass medium distributed in a broadcasting environment with limited frequencies) and an on-line 'journal électronique' (distributed on demand in an unlimited on-line environment) pose radically different issues. In terms of commercial communication, while advertising for some products and services may be banned on television or in print, yet advertisements for banned products (tobacco, pharmaceuticals) and regulated professions (doctors, lawyers) are freely available on the Internet, as Web pages today and as video sites tomorrow. While in some instances NDS may reduce the risks in relation to broadcasting (minors are de facto better protected in a securely encrypted digital environment), in others NDS might increase them (personal data are de facto less well protected in an on-line environment where every clickstream can be monitored).

Faced with new perceived risks, Member States have been tempted to regulate pre-emptively in such areas as Internet content, electronic payment mechanisms and digital signatures, raising a potential risk of refragmentation of the Internal Market. In order to provide a flexible regulatory framework for the converging environment and pre-empt the danger of refragmentation, existing Internal Market instruments may be reinforced by new cross-industry measures in such fields as consumer protection, commercial communication and the protection of minors. In a converging environment, these important and highly sensitive issues need to be addressed 'horizontally' rather than sector by sector – as exemplified by the draft Directive on the Legal Protection of Conditional Access Services, which covers the whole spectrum of services from Pay-TV broadcasting to the Internet.

An additional tool has been the extension to new services of tried and tested Internal Market instruments, such as the 'transparency mechanism' recently extended from the area of goods and standards to new services. Stressing co-ordination rather than regulation, consultation rather than formal notice, this system of preliminary reporting allows the Commission and Member States to assess the possible consequences on the free flow of services of draft legislation from a given Member State. Covering the whole spectrum of Information Society services, this mechanism has already proved its efficiency and is likely to be a crucial tool as convergence accelerates.

Conclusion: managing convergence, a need for scalable, responsive and future-proof regulation

In conclusion, the next few months will be crucial to determine the 'final mix' of regulation which may best accompany digital convergence and the emergence of New Digital Services, such as Internet commerce, in Europe. Whatever this 'final mix', it is already clear that no single traditional model of regulation is suitable to the new environment. Although most models may contribute, it is probable that a new regulatory model will be needed, something more than simply a hybrid based on different aspects of the converging sectors. Extensive consultations on this crucial issue have already begun, involving industry, Users and governments.

Overall, it may be assumed at this stage that the new environment will require muscular *ex ante* as well as *ex post* application of competition law, rather than a priori, *dirigiste* regulation. In some issues like electronic commerce, it may require adaptation of existing law (such as the uniform commercial code), rather than a total overhaul of the existing framework. It will also stress self-regulation. Self-regulation, however, should not be considered a panacea. Self-regulation can and does, in some cases, reinforce obstacles rather than contribute to the free circulation of products and services. It is better fitted to some legal traditions than to others. However, self-regulation – especially 'self regulation with teeth' and strict enforcement mechanisms – remains a powerful tool, when used in conformity with, and backed up by, the established legal framework. Its effectiveness has been amply demonstrated in the area of problematic content on the Internet[3] as well as in electronic commerce.[4] But its crucial advantage is its responsiveness, as it can often respond to technological or market change faster than traditional regulation.

In a fast-moving global environment, there is general agreement that new forms of regulation will need to be flexible and technology-neutral in order to be future-proof. In order to accompany and manage change, these will need to be minimalist, yet strong enough to enable and guarantee competition. Above all, they will need to be clear and predictable to encourage operators' investments and ensure consumers' confidence – both a particular challenge in Europe. Increasingly, they will have to take into account the international dimension. The rapid emergence of e-commerce, fuelled by the Internet revolution, has demonstrated the essentially transnational dimension of regulation. In a converging environment where borders between industries and between continents inexorably collapse, the challenge for regulators will be, quite literally, global.

As convergence gathers speed, and the rate of change accelerates, history might offer some lessons. It is widely agreed that, at the time of the industrial revolution, countries and industries which embraced change became the next century's leaders. Those who did not, fell back irremediably. At the dawn of the information revolution, the unprecedented rate of change which fuels convergence may need to be similarly embraced, and managed – on pain of leaving the field to Europe's competitors. In this environment, Europe – with its 320 million potential on-line users, its mastery of key convergent technologies in the telecommunications, digital broadcasting and electronic commerce fields, and its experience in building the Internal Market in these areas – is uniquely positioned to answer this challenge.

Notes and References

1. BBC, *The BBC's Fair Trading Commitment*, London, BBC, 1994.
2. 'Bangemann Report', *Europe and the Information Society*, CEC, Brussels, 1994.
3. Commission Communication, *Illegal and Harmful Content on the Internet*, CEC, 1996.
4. Commission Communication, *A European Initiative in Electronic Commerce*, CEC, 1997.

PART IV

THE CHALLENGE OF EUROPE

CHAPTER 11

MULTIMEDIA MULTINATIONALS: CANAL PLUS AND REUTERS

MICHAEL PALMER

Multimedia multinational groups, headquartered in France or Britain, have existed for decades – even if the term 'multimedia multinationals' is of recent vintage. In the 1980s certain prominent groups stressed the European dimension of their activities: the debate and hyperbole generated by the European Community's Directive 'Television without Frontiers' – Green Paper 1984; draft Directive, 1986; final Directive, 1989 – served as a backcloth against which various players examined the technological, cultural, political and commercial implications of the transition from an essentially national to a European and international regulatory framework; they examined issues relating to horizontal and vertical integration, to technological convergence and synergies between group assets, while looking for markets – 'niche' or 'mass' – alone or, more often, via joint ventures and with (local) partners. Television is a cultural industry and policy issue which politicians across Europe approached in often different ways but in the knowledge that the stakes and lobbies involved made it something of a Pandora's box. Once the EC Commission and the European Council of Ministers had shown that broadcasting fell within the remit of the mission to ensure free circulation of persons, capital, goods and services within the Community, existing trends within different Member States were reassessed: deregulation of national broadcasting systems, the increase in the number of television channels (public service and private sector, general interest and thematic) and attempts to foster co-productions and intra-European programme exchanges (see chapter 13) so as to offset the anticipated increased dependence on programme imports (notably but not solely from the

U.S.) were debated in a host of European forums – in the Council of Europe as well as in the Community, by trade lobbies and professional bodies as well as by non-governmental organisations, in Geneva as well as in Strasbourg and in the capitals of EC Member States. One introductory example must suffice: in France, the Communications Minister François Léotard (1986-8), who introduced multimedia or cross-media legislation (the Law of 27 November 1986), referred to the need to create favourable conditions at home so that leading French communications groups could become major players on the European stage; they were weak compared with groups like that of Murdoch, Maxwell and Bertelsmann, he argued.[1] Concern was voiced that European television – whose channels were to increase – would be increasingly 'Americanised': fears concerned programme content (light entertainment, 'wall to wall Dallas', Hollywood films and telefilms, and even U.S.-style newscasts), programme formats (to accommodate advertisers' needs), the machinations and capitalist alliances of multinational multimedia groups, and technology (in high-definition television, U.S. groups started late but imposed an industry format that Japanese and European actors ultimately adopted), (see chapter 14).

The 1990s opened with European television audiences discovering anew the impact of American television – in particular, the resources U.S. television channels devote to covering major breaking stories, set to figure high as recurrent themes on the news-agenda for weeks to come: the coverage of the 1990-1 crisis and 'war in the Gulf' saw television channels in Europe (and elsewhere) take signal-feeds from CNN and duplicate CNN news-programme formats; in France, La Cinq (the commercial television channel then owner-operated by Robert Hersant) adopted news-programme formats that broadcast CNN International: the 1985 channel founded by the Turner broadcasting company which had launched CNN in the U.S. in 1980 was monitored extensively; during the night of January 16, English-language television channels broadcast the sound commentary of CNN journalists reporting the bombing of Bagdad – 'Holy Cow!' screamed one CNN journalist listening to the bombing from his hotel window.

CNN was a relative newcomer to international broadcasting. In early 1991 it claimed to have nineteen full time bureaux outside the U.S.; in mid-January 1991, on the eve of the allied land offensive against the Iraqi forces, it had nineteen journalists in the Middle East, backed up by ninety technical and logistical support staff (in mid-1997 CNN had thirty-one bureaux outside the U.S.). The impact of CNN was such that it quickly became – in newsmen's parlance – a 'primary source' for other news-media; there was, however, head-shaking at the Americano-centric slant on international news. In France, in the months preceding the Gulf crisis, there had been concern about errors in reporting recent top international news stories (for instance, the revolution in Rumania, notably the misreporting of the charnel-house of Timisoara); (often young and inexperienced) journalists had covered events – either from the television studios in Paris or from 'on-the-spot' venues or news-centres where they had recently arrived (and were dependent on local journalists, translators and experts); there were fears such errors might be repeated in covering the Gulf crisis, and angry scenes when French authorities, like their American counterparts, attempted – often successfully – in preventing journalists from reporting the news 'straight'; French journalists resented their dependence on the authorities on the one hand, and on U.S. newsfeeds on the other. Agence France Presse (AFP) journalists in Washington even cited the White House before the Supreme Court, because their agency was refused accreditation, and access to the White House pool.

In both France and Britain, however, there were respected international broadcasters with a proven track record, as there were multimedia multinationals whose experience of operating in various national and international markets stretched over decades. Such groups including the advertising, tourism and communications complex Havas, the AFP and Reuters news agencies, the BBC and Radio France Internationale. In very different ways, and with very different resources at their disposal, these figured among the major French and British-based 'players' to develop innovative audiovisual strategies over the past fifteen years.

Canal Plus and Reuters: 'European' success stories?

Communications industry actors are more concerned with the mid- and long-term future than with their past. France and Britain, however, have a series of long-established communications groups, often with substantial international interests, who 'reinvented themselves', in the domestic, European and international environment of the mid-1980s and 1990s: they adjusted to market possibilities in the 'new world (communications) order', and the new 'European audiovisual landscape', as technological convergence and geopolitical change led them to rethink international strategies often founded on a 'worldvision' that had long reflected colonial or post-colonial thinking and ties; in the communications industry, as elsewhere, the world, for example, was often perceived in terms of markets divided into cultural and linguistic zones – English/American, French, Hispanic, Chinese, Arab and the like. These were often the starting-point for a communication company's corporate strategy. In many respects, they still are – programming and content have to be presented in the most 'user-friendly' manner for the intended public(s)/market; but there is a greater willingness than in the past to form joint ventures and partnerships with players from different cultures.

While referring to other, related actors and issues, this paper centres on Reuters and on Canal Plus, and on their television strategies and products. These are two of the 'success stories' among European communications multimedia groups of the past fifteen years. They are present in different 'niche' markets and sectors of the communications industry, and the juxtaposition of the two may seem unusual: we are concerned with a diptych, not with a comparison. To look at a purveyor of news (and news film), on the one hand and a broadcaster for whom news-programming was not a major priority, on the other, reflects, perhaps, the open-ended approach that the study of European television invites. *Perpetuum mobile*: however trite the observation, over the past fifteen years television policies and market strategies in Europe were in flux, and were often affected as much by factors outside the industry (and the continent) as within; likewise, long-established actors, for whom Europe was the major market, developed a television strategy, where before they had next to none (Reuters), while others sired via the state and a long-established communications player (Havas), a company (Canal Plus) that developed a successful formula of subscription television (programming and technology); this owed much to subscriber television systems developed in the U.S. (the Home Box Office channel, for example). There is, however, something of an irony: the success of Reuters – which predates 1984, but increased thereafter – was founded on serving the information needs of media and non-media actors in increasingly deregulated markets; the success of Canal Plus – widely seen to have been the major achievement in the audiovisual sector during the Mitterrand (double) Presidency, 1981-95, was founded initially on the support the President gave to André Rousselet, his friend and associate of over thirty years, who developed subscription television in France in – as we shall see – a favourable environment.

Both companies have the same remit – to earn money for their shareholders – but they have different 'cultures' and expertise. The different nature of the two 'beasts' makes a joint consideration of their past development over the 1984-97 period somewhat improbable. But, we would argue, the very juxtaposition of the two companies is instructive. Reuters has a computer and communications 'culture', geared primarily but not exclusively to providing information, market data and news for international 'players' in finance, the economy and the media; it subsequently 'moved into broadcasting', as we shall see. Canal Plus, sired by the French state and the then (state-controlled) Havas communications, advertising and tourism company, was launched in 1984 as France's first encoded (involving encryption and 'descrambling' of the signal transmitted) and subscriber pay-television channel. Canal Plus, a new 'player' in the French broadcasting environment, appeared at a time when broadcasting policy faced contradictory pressures: the year that saw the publication of the European Commission's Green Paper, 'Television without Frontiers', and Franco-Luxembourg arguments over satellite broadcasting, was followed by President Mitterrand's statements in favour of the launch of local television channels and of two new terrestrial commercial channels: these decisions and arguments modified the funding projections on which Canal Plus, then in its infancy, was based. In 1984, Reuters, by contrast, had already embarked on the expansion that transformed it from one of the five major world news agencies of the 1970s into the leading world vendor of financial data and systems, as well as a major multimedia player, in the 1990s. In 1984, furthermore, Reuters news agency was transformed into a public company – Reuters Holding plc – and floated on the stock exchange. Canal Plus first floated (8 percent of) its capital on the Paris Bourse in November 1987: the floating as a public company of communications corporations is itself evidence of the commercial logic and capital requirements of the highflying multimedia multinationals exemplified by Reuters and Canal Plus.

In the 1990s, both Canal Plus and Reuters occupy high positions in the *Financial Times*' annual lists of European companies ranked by market capitalisation. Reuters position in 1992 and 1996 respectively was number 48 and number 35: in the same years, Canal Plus ranked 102 and 145 – these were rankings higher than those of Havas, its parent company. In *FT* nomenclature, Reuters is listed as a publishing company – the first company of the sector, save for the British/Dutch company Reed Elsevier. Canal Plus is listed as the first of France's companies in the 'broadcasting media' sector; TF1, currently its major rival in the French terrestrial and digital satellite television markets, did not figure in the 1996 *FT* list.[2]

Consequently, judged by the criterion of market capitalisation, Reuters and Canal Plus rank among leading London-based and Paris-based companies active in both the hardware and software of the communications sector in Europe. Compared to other companies in the *FT*'s 'Europe 500' listings, both companies have a relatively small number of employees: Reuters – 14,182; Canal Plus – 969.

Both are leading players in their respective European markets, and Reuters, of course, is the leading figure in several world markets – as a vendor of financial data and transaction systems, in particular for currency markets ; Canal Plus has grown from being the leading French to the leading European pay-television company; it is the chief mainstay of the French cinema industry, prebuying over 100 films a year, and contributing to the funding of 80 percent of French movie productions.[3] It has long had close ties with Hollywood – since 1985, at least; in particular with Warner Bros, the biggest of the U.S. cinema and television production studios; in addition to its existing agreements with four other Hollywood majors, in September 1986, it signed with UPI-Pay-television (grouping three other studios), securing exclusivity transmission rights to some eighty U.S. feature films on pay-television channels in Europe. Among the wide range of its other activities Canal Plus is also a major player in the burgeoning market for pay-television in Africa, from North Africa southwards (Canal Horizons, launched in December 1991).

To state the obvious: Canal Plus is primarily a broadcaster; Reuters is primarily a vendor of news, information and data – it provides a 'news feed' to broadcasters such as BSkyB and other Rupert Murdoch-led broadcasting companies worldwide (Fox in the U.S.A., for instance). In 1983, Reuters did not have an 'audiovisual culture', *stricto sensu*; in 1984-5, it started a news-photo service; in 1990, it launched its computer-graphics division. These products were primarily intended for print media clients. In the 1990s, it expanded both its on-line and real-time services and products, and its presence in the audiovisual sector. The second part of the chapter will be centred on its television activity and, indeed, on issues raised by the integration of a range of print and audiovisual media resources and products; the first part will focus mostly on Canal Plus whose 'in-house culture' is very different; this is fashioned, in part, by the economics of the French film industry as programme supplier to television and, in addition and increasingly, by the competition for transmission rights to Hollywood films and for sports programming. For both companies, assessment of the market possibilities of the applications of research and development into various information and communication technologies is of strategic importance. This may sometimes be masked by the high profile that Canal Plus in particular, and Reuters also in recent years, have assumed in both the media marketplace and the public sphere. For example, while transmitting primarily as an encrypted channel, Canal Plus derives much of its popularity from flagship programmes, such as the news satire programme, *'Les Guignols de l'Info'* – transmitted unscrambled, and accessible to all viewers. Promotional strategies of company strategies, personalities and products intertwine; successive chief executives of Canal Plus – André Rousselet (1984-94) and Pierre Lescure (1994-?) – are prominent figures of the 'media establishment', that some journalists term the *'mediaklatura"*; Peter Job, chief executive of Reuters, is less of a 'public figure' yet his company is portrayed by specialist and general interest media alike as 'all-powerful' – the French news magazine *Le Nouvel Observateur* listed him in January 1997 among 'the top fifty world leaders'.[4]

In many respects Canal Plus and Reuters appear to be operating at opposite 'ends' of the television and information industries. In January 1984, Reuters could not be called a 'broadcaster' and Canal Plus did not exist. Today, they occupy very different positions in the multimedia multinational environment. Long seen as a gadfly, offering alternative, innovative or complementary programming, attractive to upwardly mobile professional classes tired of staid traditional television channel fare, Canal Plus makes ('in-house') very few of the programmes it broadcasts – but these do include flagship talk shows and satirical news programmes, transmitted live; Reuters, by contrast, is primarily an information vendor, processing, packaging and providing feeds of data, news and information to media and non-media clients throughout the world; it has little of a trackrecord as a 'broadcaster' – its venture into radio news broadcasting in the U.K. in the 1990s was not generally considered a success. Both companies, however, belong among the ranks of multinational multimedia companies, and – in their different ways – are high-flyers among what 'Les Guignols' dub 'The World Company'. This diversity, we shall argue, is itself suggestive of the strange hybrids or myriad-faceted rhetoric about technological convergence, on the one hand (see chapter 10), and about the global advertiser's dream (*pace* Saatchi and Saatchi of yesteryear) of 'one-stop shopping', on the other. A year 2000 positivist rewrite of Huxley's *Brave New World* (and of Orwell's *1984*?) might conjure up interactive communications in real time linking actors worldwide: multimedia multinationals strive to be 'part of the act'; television and computer programmes and information flows 'service' a networked community where, via one terminal (keyboard; screen-console-monitor), participants receive and exchange information and may conclude transactions. In such a 'rewrite', television viewers themselves include both 'couch potatoes' and proactive consumers: they choose between the channels and programmes on offer, include discriminating (or fickle) zappers and viewers who change channels ('churn') little – 'Thanks for watching us', the newscaster Henri Sannier tells his public; viewers negotiate texts, semiologists have demonstrated; they also conclude transactions – via 'teleshopping channels' , and in choosing whether to take, and renew, their subscription to a pay-television channel such as Canal Plus.

How to position oneself so as to be well placed to profit from 'technological convergence' and market possibilities is a recurrent preoccupation of multimedia multinationals: one such theme in the 1990s is 'the interface' between the personal computer and the television screen; another leitmotif is the capacity to access the Internet via television; advances in multimedia and interactive technologies make such 'dreams' – which of course act as a spur – come about. Thus an article in *Fortune*, in December 1996, found it useful to open by recalling the hype of past 'dreams': 'Forget HDTV. Forget interactive television. Forget the 500-channel universe. Instead start thinking PCTV'.[5] By this token, 'broadcasting' is an outmoded term; ten years ago, or thereabouts, 'simulcasting' and 'narrowcasting' were in vogue; today 'consumer choice', 'ease of access' and 'user-friendly' are the positive side of a coin whose obverse features the commercial nature of the information – and programme-exchange and transaction, (See Chapter 10).

One characteristic of the climate or universe in which both companies operate is common to most media multinationals; they operate in a 'culture' suffused by the language or rhetoric of combinations and concentrations, of 'Citizen Kanes' operating in a host of media, information and entertainment markets, where it is necessary to show shareholders and others proof or likelihood of success: company strategists require an understanding of both 'hardware' and 'software', of content and production, processing and delivery systems, of 'cables' and of 'cable broadcasts'. Capitalism, cultural industries and communications make for sometimes odd bedfellows. Highly capitalistic, at both start-up and expansionist phases, media conglomerates require creators, accountants, salesmen and managers, a feel for the market applications of burgeoning technologies, and a dash or more of megalomania and showbiz sense 'upfront'. The latter characteristics, for example, are often highlighted in accounts of the expansion of the company founded in 1981 by Michael Bloomberg, portrayed as the coming (or rather arriving) force among electronic information vendors, to Reuters's chagrin.[6] In France and elsewhere in continental Europe, the imagery of British and American 'media moguls' has been transposed (and modified, via the mandatory references to the 'Anglo-Saxons') to different corporate cultures. Pierre Lescure, Chairman and Managing Director of Canal Plus, employed the rhetoric of international corporate management, heavily leavened with Anglo-American terms – from finance and technology – when addressing French journalists on an economic 'question and answer' forum on French radio.[7]

There is a further corollary for the personnel and employees of multimedia multinational corporations: the calling into question of existing, albeit tried, procedures, and the development of multi-skilling know-how facilitated by the interface between new technologies and existing resources: this is a continuous process, as important for journalists in their capacity as producers and editors of copy and programme material as is identifying niche and other markets for their organisation's 'business-plan' strategists. We shall examine this further, in noting how Reuters print media journalists adapted to working for television.

Reviewing the development of Canal Plus and of Reuters over a decade or more, the observer first notes that they have done well by trying to anticipate change in fast-moving markets where long-established and new industry actors sought to do likewise. The extent and speed of the sea-change should not be underestimated. At start-up, in 1984, Canal Plus presented itself as an alternative to both the programme content and mode of reception of existing national channels in France: there were only three of them, and they were all public service. In 1998, Canal Plus is the chief shareholder of Canal Satellite (launched in April 1996): this offers subscribers a choice of seventeen channels – thematic, French and foreign. This gives some measure of the change in the television environment – in France and Europe – as television franchise holders, using cable and satellite as well as terrestrial 'off-air' delivery, and digital compression of signals, increase the range of channels (and quality of picture) on offer. Reuters, likewise, profited from anticipating changes in market conditions and opportunities. Most of its revenue – 94 percent in 1996 – comes from financial information services and systems; foreign exchange dealing ('forex') represented 45.6 percent of this – some notion of the revenues to be earned in forex, where Reuters is the market leader among information vendors, emerges from the following: global forex turnover was reckoned to be U.S. $640 billion a day in 1990, and U.S. $1.2 trillion in 1996.[8] In 1995, media products reportedly represented 6 percent of company revenue. But Reuters' television strategy, we would argue, merits attention for at least three reasons. First, adapting to changing market conditions (decline in revenue from newspapers, increase in the number of television channels worldwide), Reuters reorganised its 'television arm' (1992-3): it integrated a subsidiary, Visnews, the leading international news-film agency, into the company, thereby developing multiskilling and multimedia awareness among all its journalists. Second, building on its expertise as a vendor of financial data, Reuters launched a financial television service (1994); this is accessible on television screens and on Reuters computer terminals – thereby illustrating the television-computer screen interface mentioned earlier. Finally, as thematic television programming develops, data and news vendors like Reuters and its rivals, such as Bloomberg, compete on television as elsewhere: Bloomberg Information television is one of the seventeen channels featured on Canal Satellite's 'programme bouquet'; Reuters makes current affairs programmes for television (about Bosnia, for example), and has TV production facilities, feeding news-programmes to television channels in London, as in St. Petersburg.

One major distinction between Canal Plus and Reuters must be stressed. Canal Plus succeeded ultimately because it was 'protected' in its infancy: this protection, in its home-base market (the ties between André Rousselet and François Mitterrand, the support lent to the fledgling Canal Plus by the Havas group, the longest-established (with Hachette) of France's major communications groups), proved invaluable, especially in the period 1984-5 when adverse factors promised to blow it off course. Reuters, by contrast, had no protection other than the capital resources garnered from the prosperity achieved prior to the flotation of the company in 1984, and which its shareholders expected it to maintain, or increase. Its resources were such, in 1984, that British newspaper directors sitting on the company board were well disposed to the flotation; their own companies were to benefit from the process.

Compared to the market conditions under which other television channels (first public service, and – after 1986 – private sector) – operated in France, Canal Plus enjoyed a privileged position (see chapter 3). In March 1984, the terms of its franchise were published: Canal Plus enjoyed what was termed 'the most favoured media clause', in exchange for not carrying advertising.[9] It was authorised to broadcast recently-released feature films several months ahead of other French channels, and was given a de facto monopoly of terrestrial pay-television in France;[10] Havas undertook to acquire a 35 percent stake; the initial franchise was for twelve years.

During the next ten years (1984-94), under the management of André Rousselet, initially the chief executive of Havas, Canal Plus led the way in the use of new technologies, in developing a programming mix of films, sport and entertainment programming, and in the funding of a pay-television system that it subsequently 'exported' elsewhere – in Europe and Africa. Canal Plus continued to enjoy a protected position within its home market. A change, however, in the centre of gravity of executive power in politics led to changes in the top management of Canal Plus. The centre-right government of Edouard Balladur (1994-6) presented legislation which allowed a shareholder to acquire up to 49 percent of the capital of a private television channel: this Carignon Law (February 1994), named after the subsequently imprisoned communications Minister, Alain Carignon, enabled the leading owner-operators in the different private sector television companies (Bouygues in TF1, for instance) to increase their stake to 49 percent. New capitalistic arrangements were made for Canal Plus: Havas (23.6 percent), CGE (20.1 percent), a public utility, and the bank, la Société générale (5.1 percent) formed a joint company owning 48.5 percent. of Canal Plus. Canal Plus and Havas continued to have shared cross-holdings: Havas owned 23.6 percent of Canal Plus, and Canal Plus 8.4 percent of Havas. The aim was to ensure that no foreign group could make a take-over bid for Canal Plus. The left-leaning André Rousselet, however, did not accept the new capital structure: he resigned, and published an account of the behind-the-scenes manoeuvring, in a hard-hitting article in Le Monde: 'Edouard m'a tuer' [sic], played on the first name of the Prime Minister, and a controversial human-interest crime of the time, involving a death-bed message, 'Omar m'a tuer' [sic]. Television politics, like political television, continued in France to make headline news. Pierre Lescure, previously Rousselet's second-in-command, succeeded him as Chairman and Managing Director.

Since 1994, however, most media coverage of Canal Plus is devoted to technological innovation, the swings and roundabouts of programming, and to capitalist alliances and rivalries as Canal Plus expanded in Europe and became the first major French player to enter digital broadcasting. Within France, the television industry and business milieux continued to regard Canal Plus management highly; in December 1996, Lescure received two plaudits – he was voted 'manager of the year' by the News magazine, Le Nouvel Economiste, and 'man of the year' by the industry trade magazine, Stratégies. By year's end, he seemed well placed to head Europe's leading subscriber television group for some years to come. It is to the context and origin of the European dimension of this success that we shall now turn.

In the period between 1984-8, Canal Plus developed the technology, the programme formula, and the subscription television concept within France. The floating of shares on the Paris stock exchange in 1987 indicated the confidence of its Chairman and Managing Director Rousselet, and of Havas, as to the extent of its success. From 1988, Canal Plus formed partnerships or joint ventures with companies that introduced a 'domestic' version of Canal Plus in various national markets across Europe – in Belgium (1988-9,) Germany (1989-91), Spain (1989-90), and Poland (1995). Likewise, Canal Plus – via Canal Horizons – launched the concept via various joint ventures developed in five west or north African countries, between 1991 and 1995; Canal Horizon is also transmitted by DBSatellites whose footprint extends across Africa. A Havas subsidiary assures the satellite transmission of Canal Plus to French overseas DOM-TOMs. Industry estimates suggested that in 1995, a total of 7 million subscribers paid to watch one of the affiliate Canal Plus channels in Europe, some 50 percent of market share; other estimates, in mid-1997, argued that while the subscriber base had continually risen since 1990, a total of 3.20 million subscribers watched one of the affiliates.

Canal Plus, therefore, built on its de facto monopoly of subscription television in France an expertise that enabled it to become one of the main players in Europe (See Chapter 8). Partnerships with other prominent French and European communications conglomerates, especially in the fast-moving industry politics of television, are subject to continual stresses and strains, in the search for capital, market advantage, and as new commercial applications of technologies come on-stream. Canal Plus developed partnerships with other major communication industry actors in France – Havas, of course, but also Pathé, and the water utility, la Compagnie Générale des Eaux, for example – as elsewhere in Europe; indeed in France, where in 1997 'la Générale des Eaux' became the leading shareholder in Havas, there were reports that Canal Plus would withdraw completely from Havas. The situation appeared even more complex in Germany, where Canal Plus founded in 1989 the subscriber television channel Première – taking a 37.5 percent stake – with Bertelsmann, considered by many industry estimates to be the number one communications group in Europe, and among the top three in the world. In 1996, a succession of volte-face between March and September saw a brief joint venture between Havas, Canal Plus, Bertelsmann and Rupert Murdoch unravel when Murdoch broke with Bertelsmann and formed what itself proved a short-lived alliance with the rival leading German subscription television group, headed by Leo Kirch. Meanwhile, in May, and of more lasting significance, Bertelsmann merged its audiovisual interests with the leading Luxembourg-based commercial broadcaster, CLT, in which Havas had a 20 percent minority stake. In June 1997, Canal Plus announced its withdrawal from Première, which CLT-UFA and Kirch would jointly control; in part compensation, Canal Plus was to acquire the Kirch stock in the Italian digital programme bouquet operator, Tele Più, which had a monopoly of subscription television in Italy; Canal Plus management spoke of the complexity of the over-crowded German market. In France itself, Rupert Murdoch reportedly explored the possibility of entering the subscription television market; he renounced, seemingly because Canal Plus had market dominance. Canal Plus, meanwhile, was concerned in 1994-6, with the advent of digital transmission, with placing orders for the manufacture of the necessary technology (the 'Seca' decoders, developed with Bertelsmann), and with forming consortia of television channel operators, whose programmes were to be transmitted by satellite as part of the 'package' or 'bouquet' of channels , accessible or available via a 'Canal Satellite Numérique' decoder. It is to the digital television market in France, where Canal Plus became the market leader in 1996-7, launching Canal Satellite in April 1996, that we shall now turn.

Technology was central to the success of Canal Plus, in the mid-1980s, when France (and Europe's) first viable pay-TV channel used technologies permitting the transmission and 'descrambling' of encrypted programmes, on the one hand, and the management of subscriber payments, on the other; again, such expertise was invaluable when Canal Plus invested in research and development (FF 100 million, prior to launch) and ordered the decoders in preparation for digital television 1996 and Canal Satellite's 'bouquet' of channels .The relation to television of the viewer as a paying subscriber, as opposed to the licence-fee payer, is that of a consumer expecting value for money, 'here and now': the contractual relationship is like a market transaction, for Canal Plus, Canal Satellite, and pay-TV operators. Digital television increases the range of attractive programming and consumer choice: in P. Lescure's words, 'digital TV is not another kind of television, but a different way of consuming television'; consumers pay a monthly subscription to access the high-quality (in picture and content) channels of particular interest to them. This reasoning extended the notion of paying for a subscription to a television channel, whose novelty in France in 1984 cannot be sufficiently stressed. The overall aim of the Canal Plus strategy had not changed: to so position itself as to be well placed to offer at competitive prices a wide range of attractive high quality programming for which television consumers would willingly, and regularly, pay; this meant in 1997, as in 1984, developing the commercial applications of state-of-the-art technology; and industry alliances so as to be a – if not *the* – major player in subscription television in France, and in Europe.

Canal Satellite was the first (of three) digitally-compressed and satellite-beamed 'bouquets' of television channels to go on the market in France in 1996: the others were TPS, whose backers included leading commercial private sector and public service channels (such as TF1 and France Télévision), and the financially more modest AB SAT. Heading consortia promising thirty or more channels, available on high-definition television screens, Canal Plus, in short , embarked on what some called the new generation of subscriber television; it was well placed in France, and indeed elsewhere in Europe. In September 1996, Canal Plus announced the (complex) terms of a merger with the South African group Nethold: Nethold was present in subscription television channels and consortia and channels in Italy, Benelux and Nordic countries. Canal Plus would reinforce its position as the leading subscription television group in Europe: weeks later, in December, Canal Plus also announced a joint venture for a satellite-delivered digital programme bouquet of subscription television channels in Spain (December). Save for Britain, after June 1997, Germany. Canal Plus was indeed *the* – major player in subscription television in major European markets.[11] But the number of powerful rival players continued to grow, (See Chapter 8).

Programme and technology investment costs, however, were seen by some to be prohibitive: a high entrance ticket to a potentially crowded market led even Bertelsmann and the CLT to withdraw briefly from the nascent digital television 'landscape' in Germany. Alone or with local partners, Canal Plus spends ever more on acquiring the rights to the first television showing of U.S. studio productions (such as MCA/Universal and Columbia/Tristar) and of live football (in France, as in Spain, etc); management speaks of programme synergies across Europe where it is present, but admits that, unlike the U.S., European markets remain distinctively national.

The success of Canal Plus, like that of Reuters, made it the target on which competitors set their sights. Both companies encountered a stiffer competitive environment in the mid-1990s than in previous years. In digital television – unlike analogue terrestrial subscription television in 1984 – Canal Plus faced severe competition within its home base-market. Canal Plus has vast resources – its cash-flow was some 25 percent of its turnover – and an expertise or know-how in managing a subscriber base of 4 million. The first to enter the market, Canal Satellite transmitted from April 1996 a digital 'bouquet' of a minimum of seventeen television channels, including cable channels, films and football on pay-per-view. Nonetheless, the exercise was difficult. First it sought not to kill the goose that had lain the golden egg: Canal Plus had succeeded as a subscriber television channel in France by offering a programme formula sometimes expressed thus: 'exclusive live coverage of top football matches plus recently released Hollywood films'; the programme bouquet offered by Canal Satellite was not to undermine this subscriber base; thus, the programming formula initially developed by Canal Plus and Canal Satellite saw the latter play a complementary role (in sports programming, for instance – a second top-flight football match, rugby and formula one motor racing). Second, the other major player of the commercial private sector television industry in

France, TF1, sought likewise to enter digital television: it feared that the development of themed television channels would lead it to lose viewers and advertising revenue accordingly (its market share, which was 40.7 percent in 1987, was 35.4 percent in 1996).

Following a series of often abortive negotiations involving public and private sector channels (1994-7), TF1 formed an alliance with the public service corporation, France Télévision, and other major television and telecoms groups and public utilities – France Télécom, M6, la Lyonnaise des Eaux, la CLT: put together in haste, and launched in December 1996, the programme bouquet of TPS was characterised by some industry experts as judiciously placed between what Canal Plus and Canal Satellite offered, at a price less than that of the two together. In early 1997, both Canal Satellite and TPS had reason to be satisfied; but it was clear that the competition would prove severe and eat into the substantial capital reserves of each consortium – Canal Plus had reportedly invested FF 1.3 bn in Canal Satellite and reckoned on three years of losses totalling 500 million. The viewing – and paying – public of satellite channels (digital, and other) was reportedly the gainer; the range of programming on offer was such that while subscribers to Canal Plus were relatively upmarket, subscribers to satellite television channels included minority interest, less affluent publics – including Arab-speaking communities wanting to watch Maghreb /North African channels, while Canal Satellite claimed subscribers among the less affluent social categories who had not been attracted by cable television offerings but found the picture quality of digital television and programme content sufficiently attractive to subscribe.[12]

In France, by mid-1997, the complexities of the capital structures of the communications industry conglomerates, of which the television industry was part, could be simplified thus: a duopoly was emerging. In April, the Compagnie Générale des Eaux increased its stake to become the leading shareholder in Havas and, via Havas, in Canal Plus. Facing it, another conglomerate took shape: these included a further communications infrastructure and water resources group, la Lyonnaise des Eaux, Bouygues – the construction company owning 39 percent of TF1 – and the two private sector television channels, TF1 and M6; the members of this conglomerate together funded TPS, in conjunction with France Télécom, France-Télévision and CLT-UFA – the grouping of the audiovisual interests of Bertelsmann and the Luxembourg group , both of which were previously Havas 'allies'. While the toings and froings, alarms and excursions, between the different partners were set to continue, it was evident that Canal Plus would not enjoy in France in digital television the same relatively free run that it had had in subscriber television.

Television news, views, current affairs and information

Television news-film provision and corporate strategies

Both Canal Plus and Reuters were proven successes by 1990. Both rethought their strategies towards news on television, and news and data feeds for television, during the decade. They approached the question from different perspectives and cultures and with different aims: Canal Plus was a broadcaster, whose forte lay in novel entertainment (first television showing of recently released Hollywood studio films in France, etc.) and live coverage of sports events; founded in London in 1851, Reuters is a 150-year-old news and data agency, acting as a gatherer, processor, retailer and vendor of information to media and non-media outlets. As stated earlier, one is a broadcaster, the other provides news feeds to broadcasters. Here also, however, the situation grew more complex in the 1990s; Canal Satellite's 'programme bouquet' includes thematic and general news channels for news junkies, including CNN International, the TF1 subsidiary LCI, and the television channel launched by Reuters' rival, Bloomberg information TV; Reuters ventured into owner-operating radio news stations in London, and in providing news and current affairs programmes to television channels across the world; above all, it integrated the Visnews film agency, the biggest purveyor of news film worldwide, into its media operations, and created Reuters Television.

The provision of news and current affairs programmes was not a programme priority for Canal Plus; at start-up, in 1984, its news division numbered about ten people. Yet in the context of news-presentation techniques elsewhere on French television in the mid-1980s, it was an innovator. The three journalists heading the Canal Plus news-division – Jean-Louis Burgat, Erik Gilbert and Federick Boulay – were proven professionals, who had previously developed on the (then) public service channel TF1, a novel (on French television) current-affairs programme concept ('7/7'). Furthermore, on Canal Plus in 1984-5, they launched a system of regular bulletins of news-updates (short subjects), dovetailing within live entertainment/discussion programmes, which at the time was new to French television. 'We were the first (French) channel to introduce news-flashes in live programmes', states a Canal Plus programme director. Its 'TV news-in-brief' format was adopted later by other channels aiming at a 'young' audience; one such channel, M6, entitles its prime-time news bulletin 'six minutes', consisting of clips, one of which is captioned 'vite!'. Canal Plus transmitted early in the morning (French time) the prime-time evening newscast of the U.S. channel, CBS. Another Canal Plus programme director dates the beginning of a commitment to in-house current affairs programmes on the channel to the recruitment of talk show hosts in the mid-1990s. Innovative treatment of news and current affairs programming was part of the Canal Plus formula to appeal to a youngish, upwardly mobile and well-educated public. It developed 'event ' journalism, buying up major documentaries and current affairs programmes, made by others: for instance, it was the first French channel to broadcast (in prime-time) the British five-part documentary about Yugoslavia, 'Death of a Nation'.

News-handling, news-packaging

Journalists are very much creatures of the instant, concerned with the current assignment, the current issue, the implications of the latest news development for the story they are writing, or for the production on which they are working. News, like other programme content, is – among other things – a commodity; and, as a programme genre, it is much like a 'feuilleton', with a scenario and 'dramatis personae'. Reputable news organisations and broadcasters negotiate the tensions between the packaging of news – which is itself only part of a larger 'package' – and the gravity (and diversity) of the situations that they report; their professional reputation – and sometimes colleagues' lives – are at stake. To convey some of the breathless and competitive nature of this process, we shall include remarks by journalists observing the processes of news-production – their own output and that of colleagues, and the 'in-house' debates they provoked. Newsfeeds and services, and specialist television news channels increased in the 1990s; Reuters TV, providing news-film to channels worldwide, was part of this process, of which CNN (International) was the standard-bearer, and to which BBC World, Radio France Internationale, and other established British and French news-organisations sought to belong. We shall centre on television news and news-film coverage of Yugoslavia and of Russia – two of the major leitmotivs of media coverage of European/international affairs, in the early 1990s – and on how Reuters print media journalists adapted to working with colleagues 'thinking television'. Again, we must first refer to CNN.

Both at the time, and in retrospect, the impact on Europe's broadcasters of CNN coverage of the Gulf War crisis and aftermath (1990-1) drove home lessons that the self-same broadcasters had started to learn in 1986 (CNN's thirteen-hour live coverage of the explosion of the U.S. spacecraft 'Challenger'), and which CNN coverage of Tiananmen 1989 and the abortive coup against Gorbachev (August 1991) had confirmed: CNN became a player in the provision and broadcasting of television news worldwide; existing providers of international news-film and related products had to adapt accordingly.[13]

From little acorns great oak trees grow: within Reuters, the Gulf War crisis helped spur the launch of the computer graphics news division. CNN notwithstanding, little news-film came out of Iraq: computer graphics 'go' where news cameramen may no longer tread; provided they have reliable data, computer graphics editors can work in any locale or venue – thus, in recent years, computer graphics from Reuters about conflict in Iraq, ex-Yugoslavia, or Russia, are produced in its offices in London, Paris and Sofia.

Three factors led Reuters to reassess strategies for the provision of news-film for television channels worldwide: advances in computer, satellite and telecommunications technologies, geopolitical developments, and the burgeoning markets for feeds of international news-film. The amount of news-material generated worldwide by the Gulf crisis and war seems to have represented something of a quantum leap; it invites comparison with the emergence of U.S. news media as purveyors of copy about international stories at the turn of the century – the U.S. conflict with Spain (Philippines, Cuba), the Russo-Japanese war and 1905 Russian 'revolution'. A Reuters in-house magazine lists fifty bureaux mobilised by the coverage of the Gulf War; its news editorial 'quality control unit', assessing the product of Reuters, other agencies, and CNN, wrote of the persistence and prominence of the same prevailing international news agenda, months on end.

In 1991, Reuters was the majority shareholder in Visnews: the latter was the leading supplier of international news-film to broadcasters worldwide: in July 1992, Visnews (founded in 1957) claimed to be used by over 400 broadcasters 'in almost every coverage where television exists our coverage is seen on an estimated 470 million television receivers throughout the world'; it had thirty-four bureaux and some 400 camera crews.[14] In 1992-3, Reuters acquired outright control of Visnews, rebaptised the concern Reuters Television (RTV), and sought to integrate Reuters and Visnews bureaux worldwide. The logistics of this 'merger' required print and broadcasting journalists to work together; at the same time, in related developments, Reuters diversified into operating local radio stations in London, and providing newsfeeds and current affairs programming for television channels in London, Moscow and elsewhere. These developments led journalists to develop what news-managers or executives call 'multiskilling'. We shall now look at some of the competitive pressures, and 'cultural shocks', experienced by journalists as a result.

Multiskilling: producing material for Television (from Yugoslavia)

'Think visuals: we've entered a wider world': thus did a Reuters 'quality controller' – known familiarly as a 'quack' – enjoin Reuters' correspondents worldwide, used to producing text (and photos) for computer screen-delivered services, to adapt to working continually hand-in-hand with their Visnews colleagues who were now Reuters' employees. During the six months or so prior to the effective implementation of the 'integration' of Reuters and Visnews staff (July 1993), journalists discussed how to nurture the multiskilling required in preparing the logistics of the coverage of a story for both television and text clients. Journalists used to producing copy for newspapers worldwide had to realise that when they covered a story they should allow for the requirements of the cameraman who was filming alongside them: 'the full incorporation of RTV compared with the old looser Visnews connection means much more careful co-ordination if the multimedia concept is to work'.

Television requirements took precedence: 'set up a feature to meet TV demands – good visuals first, last and always – and the text will take care of itself. The other way around doesn't work. Don't set up a feature and take TV along. Involve TV in stories from the start. Some may work for TV, some not . When a story breaks we share resources – cars, charters, sat. phones – and move in together. Correspondents are learning to place themselves by the RTV camera at news conferences. Why? When the subject answers a RTV question he is facing our camera. So we co-ordinate on questions with the RTV crew. And television might be working on something else that needs a soundbite. Doorstepping VIPs? – work with the TV crew and get that quick entry or exit quote on camera. TV has a wonderful institution called a fixer or producer, in RTV a co-ordinator. RTV co-ords have a wide range of contacts and are terrific at quickly and efficiently moving the earth to get a news-team on to a breaking story. Use their talents to set up cover and relieve journalists to concentrate on writing and reporting'.[15]

In January 1993, the co-ordinator of the television, text and photo services of Reuters intended for media clients began logging daily entries on how RTV was performing against the competition. One of the top on-running themes of the then international news agenda was the violence and conflict in what became known as 'ex-Yugoslavia', and related diplomatic developments in Europe, North America and Asia. At the time, many French television viewers watched the prime-time news (at 8 p.m.) on either the private sector TF1 or public service France 2 newscast, sometimes zapping with the satirical news programme (centred on a spoof on the TF1 newscaster 'PPDA') on Canal Plus *Les Guignols de l'Info*. Out-in-the field, in Yugoslavia, as elsewhere, journalists and camera crews sought to cover the fighting and linked developments: in particular, Reuters, WTN and – from November 1994 – APTV competed to feed the EBU Eurovision exchange of electronic video newsgathering material; Reuters collated film for its own VisEurope. Thus, the report dated Thursday April 1 1993, filed by the quality controller under the heading 'Reuters television', began thus:

> Reuters had a beat of more than three hours on first word that refugees had been killed in a stampede to get out of the besieged Bosnian town of Srebrenica in a U.N. convoy. RTV, covered by Miki Stojicic and Dusan Popov fed from our dish in Belgrade, included pictures of two victims who had suffocated in the back of trucks. Sasa Kavic's scenes of the refugees arriving in Tuzla were fed live into Eurovision and at the same time to VisEurope – to widespread acclaim from European Broadcasting Union members and Visnews subscribers.[16]

Lives are risked, and injuries – sometimes fatal – incurred, so as to cover and transmit stories. Martin Bell, covering Yugoslavia for BBC news, subsequently wrote of the excessive dangers incurred by correspondents in the field, urged on by news/editorial headquarters, so as to cover dramatic breaking stories fast. Discussing 'the competitive nature of the TV news business', he centres on the competition between WTN and Visnews/Reuters TV:

> They operated under separate rules, devised by the European Broadcasting Union, whereby they would offer the images of the day's events on the Eurovision News Exchange – a market controlled by a cartel of national broadcasters. On the basis of the agencies' pictures and their local producers' promotion of them while they were as yet an unseen commodity, one side's edit would be accepted, and the other's rejected – and most of Europe would use one sequence of images (the national networks which were already in place, such as ourselves and TF1 of France, of course had a much freer hand, and would also trade images with each other). In the agency game there was a winner and a loser, with many a tear and tantrum at the feed point – from the men as well. The pressure on today's losers to become tomorrow's winners, by venturing that half block further where the fighting was thickest, was clear and unconscionable. Head office was urging them to greater heroics.[17]

Bell relates the circumstances of the coverage of the fighting in Sarajevo (and of 'snipers' alley'), and his attempts to organise a co-operative pool of coverage by the competing agencies; this operated for a brief period but came to an end, such were the competitive pressures (notably when APTV entered the fray). Reporters in the field had to acquire the reflexes of multiskilling and cooperation between print, radio and TV crews, on-the-job, in 'the heat of the moment'. Reuters noted approvingly how its different teams in Yugoslavia – including the (American) reporter Kurt Schork, who, albeit less than Bell, became a household name in Britain – worked well together. In December 1993, AFP and WTN spoke favourably of cooperation and synergies between their respective bureaux in Belgrade, Zagreb (and elsewhere): WTN had news-film crews, unlike AFP, and appreciated the daily phone contacts and updates between the two – 'mostly information: where, who, what, how, when' – and access to AFP' s 'wires' of international news: forward planning arrangements benefited likewise.

The market for news-film

Competition to provide news-film for the growth in the number of television channels worldwide intensified throughout the 1990s. Reuters' transformation of Visnews into the agency's 'television branch' reflected the growing market for television channels wanting 'feeds' of news film. An in-house feasibility study of the market for television news-film, conducted in 1994 by one of the major players, described the situation thus: in Europe, in the past, there were relatively few major broadcasting companies, and most of them produced either individually or by working together (the EBU's Eurovision exchange, for example) enough material for their purposes; even today (1994), production of news-film for television 'majors' is characterised by high added-value (exclusivity, subjectivity) criteria that run counter to the traditional functions of a news agency (exhaustive coverage, 'agency' news-reporting style). The study argued that a sea-change was occurring – not just in Europe, but worldwide: 'in the future, most TV channels will have fewer (financial) resources than their predecessors; they will have to buy most of their programmes for much less than the cost of in-house production; competition will itself change as specialist or thematic channels proliferate'.

According to this feasibility study, standardised products, reusable and interchangeable, were to be delivered by a 'mass' distribution system of programme feeds to all manner of television channels; in-house productions would have to cover costs via repeats and sales. It was anticipated that the demand for programmes was so great that quality criteria would suffer: 'this will reflect on the demand for news-film products: TV news departments will have limited resources and will have a public service function compared to the entertainment role of most of the programmes TV majors will carry. The market for news and current affairs programmes will not increase in proportion to the number of television channels'. As an indication of the 'consumerist' trend that characterised the growth of the number of television channels, the aforementioned study cited the rise of teleshopping: 'one of the 600 Italian TV channels is dedicated to consumers using television to buy carpets'.

The same study noted how ReutersTV, distributing news-film worldwide by satellite, was highly appreciated whereas the number of news-film reports offered by the EBU's electronic video news-exchange arrangements was falling fast. Reuters and AP appeared particularly well placed to respond to the market for television news-film among TV channels who devoted few 'in-house' resources to news; channels like France's M6 – whose-prime time news-bulletin of brief subject-sequences is called 'Six minutes', as mentioned earlier – want outside suppliers to provide 'news kit' programming, i.e., video items ready for broadcast, commentary in English available if so desired, news-film available with or without sound-track, etc. APTV, attentive to the needs of broadcasters worldwide, stated that 'sound-bites and direct quotes', should be both translated into English and available in the (vernacular) language in which they were said: there was little point in translating, say, the comment of a German tourist mugged in Miami, from German into English and subsequently back into German (if used by a German television broadcaster). The feasibility study pointed out that channels broadcasting to publics straddling several countries or cultures had different news agenda and requirements from those of 'nationwide TV news bulletins': thus, commenting on the non-fiction programming of Arte, it observed:

> paradoxically, because of its double nationality, the ARTE '8 1/2' news bulletin includes more international news than the newscasts of France's other channels. '8 1/2' provides German TV viewers, who are used to a larger number of international news-stories than their French neighbours, with an abundance of reports and analyses of news-stories from parts of the world with which they are unfamiliar – such as (sub-Saharan) Africa, North Africa and South-East Asia.

The study pointed out that at the time (mid-1994), Arte used news-film from the EBU-EVN, WTN and ReutersTV; worldwide, Reuters had a competitive edge with its existing market of feeds to 650 television channels in eighty countries. In 1994, RTV had thirty-eight bureaux, and could call on the resources of the 118 other bureaux of the agency; it had news-exchange agreements with the BBC, NBC, CNN and Reuters Financial TV, and with the economic news channel of the Mexican television company, Controle Televisa. RTV had 400 journalists and could call on the 11,000-plus news-staff of the parent agency; it stated that it broadcast 6,000 hours of programming a year (news, current affairs magazines, and 'à la carte' programmes). It was the market leader worldwide (with the important exception of the U.S.A.).

Beyond such assessments of respective strengths and weaknesses as competitors in the provision of news-film for the growing number of television companies and channels, there was a perception in some quarters that international or transnational news agencies and broadcasters were each 'treading on one another's patch': the market for news-film worldwide was such that established players in the production, transmission and/or distribution/delivery of such material, were themselves converging, developing partnerships or accentuating traditional rivalries, as the case might be. As noted in the above references to news-agency competition in Yugoslavia, the leading U.S. agency AP, – 'which started with the written word in 1848 and expanded into photographs in 1927 and voice in 1974[18] – launched APTV, 'reporting the news in moving pictures', in November 1994. Entering production and television broadcasting from a different 'culture', Bloomberg L.P., the economic and financial news and data agency launched in New York in 1981 by a former employee of the New York bank Salomon Brothers, diversified in the mid-1990s into the provision of programming for financial television channels, and formed partnerships in national markets with general news agencies – AFP in France, EFE in Spain, ANSA in Italy, etc; these provided it with feeds that it used in transmissions live out of London; for instance, from 1996, AFP provided Bloomberg with feeds and French-language programming for thirty minute news bulletins, which Bloomberg transmitted via the French cable Télécable and as one of the Canal Satellite 'bouquet' of television channels. At the same time (in fact, over several years), AFP discussed with another major international vector of news, the news-film agency Worldwide Television Network (WTN), possible Cupertino. This move made abundant sense: Reuters TV, calling on existing strengths of the agency's text and photo networks, appeared to enjoy logistical advantages in covering the world's news hot-spots (including at the time ex-Yugoslavia, CIS (ex-USSR), South Africa), to the detriment of the news-film agency WTN and the news-agency AFP; in November 1996, AFP and WTN agreed to share resources (news, logistical, commercial – shared offices, for example, in Beirut and Havana).

Reuters and Bloomberg derive substantially more revenue from their non-media than from their media clients, yet appreciate the 'high profile' television brings (and because broadcast channels and stations are a growth market, unlike newspapers). In short, data vendors and international news agencies – whether their forte is in general or financial news – felt they had to be present in television (and, indeed, in various on-line and multimedia markets); and broadcasters, such as CNN, diversified into activities where their 'product' is akin to that of a news agency: CNN on-line material distributed via their website is edited and presented just like the copy of a news agency; AFP staff preparing teletext material (similar to the BBC's Ceefax) and sound and television footage (aided by Bloomberg's logistical support) for Bloomberg television, broadcasting (via cable and satellite) from London, note how their 'copy' and presentational skills have to be more incisive than agency traditionalists might expect.

In this complex and continuing process of business plans, company rivalries and alliances, technological developments, and the search for market niches, some of the actors involved were well-established players in the production and distribution of international news; others were new players in the provision of financial news; all sought to find a market in the expansion of live continuous television news, that – in the U.S.A., as of 1980, and in Europe and most other world regions, as of 1990 – was symbolised by the expansion of the broadcasting companies associated with Ted Turner: CNN and, especially, CNN International. The impact of 'live' television broadcasting, or rather the continuous up-dating, of news, transmitted via cable and/or satellite, by CNN, cannot be overstated: its impact was considerable on information vendors and transnational broadcasters alike: in Europe, Euronews (launched in 1993), and in France, the TF1 subsidiary LCI (launched in June 1994), were presented as 'adaptations' of (or reactions against) the CNN concept for European audiences ; similarly, Rupert Murdoch's subsidiary 'Skynews', beamed by cable and satellite across Europe, transposed the live/continuous concept for European audiences. However, despite the impact of the CNN 'model', the channel depended heavily on feeds of video news-film from outside suppliers.

Competition between international news organisations – whether agencies or broadcasters – intensified from the mid-1980s to the mid-1990s, just as did the competition between subscriber television groups in Europe: the provision of news-services and feeds, however, generates less revenue than subscription television. In 1997, CNN was considered one of the few to be turning a profit. And even this leading world broadcaster in the provision of continuous television news in the mid-1980s was reckoned to face serious competition from some of twenty other international news vectors of the mid-1990s. From 1996-7, CNN International regionalised its services – partly in response to the growing competition from the likes of MSNBC, Rupert Murdoch's News Corp (Fox News Network in the U.S.A. and Sky News in Europe) and BBC World. Regionalisation involved broadcasting non-English language programmes – for instance in April 1997, CNN launched a twenty-four-hour Spanish service, broadcast from its Atlanta headquarters – and strengthening staff resources in London and Hong Kong. Europe was the venue of severe competition for 'market-share' between English-language news-services where Sky, CNN and BBC World appeared as the market-leaders. For instance, in April 1997, after two years in Europe, BBC World claimed an audience of 30 million homes out of a worldwide viewership of 50 million homes in 174 countries and territories; the BBC had a total of 250 correspondents worldwide.[19]

French news organisations with international ambitions feared they might be the ghosts at the feast. Plans to launch a 'CNN à la française', supported by the chief executive of Radio France Internationale, Jean-Paul Cluzel, were shelved in May 1997. On the other hand, the CNN 'model' was constantly referred to – by the financially troubled Euronews (based in Ecully, near Lyon, and transmitting Europe-wide (and to North Africa) in five languages, and by the TF1 subsidiary, LCI.

International news agencies have substantially greater experience in tailoring a 'world news budget' to the requirements of different world regions, and in different languages. While proving a sometimes difficult customer, Rupert Murdoch appreciated the news-services, financial acumen and technological expertise of Reuters: he sat on the company board in the 1980s. And CNN executives appreciated the breadth of the international coverage of AFP – 'there are certain places in the world where AFP owns the story', remarked a CNN senior national editor for CNN domestic, in 1995. Other CNN executives observed, in 1996: 'all agencies make mistakes (especially in the era of real-time and market-moving news)'.

In 1994, according to one industry estimate, CNN used material from its own network of nineteen bureaux worldwide (excluding the U.S.A.), and from the following agencies, WTN, Reuters TV, Eurovision (of which CNN was a member), Arabvision, and the Asian agency AVN. CNN, like the major U.S. networks, found RTV and WTN largely sufficient for their purposes: RTV, for example, transmitted from ten to twelve videos (lasting two minutes each) per day; they covered 'hot news' subjects of general interest and subjects of 'regional' interest – transmissions on Asia, on Latin America . Transmission costs (by satellite) were still hefty – some U.S. $1000 for ten feet of film; accordingly, CNN found it more advantageous to use agency news-film (for non-U.S. coverage); CNN was more a consumer than purveyor of news-film worldwide.

Technology, finance – i.e., anticipated investment costs and rate of return – market conditions and company strategies are, in this field as in others, fast-moving. For example, in mid-1997, CNN had thirty-one overseas bureaux (up from nineteen in 1994) and was the first U.S. media group since Fidel Castro had acquired power in Cuba to open a bureau in Havana. International news and data organisations developed their multi-media, television and on-line strategies while attempting to assess the implications for their company, competitors and the market, of the spread of the Internet. The 'convergence' of the television screen and the personal computer, as the terminal or delivery-point to the end-user, excited industry experts. Reuters launched its Financial TV service in 1994, enabling clients (traders, bankers and currency operators, in the main) to monitor on their computer and television screens the connection between real-time live coverage of a 'market mover' – a speech by the chairman of the U.S. federal reserve board, Alan Greenspan, for example – and price movements worldwide. In Europe, international purveyors of financial news and data developed feeds to broadcasters or entered broadcasting themselves. Most of the leading news organisations and information vendors were headquartered in the U.S.A. or Britain.

Reuters – absent from television in 1991 (save indirectly, via Visnews) – was seen by 1994 as a major purveyor of television news film: its brand image benefited accordingly. Established agencies moved from their traditional role. Previously limited to acting as footage wholesalers, as international newsgathering support systems for broadcasters, and as syndicators of broadcasters' material, they moved to providing cost-efficient programming for broadcasters, seeking not to compete with their broadcasting clients, but to act as complementary service-suppliers. A WTN deputy managing editor expressed matters thus: 'broadcasters are increasingly relying on agencies for frontline coverage; the agencies, expansion has allowed broadcasters to cut back on protection coverage'. One trade press journalist observed in 1994: ' WTN tends to focus more on entertainment and lighter news and features information than Reuters, a lucrative area given the range of broadcasters now competing for ratings around the world'.[20]

Conclusion

Information and programme flows have increased prodigiously: AFP produces more than 2 million words a day; Reuters more than 27,000 pages of data each second; the Chairman and Managing Director of M6, Jean Drucker, observes: 'every single TV channel in France broadcasts more interesting programmes than anyone can possibly watch'. In the 1980s, in France, some television industry figures claimed that, as channels proliferated, there would be a shortage of programming; in the 1990s, the fear is – 'how can the TV viewer possibly absorb all the programmes on offer and at what price, social as well as economic?'

In 1998, Canal Plus is the market leader in Pay-television in Europe, as is Reuters in the provision of general and financial news, data and attendant support systems, worldwide. Both are in 'the added value' market: Canal Plus invested in high-quality programming and delivery systems to consumers willing to pay for quality programming; Reuters, known as a reputable international news agency for over a century, invested in the 1960s in developing systems and services for international finance and the electronic marketplace: in the 1990s, the profits thus made serve to fund development of media services and expansion into television. Canal Plus became in a very brief period 'the Reuters of the pay television scene in Europe'; a former chief executive of AFP called Reuters the 'IBM' of the news agency world (at a time when IBM was *the* computer industry reference).[21]

In the competitive environment of multimedia multinational players, Canal Plus and Reuters each experience occasional reverses, as rivals (or sometime allies) consider them the lodestone that they must emulate, or beat. This 'diptych' highlights different facets of corporations that cannot be compared, but in which journalist and non-journalist personnel fashion a corporate or in-house culture that highlights multiskilling, client satisfaction and the continual search for new markets. In very different ways, both companies illustrate how, over the past twenty years, the ethos of the transaction, and of paying the market price, has replaced, or emerged alongside, that of information and entertainment programming as a public good or service, in France, Britain and elsewhere.

Notes and References

1. Interviewed in *Le Monde*, 15 September 1987. J. Tunstall and M. Palmer, *Media Moguls*, London, Routledge, 1991.
2. 'FT 500', *Financial Times*, 10 February 1993, 24 January 1997. TF1 was the first public service television channel in Europe to be privatised.
3. In France's regulated system of support for the film industry, Canal Plus is required to spend 12 percent of its turnover on French and European films, in return for the right to broadcast its encrypted subscriber service – including films – months ahead of other channels. Of the FF. 2.7bn funding of French films in 1995, Canal Plus contributed FF 912m, and France's other television broadcasters FF 449m. *Financial Times*, 7 May 1997.
4. *Le Nouvel observateur*, Paris, 30 January 1997.
5. F. Rose, 'The end of TV', *Fortune*, New York, 23 December 1996.
6. M. Bloomberg's own account, *Bloomberg on Bloomberg*, New York/London, John Libbey, 1997. Excluding transactional and media services, Reuters's and Bloomberg's revenue growth between 1993 and 1995 was put at 32 percent and 93 percent respectively. Market data Industry, *Financial Times*, 14 March 1997.
7. P. Lescure, interviewed on 'Questions orales', Radio classique, January-February 1997.

8. 'Illiquid lunch', *The Economist*, 30 March 1996; Waters Information services, Market data industry survey, *The Economist*, 14 June 1997.
9. In 1985 it was authorised to carry a small amount of advertising: Canal Plus was then perceived to be in difficulties. In 1997 its proven commercial success, as well as the pressures from rival broadcasting groups (led by TF1), led some right-wing (UDF-RPR) MPs to urge that Canal Plus should no longer carry advertising. See 'Le développement de Canal Plus pourrait être freiné par les députés', *Le Monde*, Paris, 20 March 1997.
10. 'Le statut de Canal Plus', *Le Monde*, 31 March 1984; M. Palmer and J. Tunstall, *Liberating Communications*, Oxford, NCC Blackwell, 1990.
11. This account is based on various industry and trade presss sources, news magazines and *Le Monde*. See, for example, 'Televisions: 1000 chaînes et après', *Enjeux Les Echos*, December 1996.
12. 'La guerre du ciel', *Télé Obs, Le Nouvel Observateur*, 17-23 April 1997; 'Aujourd'hui Communication', *Le Monde*, 29-30 December 1996.
13. Visnews, the news-film agency then owned by Reuters, NBC and the BBC, competed against CNN in providing footage of events in Moscow in August 1991.
14. Visnews publicity brochure, July 1992.
15. World Media Comment (WMC), 3 March 1993, Reuters corporate archive, London.
16. WMC, 1 April 1993, Ibid.
17. M. Bell, *In Harm's Way*, London, Hamish Hamilton, 1995, 63.
18. *Editor and Publisher*, New York, 16 October 1993.
19. Hugh Williams, BBC Director of Channels, quoted in *International Herald Tribune*, 23 April 1997.
20. S. Busfield, 'Agency on the make', *Broadcast*, London, 4 November 1994. In 1998 AP acquired WTN.
21. H. Pigeat, *Le nouveau désordre mondial de l'information*, Paris, Hachette, 1987.

Chapter 12

The Europeanisation of Programming

Alex Taylor

Having earned my living for the last seven years in France producing and presenting various programmes about Europe on French radio and television, I have decided to take the easy way out and interpret the prescribed title in the practical sense of 'the way the French and British media talk about Europe'. My experience of French television is hands-on, that of British television much more passive as a viewer, and I would like to emphasise that all that follows is of a purely subjective nature. I have also taken the very easy road of understanding 'Europeanisation of programming' to mean 'more and more programmes about Europe', but this is in practical terms what it generally comes down to for programme makers.

Prior to getting my first permanent job on French television, I spent ten years between 1980 and 1990 attempting with varying degrees of success to earn a living. This ranged from doing a regular gardening chronicle in rhyming alexandrines on local Parisian radios to trying my hand at taming dromedaries in a circus. Whenever I tried to get more serious jobs, I was always told in more or less polite terms – 'Why should we take someone foreign when we can get a French person to do it?'

Then came the 1990s and, to cut a long story short, after ten years of 'galères' which did however enable me to get a lot of experience and meet a lot of people, all of a sudden in February 1990 I came across a person who actually wanted someone audibly and visibly foreign to present a new TV programme.

The programme *Continentales*, the brainchild of Michel Kuhn, a very enthusiastic university teacher and television producer, keen on giving French television something of the educational television that had impressed him in other countries – Germany, for instance, was producing some 2,600 hours of it every year, British television 1,800 hours, and, when you consider that the equivalent figure for French television was in the region of ninety-six hours per year, there was indeed scope for development (see chapter 7). And so it was that *Continentales* started off as a bit of a hotchpotch of predominantly bought-in material, the only common feature of which was that it could all loosely be grouped together under the pretext of being 'pédagogique'. Anyway, it gave FR3 a very cheap way of filling in two and a half hours of its morning schedules. And so it was that every morning I guided the viewer through what must at times have appeared a somewhat baffling array of spelling lessons, maths, cultural debates about the War and explanations of the function of the earlobe with a Quebec accent.

The first hour of our morning show was, however, for the whole team, by far the most exciting. This was *L'Eurojournal* – which consisted of five 10-minute extracts from British, German, Russian, Italian and Spanish news bulletins, some coming from the main bulletins of the previous evening, some recorded barely an hour before we went on air – all of which, thanks to an incredibly enthusiastic and efficient team of translators, got subtitled at breakneck speed. We even became so hooked on the adrenaline, we would record the RAI's 8.00 o'clock morning news and it would go out translated into French some forty-five minutes afterwards.

Another peculiarity of this already rather untypical programme was the decision – mainly for budgetary reasons – to produce it outside Paris in one of FR3's decentralised stations, at Nancy, even though it was shown all around France, – and, incidentally, all around Europe too, as the *Eurojournal* was retransmitted by TV5; this led amongst other things, to a surprise conversation with a Russian presenter of *Novosti* who rang up to tell me she often watched herself in Moscow with French subtitles.

My role was ostensibly to be the human face between the news blocks, although my links often provided valuable seconds while the frantic translators installed their floppy disks in the subtitling machine up in the gallery. I decided to put this airtime to use by giving 'words' of general use which would come up in the subsequent bulletin, or explaining, for example, rather arcane local practices, such as why British MPs divide off into the 'ayes' and the 'noes'. This conveniently reinforced the 'educational' nature of the programme and incidentally helped us keep our independence from the 'rédaction' of FR3, who would doubtless otherwise have interfered with the editorial content.

A month after my arrival on the show in June 1990, Saddam Hussein obligingly invaded Kuwait – I say this because it worked wonders for our viewing figures, since this was back at the turn of the decade when no one in France had cable – let alone satellite (see chapters 8 and 9), and had never seen what a foreign news bulletin or newsreader looked like. We were therefore showing 'the whole of Europe watching the situation develop' at the same time as other French channels had to content themselves with a mixture of badly dubbed CNN or French generals endlessly discussing maps. It got the programme a lot of encouraging press and catapulted our viewing figures. One morning – the only one ever! – we even managed to beat Pierre Bellemare and Maryse selling sewing machines on TF1's early morning teleshopping show, getting some 3 million viewers.

A few months later I became producer of *Continentales* and decided that as we had already shown everything 'educational' produced in French, it would be best to concentrate on the 'European' aspect, following the hour-long *Eurojournal* with one and a half hours of *Euromag* – news magazines and reports from over 100 or so European channels, everything shown in the original version with French subtitles. The French are slightly less reticent about the use of subtitles than the British, being more accustomed to reading them at the cinema if not on their television screens, but the big channels still steer clear of any subtitling at all anywhere near prime-time. As regards content, 'Panorama', 'Assignment', 'Dispatches', 'World in Action' were some of the British purchases.

The daily schedules were organised according to countries. Monday would be British and Irish television, Tuesday German, Dutch and Scandinavian, Thursday Italian and Spanish, and Friday Russian and anything from 'the East'. One programme more than any other brought home to me the 'Europeanness' of the show – broadcasting reports about the war in Croatia, we had viewers watching via TV5 phoning in from all over the continent to give their views on the situation in the Balkans.

Over the next four years we did a total of 1,500 Continentales programmes, and in the last two years, the daily two and a half hours were split into two parts, l'*Eurojournal* going out in the late evening to give us an audience comprising the more inquisitive late-night viewers and French business people back home late and eager to catch up on the news.

Ratings for the show generally had very little to do with the content, depending solely on what FR3 had shown beforehand – we reached dizzy heights of almost a million at 12.30 one evening (which was even later than usual) as a result of coming just after the umpteenth repeat of *Gone with the Wind*.

The one-and-a-half hour *Euromag* section still went out at 8.00 in the morning, which is, contrary to what might be thought, an ideal time for any television producer, because there was at the time no pressure whatsoever to get ratings, and contrary to other people in charge of programmes I was able to base choices entirely on what was interesting without systematically putting out what would 'please'. To show how content-based ratings are, on the other hand, it must be said that one of our highest 'scores' came the day we showed an unusually risqué Dutch report about sado-masochistic sessions in Amsterdam brothels. There was, however, no pressure to repeat these audience peaks.

But *Continentales* – which between 1992 and 1994 actually consisted of nine slots a week (we also did a 'best-of' each Saturday evening) despite being on the margins of the station's main prime-time, was frequently cited as being among the three best-known programmes on France 3. During this time we covered many special events like the putsch in Russia which we followed live as it was seen on Russian television. The magazine part also gave insights through magazines such as *ZAK* from the WDR in Cologne into the after-effects of the German reunification, aspects of which the two-minute cameo pieces provided for French television's evening news bulletins could not possibly convey in any depth. (French news has since the beginning of the 1990s become increasingly 'hexagonal' as the main '20 heures' on TF1 and France 2 run side by side and vie desperately for viewers – to the point where they even keep an eye on what the others are showing, changing the running order at the last minute to take advantage of 'boring bits' on the other side). In this context it is hardly surprising that foreign news is squeezed in among the more attractive bits, like football or more accessible features from 'la France profonde' (rural France). John Simpson would certainly be even more dismayed than at the BBC about the 'squeezing out' of foreign items on French television, and if in his recent comments he reacted with some alarm to the idea of sending popular figures like Ulrika Johnnson to cover foreign stories, no such idea has even found expression in France.

After *Continentales* in 1995 I was asked to conceive, produce and co-present a new daily programme, this time for Arte, the Franco-German cultural channel. Arte has had a great deal of trouble establishing itself as a watchable television channel, mainly because, contrary to any other existing media, it is the result of a political treaty signed at the time between Helmut Kohl and François Mitterrand. This is a long way from the origins of Channel 4 in Britain. Decisions were for a long time – and in some cases still are – made according to a political agenda, which does not always cater to the needs of good programme making. I was obliged to take on two secretaries for example, one French, one German, not because we needed two secretaries but because the balance had to be maintained in the employment of French and German nationals. Higher up the scale, this same process considerably bogs down any decision making, engendering a good deal of traditional Franco-German hostility between two people trying to do a job one could do perfectly well on his or her own.

The brief for *Confetti* was to produce something 'lightweight' and feature-based about Europe. I should have known from the beginning that this would be a much harder nut to crack than the ostensibly far more serious *Continentales* – and this from the dispute about the way to translate the French word '*léger*' for the German version of our press brochure. As the concept doesn't apparently exist in German, it was decided after three days of acrimonious debate to settle for the ungainly 'augenzwinkernd' ('that makes your eye twitch').

We did 250 *Confetti* programmes – a daily half-hour tour of the 'human side of Europe' consisting of two-thirds bought-in material and one-third specially commissioned reports which were carefully distributed equally amongst French and German production companies in order to pacify Arte's ferocious need to keep the peace between its two poles. (I even had to take on two employees, one German, one French, for several positions where one would have been perfectly adequate – the result of which was that two semi-occupied people ended up squabbling about who would do what, which illustrates in its own way the traps of so many European ventures.)

The commissioned material in *Confetti* concentrated, for example, on different people throughout Europe presenting their homes, or 'wedding ceremonies throughout Europe' or '6.00 am in the streets of Berlin, Barcelona, Birmingham' etc. All this with the perhaps rather naïve ambition of rendering Europe more 'sympa'.

Confetti was quite successful in Arte's terms but fell victim to the intense friction within the Strasbourg offices between the two partners – the French for whom Arte is one terrestrial channel among five others needing something to attract viewers, the Germans for whom it is a real intellectual and cultural oasis amongst the twenty or so commercial channels showing soaps and game shows. However, the programme did win a few prizes, including one in Germany itself for 'innovative' television, being the first European magazine presented simultaneously (if rather maniacally) in both French and German.

After this, I spent a year on the new French educational channel La Cinquième doing the *Eurojournal* once again, and subsequently a new programme *Euroclic* – where each day we would look at a particular issue affecting different countries throughout Europe through a mixture of extracts from television, press and correspondents from the country's media live in the studio.

Based on this experience, I have to admit that talking about Europe on French television has been at best an uphill battle. To illustrate what I mean by this, if ever there was a 'European, pedagogical and cultural programme', it was *Continentales*, but I very soon learnt, as presenter, that there were three words I should on no occasion say on the air – '*pédagogique, culturel*, and above all – *européen*!' Being English helped me get away with this last one as I often substituted the slightly more affectionate 'notre continent'.

The truth is that despite impressions often to the contrary, especially in Britain, the French are far from being the rampant Europhiles their leaders would like them to be, and 'Europe' is as hard to sell here as anywhere else.

As further evidence of this, I now do a daily European press review every morning on France Inter, the French equivalent of Radio 4. If I start off by saying something like 'France is once again in the headlines' or 'Chirac's attitude is heavily criticised in the *Frankfurter Allgemeine Zeitung* this morning' all the French journalists having breakfast in the studio are instantly agog. If, however, I start off with 'The problems of the Italian government are the lead in *La Repubblica*', it is generally the moment everyone puts the dirty coffee cups back on the trolley. On the day of writing this, bang in the middle of France's legislative elections, one of the main journalists on France Inter reacted with incredulity when I told him that there was also an election going on at the moment in Ireland!

This to me is very symptomatic of the general state of affairs. After seven years of broadcasting about Europe in the French media I must admit it would be difficult to be anything other than pessimistic about the interest these issues hold – but then why should they be interested in Europe? It seems such a hotchpotch of small countries, all speaking different languages and with immensely complicated political set-ups and, worse still, everyone seems to spend their time constantly bickering with each other. No wonder that with resources few and far between, and pressure on viewing figures intense, television channels would rather send their correspondents to 'big' places like the U.S., Russia or Africa. Even at Radio France Internationale it needed a lot of persuasion to obtain a regular correspondent and a shared bureau this year in Berlin, the 'future capital of Europe'.

However, all this, it has to be said, is infinitely more impressive than the coverage of Europe in the British media, admittedly victim of the anti-European feeling during the final term of Conservative government. Where is the European press review on the *Today* programme on Radio 4 for example? There has never been any equivalent attempt at giving British viewers a European view of the news, not even of British news (except right back on BBC Educational television in the

1970s, and this with half an hour of extracts from French and German television once a week. Europe is confined to programmes like *Eurotrash* which seem to deliberately try to cash in on any European stereotyping available, with much play made on the way funny foreigners try to speak our language. I find Antoine de Caunes, for example, very talented in French, much more cloying and down-market in English where facility is all that seems to be required of him. There are the occasional forays by Channel 4 such as *Europe Express* or when they asked different European journalists – such as Christine Ockrent – to make a film about the state of different countries. (This is not the case, incidentally, on BBC World Service, especially radio, which puts out the best European programme I have heard every morning with *Europe Today*, but I wonder who can actually listen to this, as even in Paris I only get snaps of it through the crackles on my short-wave radio at around 5.30 a.m.)

I would say that things can only change for the better – but that it would make it a whole lot easier for us broadcasters if the politicians made Europe a more attractive concept to sell. Is it any wonder that we send our correspondents and film crews far and wide around the globe rather than to Brussels to cover yet another faceless meeting of terse ministers squabbling about cod quotas? As long as the people who run Europe do not seem to actually like the place as a concept, it is very difficult to make attractive programming out of 'our continent'.

CHAPTER 13

BROADCASTERS' INVOLVEMENT IN CINEMATOGRAPHIC CO-PRODUCTIONS

ANNE JÄCKEL

In the new multimedia age, the traditional argument that cinema audiences have declined as a result of the advent of television has receded behind the new value given to film libraries by the proliferation of television outlets. Those who, along with former French Minister of Culture, Jack Lang, feared that 'the art of the twentieth century' was in danger of disappearing before the arrival of the twenty-first century, should be comforted by circumstantial evidence showing that cinema audiences have been steadily increasing in Europe in the early 1990s as a result of the multiplex boom, and that video renters and specialised film channel viewers tend to be more frequent cinema-goers. With a fast-expanding market for feature films, the 1990s have seen a remarkable increase in the level of production in most of the world's leading film-producing nations. In the European Union, the number of feature films produced has risen from 518 in 1990 to 646 in 1996,[1] and the number of films co-produced or co-financed by partners from different countries has increased from 131 in 1990 to 229 in 1996. Most European broadcasters are now involved in film production. Some have even entered the field of theatrical distribution. Whether large international players (Canal Plus) or small regional channels (S4C), they tend to take a positive view of the cinema as an important showcase for the films they help finance.

Considering the sustained importance of film in the new multimedia environment, this chapter investigates the extent to which the challenge of Europe has influenced and continues to affect the involvement of British and French television companies in film financing. Traditionally, the British regulatory approach has favoured television at the expense of cinema while French audiovisual policy privileges the latter. This difference has been crucial to European debates over the adoption of a common audiovisual policy. Today, both the European Union's Directive 'Television Without Frontiers' and the Prague Resolution on public service broadcasting of the Committee of Ministers of the Council of Europe require broadcasters to commission independent productions. These provisions have been interpreted and implemented differently in France and in Britain. As network competition for broadcasters intensifies, the terms of trade between broadcasters and independent producers are becoming a crucial issue for European cinema. The chapter also explores the extent to which recent trends in British-French cinematographic co-productions can inform future developments.

Institutional, industrial and cultural differences

In France, film is considered as a matter of national importance that justifies government intervention. The privileged place given to cinema in the country's culture is reflected in the government's generous budget allocated each year to the CNC and in regulatory measures which require broadcasters to invest in feature films. As a result, film production is more lucrative for French companies than it is for most of their European counterparts. Film also has a different status and, over the years, there has been some reluctance on the part of French talent to work for television which has been considered as minor if not degrading work, although the trend is gradually changing.

By contrast, the British film industry has willingly diversified towards television. In the past, film companies such as Rank, EMI and Granada made substantial investments in commercial television. Britain has a long-established tradition of British directorial talent given a chance to work in the television drama departments of both public and commercial channels, and, British actors, scriptwriters and film makers regularly work for television.

Recent history of television involvement in feature films before 1990

A 1981 BFI Report on British Cinema concluded that 'even without a state-regulated system for re-directing a percentage of TV revenue into feature film production, in the 1970s, the television industry [had] steadily increased and consolidated its relationship with the British film industry.'[2]

The withdrawal of American investment from British film production in the early 1970s no doubt also played a considerable part in the fact that, by the end of the decade, television was being seen as a potential saviour for British film companies. The saviour came in the form of Channel 4 – a unique television channel – charged by an Act of Parliament 'to provide a distinctive service to British audiences' and required to 'encourage innovation and experiment in both form and content' and to cater for interests not provided by ITV. Channel 4 was not the first television company in the U.K. to commission feature films. A few of the existing commercial ITV companies had already started to invest in film productions, albeit on a small scale, but the arrival of Channel 4 marked a definite break with the existing British broadcasting system in several important ways:

1. From the outset, Channel 4's role of commissioning editor was to provide finance for programmes made by independent producers (see chapter 6).
2. Channel 4 embarked on a long-term policy supporting low-budget production, the main emphasis being on British talent and contemporary subjects.
3. All films, whether made for the large screen or for television, had 'cinematic values'.

Channel 4's involvement in film had a considerable influence on the general perception of British cinema (both in Britain and abroad). Moreover, the international commercial and critical success of major films such as *My Beautiful Launderette, A Room With a View, Letter To Brezhnev* and *Mona Lisa*, encouraged the involvement of other British broadcasters in film financing.

Ian Johns is right to point out that, 'this burgeoning source of funding [lay] more in market forces than philanthropic zeal,[3] but the fact remains that, over the last decade, Britain's thriving television industry greatly contributed to support a high-profile but less than healthy British film industry and helped it survive the considerable blow suffered after the abandonment of the Eady Levy (see chapter 6) and the ending of capital allowances after 1985 (not to mention the downfall of Goldcrest and the decline of the dollar).

Whilst in Britain the interests of the film industry were largely ignored for almost two decades by successive Conservative governments (with twelve Ministers for the Arts in twelve years), in France, ever since 1958 when General de Gaulle entrusted André Malraux with the responsibility of 'State Minister in charge of cultural matters', the commitment of the Ministry of Culture (amongst others) to cinema has remained infallible.

In the early 1970s, the difficulties experienced by the French film industry led the government to turn to broadcasters to help revitalise the film industry.[4] Among the broadcasters' new obligations, under a convention signed between the Ministry for Cultural Affairs and the ORTF in 1971, were a regular annual increase of 10 percent for the price of purchasing rights and a growing involvement in film financing with a contribution of FF 10m per year to the French film Fund (*le Fonds de soutien*) which represented, at the time, the major source of finance for French producers by providing them with an automatically accessible aid (*l'aide automatique*).

After the dismantling of the ORTF into three channels in 1974, broadcasters were subjected to further regulations destined to help cinema.

In the 1980s, the Socialist government of François Mitterrand placed great faith in cultural policy and its charismatic Minister of Culture, Jack Lang (1982-6, 1988-92), was fully committed to a programme of state intervention in the film industry. Not only did he secure a large increase for cinema in his budget, but he also introduced a new system of tax shelter (SOFICA), credit facilities (IFCIC) and extended the benefits of his generous film policy to foreign directors (Wajda, Skolimowski, Loach, Kurosawa, Tarkovski, Khleifi).

At the same time, large powerful and competitive groups (Gaumont, UGC, Pathé, Chargeurs/AMLF) were able to develop. By being capable of investing heavily in both French film production and distribution, they played an important role in the promotion of cinema.

As far as broadcasters were concerned, a new law obliged public broadcasters to allocate a minimum of their annual net turnover to cinematographic production, while private channels had to meet different quantitative requirements. By January 1991, all national unscrambled terrestrial channels had to allocate 3 percent of their turnover to film production (Decree No. 90-66, 17 January 1990).

In order to ensure the independence of producers from broadcasters, the 1990 decree indicated that:

1. The channels could only co-produce films through a subsidiary exclusively dedicated to such activities. (The major broadcasters had already set up subsidiaries: TF1 Films Productions in 1980, Films A2 in 1981, FR3 Films Productions in 1984).
2. The contribution of the channel could not exceed 50 percent of the film budget or of the French share of the budget.
3. The contribution of the co-production could not exceed the channels' rights. A separate feature-film investment law applied to Canal Plus, whereby the pay-television channel had to invest 20 percent of its turnover in film acquisition, 10 percent of which for French films.

So, despite opposite approaches to the audiovisual sector, French and British broadcasters were already greatly involved in feature film financing by the beginning of the 1990s.

Growth of television involvement in feature films in the 1990s

For a brief period in the early 1990s in Britain, the uncertainty created by the Broadcasting Act of 1990 and the changing in the composition of the ITV companies' levy payments to the Treasury resulted in a virtual withdrawal by ITV companies from British film production. However, their desertion was short-lived. Granada returned to feature film production in 1994 with *August* and *Jack and Sarah* and in 1996; the leading ITV companies announced their intention to develop films for the ITV Network and to invest £100m in British feature films before the end of the decade. Rivalry for television premières among broadcasters led the new terrestrial Channel 5 to consider setting up a film production arm if its launch in February 1997 proved successful enough.

As for the BBC, the theatrical success of films such as *Enchanted April, The Snapper* and *Truly, Madly, Deeply*, produced for the Screen One and Screen Two strands – and only released theatrically after they had had their U.K. television première – encouraged the Corporation to engage, in 1993, in a policy of making ten feature films designed for theatrical release, with an annual budget of £5m. The BBC backed four films in 1994 and six in 1995. The twenty-one films that went into production in 1996, with an input of £45m from the various arms of the BBC, made the public broadcaster, the most active funder of U.K.-produced films that year.

If, in the late 1980s, BSB (British Satellite Broadcasting) had made a small impact on the British film industry (by backing a small number of films and joining the consortium of investors financing David Puttnam's company, Enigma), after its merger with Sky Television in 1990, BSkyB was only notable by its absence from the film financing scene during its first few years of operation. Under pressure to generate more home-produced programming from the ITV channels which maintained that BSkyB should be subject to the same rules as they were (which included a requirement to meet EC programming quotas), BSkyB's management decided in 1993 to buy pay-television rights to a number of high profile films such as *Howard's End* and *The Crying Game* (backed by Channel 4) which they saw as potential audience-winners for the channel. The refusal of Channel 4 – which insisted on retaining the television première on the films itself – led BSkyB to turn to British Screen for products.

The subsequent £6m deal struck between BSkyB and British Screen gave BSkyB first rights to British Screen-supported movies and opened up a significant new source of finance for British producers. In 1996 BSkyB backed twelve features, all but two through its output deal with British Screen. By 1997, BSkyB had invested in about forty British Screen films.

Prior to 1994, British Screen and Channel 4 had been regular co-investors in many projects but the deal angered Channel 4 so much that its management declared they 'would never work with British Screen again' and, effectively, their collaboration temporarily stopped. (Channel 4 rightly protested that commissioning films and getting involved in the pre-production stage as they did, represented much more than merely acquiring them.) However, it has not stopped Channel 4 continuing to invest in feature films. Indeed, by providing a mixture of equity and television rights, Channel 4 has been, in the first half of the decade, the most active financier of British films. (Channel 4 invested £22.5m in twenty films in 1995, and £17m in seventeen films in 1996). The 130 films backed by Channel 4 between 1990 and 1996 include the internationally acclaimed – and internationally-financed – films of Neil Jordan (*The Crying Game*), Mike Leigh (*Secrets and Lies*), Peter Greenaway (*The Pillow Book*) and Ken Loach (*Carla's Song*). Most of the prestigious Film on Four projects are co-financed with other television companies and/or film producers.

In the mid-1990s, David Wood asserted that 'disenchantment with British Screen' had led Channel 4 to look for 'fresh sources of finance with far reaching results.' He wrote: 'a new set of partnerships have emerged that have enabled the channel to get involved in glossier, bigger budget productions. Films funded by wealthy US distributors or U.K.-based entertainment groups such as Polygram Filmed Entertainment enable Channel 4 to bask in the reflected glory of hit films without taking the financial risks.'[5]

Indeed, the number of films with a budget of £5m and over-backed by the channel has risen from two films in 1995 to five in 1996 and Channel 4's film budget for 1997 has been set at a record £22m, as part of a four-year plan (1996-9) to invest £100m in film production. However, if Channel 4 is effectively seeking new partners, its Drama Department – responsible for backing *Four Weddings and a Funeral* and *Shallow Grave* – remains faithful to the distinctive risk-taking film policy which has enabled the Channel to move in 'where other broadcasters feared to tread': 'Looking at films in purely financial terms does not make a lot of sense to us. We do not take a commercial view about what the channel should commission in order to get a good return; half of the 13-14 films we commission each year are by people who are making only their first or second film' remarked former Head of Drama, David Aukin.⁶

One thing is certain, the international success of 'British' films such as *Four Weddings and a Funeral*, *The Madness of King George* and *Trainspotting* (a £2m film solely financed by Channel 4), has given a new confidence to investors both in Britain and abroad.

In France, almost all films agreed by the CNC between 1990 and 1996 benefited from some 'structured financing' whether in the form of automatic aid, advance on receipts, support from the SOFICA or contributions from television channels. In 1996, French producers contributed 24.2 percent of film financing (26.6 percent in 1995), foreign producers 10.2 percent (12.3 in 1995), the automatic and selective aids, more than 13 percent, the SOFICA, 4.8 percent, and television channels more than 40 percent (co-productions and pre-buys). Between 1990 and 1996, the share of feature film financing by French broadcasters has more than doubled. In 1996, their contribution to French cinema represented FF 1.2bn via their subsidiaries (TF1 films production, France 2 Cinéma, France 3 Cinéma, La Sept Cinéma, M6 Films) or directly (Canal Plus).

Whenever broadcasters have failed to comply fully with their obligatory commitment to French cinema, the CSA (Conseil Supérieur de l'Audiovisuel) has been prompt to remind them of their obligations. On the whole, broadcasters have not shown much resistance in investing in film production since their involvement as co-producers gives them the right to show the films earlier. A special Convention applies to Canal Plus, allowing the pay-television channel to broadcast films after one year.

Canal Plus's obligatory commitments are limited to the acquisition of rights. Since 1993, 60 percent of the amount the channel spends on acquiring rights is to be dedicated to European works (45 percent of which to French-language films) (Article 13 of the 20 July 1992 decree). Over the years, Canal Plus has developed an array of partners in the independent sector and, since 1990, it has its own production company, le Studio Canal Plus, with wholly – and partly-owned subsidiaries. Of all French broadcasters, Canal Plus has made the largest contribution to cinema. From a mere 8.3 percent in 1990, it went to 20.6 percent in 1996 of all investments in French films agreed by the CNC. The Channel invested FF 678.5m in 107 titles that year and pre-purchased all French-initiated films with a budget over FF 13m. Up to 1997, Canal Plus was the only pay-television outlet for new French films and virtually all French producers relied on the company to provide part of the finance for their films through pre-sales. However, in 1997, such a vital source of funding is no longer guaranteed following the arrival of a competitor, the new French pay-television group, Television Par Satellite. TPS is a joint venture between France Télécom, France Télévision, TF1, M6, Lyonnaise des Eaux and CLT-UFA. Canal Plus has said it will not do business with French producers who also sell their films to TPS. Canal Plus's virtual monopoly in France for many years has enabled the company to expand both horizontally and vertically. Aware of the arrival of potential competitors, at the end of 1995, Canal Plus had launched, with Chargeurs (20 percent) and Compagnie Générale des Eaux (10 percent), a digital satellite television pay-per-view service, Canalsatellite (for films and special events). Today, French independent producers await anxiously the outcome of the confrontation between TPS and Canal Plus.

With the television channels setting up their own subsidiaries to produce feature films (and access the various French support mechanisms) and establishing 'special links' with several large (TF1 with Gaumont) and small (France 2 and France 3 with Téléma, Arte with Les Productions Lazennec) film production companies, the 'independent' status of producers has become an important issue in the French film community today. Integration may be good in terms of economies of scale and efficiency in the production process but it can have negative effects on the non-integrated operators and the diversity of programmes offered to consumers. In June 1997, Hervé Bourges, the President of the CSA, publicly expressed his concern over the effects of 'concentration' on 'creation' but, as far as economics is concerned, the CSA has little regulatory power.

In the first half of the decade, the free television channels have regularly increased their investments in French cinema. In 1996, their subsidiaries invested FF 527.3m in eighty-three films, a rise of 4.4 percent on the FF 504.87m invested in sixty-five films in 1995. The biggest contributor was TF1 with FF 186.5m, followed by France 2 (FF 149.15m), France 3 (FF 97m), M6 (FF 50.95m) and Arte (FF 43.8m).[7]

However, investment and production figures only provide a limited view of the situation. The picture is far from uniform and a close analysis of the films co-produced by the French channels and their subsidiaries reveals significant differences between the channels (reflecting each channel's identity).

Since 1993, private channels M6 and TF1 tend to co-produce fewer films and to select large-budget projects with a strong popular appeal. TF1 Films Production's average input in a film's budget is also higher than that of other channels (FF 14.3m in 1995).[8]

A 1997 CSA report on films co-produced by French broadcasters emphasises the role played by French television channels in the [re]-emergence of a popular French cinema. French comedies – and huge box office domestic hits – such as *Les Visiteurs, Les Trois Frères*, and *Le Bonheur est dans le Pré*, as well as costly historical melodramas like *Germinal, La Reine Margot, Le Hussard sur le Toit* and *Les Misérables*, were all co-produced by French television companies.

Public channels France 2 and France 3 have a more diversified co-production policy. As well as investing in large-budget pictures which highlight the French film heritage *(The Lover, 1492, Germinal, La Reine Margot)*, they often co-produce small-budget 'Auteur-films' (France 2 co-produced Resnais' *Smoking* and *No Smoking*, and Pialat's *Le Garçu*; France 3, the two Rivette's films on *Jeanne la Pucelle* and Chabrol's *Betty* and *L'Enfer*) and debut features (France 2 co-produced Arnaud Desplechin's *La Sentinelle* and Gaël Morel's *A Toute Vitesse*, and, France 3, Christian Vincent's *La Discrète* and Agnès Merlet's *Le Fils du requin*).

France 3 Cinéma, with twenty-six films co-produced in 1996 (twenty-one in 1995) and La Sept/Arte with eighteen films in 1996 (twenty-one in 1995) were the channels which co-produced the greater number of films, although their average contribution was lower (FF 5.7m and FF 2.4m respectively) than that of other channels. All channels regularly invest in first feature films. All terrestrial channels with the exception of the Franco-German Arte are increasingly investing in films with a budget over FF 40m.

Europeanisation of broadcasting and cinema

Arte/ la Sept Cinéma

'The cinema on Arte is an Act of Faith', declared Jérôme Clément, the Chairman of Arte/ La Sept Cinéma. 'To new talent, the cultural channel gives the possibility of making their film début and to meet their public. To talent all over the world – young and established directors – which emerges or re-emerges here, in France, in Europe and beyond, Arte represents a natural partnership.' [9]

After the screening of *Wings of Desire* on 11 October 1992, *Cahiers du Cinéma*'s Charles Tesson reflected that Wim Wenders' film was an apt metaphor for Arte, 'a channel fallen from the sky, brutally parachuted onto the terrestrial network and decided from above'.[10]

'Like a magic wand', a meeting between Chancellor Kohl and President Mitterrand in 1990 had sufficed for another wall to come down. Funded by the French and German governments, the Franco-German channel aimed to produce and broadcast television programmes of 'a cultural and international nature' and to 'promote mutual understanding and unity among the peoples of Europe' by acquiring, commissioning and co-producing dramas, documentaries and films. Five years after its official launch, Arte's reputation as 'a purveyor of high quality programming' is well established. La Sept Cinéma's annual budget may be derisively small (FF 44m in 1996, for eighteen films) but, for young film-makers and more experienced European 'Art-house directors', it has become an important – if somewhat symbolic – source of finance for independent projects.

To date, La Sept Cinéma has been involved in 118 films, which include films as thematically and aesthetically different as *The Baby of Macon* (Greenaway) and *Etat des Lieux* (Jean-François Richet), or *Bambola* (Bigas Luna) and *Ulysses' Gaze* (Theo Angelopoulos). It has been estimated that 'more than 20m people watch Arte regularly, spread throughout France (15m), Germany (4m), Switzerland and Belgium. These people are usually highly-educated viewers who travel abroad, understand foreign languages and enjoy reading, museums, exhibitions, opera, concerts and theatre.'[11]

If these 20 million people fit to perfection the definition of an audience endowed with cultural capital (Bourdieu), a brief survey of some of the issues addressed in the films co-produced by the channel so far does not infer an élitist bias. Among the wide range of issues covered are exploitation (Tran Anh Hung's *Cyclo*) and child abuse (Christine Carrière's *Rosine*), religious fanaticism (Merzak Allouache's *Bab El Oued City*), immigration (Youssef Chahine's *L'Emigré*) and racism (Karim Dridi's *Bye Bye*), political terrorism (Lucian Pintilie's *The Oak* and Alexei Guerman's *Khroustaliov, Ma Voiture*), youth alienation (Mathieu Kassovitz's *La Haine*) and sexual difference (Alain Berliner's *Ma vie en rose*).

On a shoe-string budget, the Franco-German channel has been able to fulfil its remit as 'a network devoted to intelligence' and 'a point of access to knowledge, learning and culture' by supporting creative talent and engaging in innovative programming such as its thematic evenings (which include a feature film) and the widely acclaimed series, *'Tous les garçons et les filles de mon âge'*. The series led to the subsequent theatrical release of – and prestigious international awards for – André Téchiné's *Les Roseaux Sauvages*, Olivier Assayas' *L'Eau Froide* and Cédric Khan's *Trop de Bonheur* (1993).

If commercial awareness was behind the co-production Agreement signed in December 1995 between La Sept Cinéma and Arte Germany to develop more prestigious productions (with prime-time viewing and box office potential in mind), the first co-production directed by Lars von Trier augurs well, judging by the number of international awards bestowed on *Breaking the Waves*.[12]

In assessing the results of La Sept Cinéma/Arte since its inception in 1992, it seems fitting to endorse Thierry Leclercq's opinion that 'even those who were considering the initiative as "elitist" and/or "boring" must recognise that the channel has found a niche where television is synonymous with quality and intelligence'.[13]

There is little doubt that without sustained public support for 'quality programming' in general and 'quality film producing' in particular, the channel would have had little chance of surviving in the competitive environment of the 1990s. No other channel has contributed so much to European talent in such a short time, even if its limited resources render its position extremely fragile.

Other French channels

The other French channel which can also claim to have played a major role in the Europeanisation of French broadcasting is Canal Plus. Whether one takes into account the number and the range of European projects the channel has supported over the years, or its efforts in both finding a market for French films in Europe (Jeunet & Caro's *The City of the Lost Children*), and showing non-English language European productions in France (Gérard Corbiau's *Farinelli*, Gianni Amelio's *Lamerica*), the achievements of Canal Plus are noteworthy. As far as the other French public channels' investments in co-productions involving European partners are concerned, they tend to reflect the overall French pattern of production.

Up to the mid-1990s, French broadcasters have tended to invest in French-language productions, both because of regulatory requirements and a marked preference by television audiences for domestic films (along with American movies). However, one broadcaster stands out in its international output in the last two years, private channel M6 which has shown a strong bias towards ambitious projects shot in English. In 1995, M6 co-produced Nils Gaup's £8.2m-budget film *Grand Nord* with Norwegian and American partners and Steve Barron's £15.5m *Pinocchio* with British, German, Czech and American co-producers. In 1996, the channel co-produced another English-language film, Anne Goursaud's *Love in Paris* (£10m).

If TF1 Film Production is noticeable for its lack of involvement with European partners (with the exception of its participation in Polanski's *Death of the Maiden* in 1994) during the period 1990-6, Ciby 2000, the subsidiary of the Bouygues group – the successful bidder for the 1986 privatised TF1 – has developed a reputation for financing the prestigious projects of reputed international directors such as David Lynch (*Twin Peaks*), Jane Campion (*The Piano*), Bernardo Bertolucci (*Little Buddha*), Pedro Amaldovar (*High Heels*), Martin Scorsese (*Casino*) and Mike Leigh (*Secret and Lies*). Ciby recently set up a new television production arm, Ciby Fiction, to produce English-language fiction (and to fulfil its European quota requirement); one of the company's first projects was to make a six-part series based on Kusturika's *Underground*.

Internationalisation of European film production

Bouygues's Ciby 2000 was not the only French company with global ambitions to have made a foray in Los Angeles. Le Studio Canal Plus also developed 'an American policy' based on a close collaboration with two leading U.S. independents, Arnon Milchan (Regency) and Mario Cassar (Carolco), which led to the productions of, among others, James Cameron's *Terminator II*, Reny Harlin's *Cliffhanger*, Oliver Stone's *JFK*. After the bankruptcy of Carolco (in which Canal Plus had a 12 percent stake) in 1994, Canal Plus decided to end its production activities in the United States and concentrate on Europe.

If Canal Plus and Bouygues's ventures in Hollywood have ended in failure, both concerns have gained high levels of visibility and acquired international recognition (and partners) as a result of their ambitious international film policy. In 1996 Canal Plus announced the setting up of a joint venture with Sony Pictures Entertainment (SPE) to develop a production structure in London aimed at developing and producing English-language European productions with budgets between U.S.$5m and U.S.$15m[14] and Bouygues has set up a sales operation in London (Ciby Sales). Other French conglomerates (Chargeurs, Pathé) have also set up companies in London. Indeed, after the mid-1990s, London seems to have become '*le passage obligé*' for the major European players, responding somewhat belatedly to the wishes of former BFI director, Wilf Stevenson, for Britain to become 'the Hollywood of Europe'.

According to BFI records, the number of British-based American films trebled between 1992 (a mere seven) and 1994 (twenty-one). There were eighteen such films in 1995, and 21 in 1996. Their average budget has remained stable around £13m while the average British film – defined by the British Film Institute as a film 'where the cultural and financial impetus is from the U.K. and the majority personnel is British' – still costs less than £2.5m.

For Terry Ilott, one of 'the worst aspects of the American stranglehold' on the British film industry is the fact that 'the American companies in London, even run by Brits, regard the U.K. as a market and nothing more ... They put all their resources into maximising revenues from the territory while holding back from any meaningful engagement in what may be called "citizenship issues".[15]

In addition to their traditional alliances with British companies, 'U.S.' investors are now regularly investing in 'foreign' English-language productions shot in Britain. In 1996, for example, Sony was involved in Luc Besson's *Fifth Element*, and Summit in the German-American *Prince Valiant*.

In 1990, Simon Clayton reflected that, 'given sufficient common purpose and political will', Britain might soon be in a position to establish its own industry 'as a conduit, manufacturing American films for the European market and vice versa, and be able to skim enough from the top to increase indigenous production'. 'Our home market was never big enough to allow us to do this,' he wrote, 'the European market will allow us to challenge the U.S., at long last, in its own markets, with a brand new product: the English-speaking European film'. [16] In the 1980s, French film-makers had already started showing a growing interest in making English-language films (*The Bear, The Big Blue*). By the beginning of the 1990s, confirmed directors with an international reputation, such as Jean Jacques Annaud (*The Lover*), Louis Malle (*Damage*) and Luc Besson (*Leon, the Fifth Element*), were prepared to brave French legislation to shoot their films in English with British partners.

The trend in international English-language movies shot in Britain is set to increase with the introduction of a National Lottery's award of £85m made in 1996 by the Arts Council of England to the British film industry (over five years) and new tax measures in 1997, making Britain a more attractive place for film-making.

However, if the French example is anything to go by, these large-budget and expensively-promoted 'European' movies made to appeal to international audiences may respond to the operators of multiplexes and their prefabricated mass audience but they rarely address European-ness or European issues (let alone British or French contemporary ones).

Europeanisation of British film production in the 1990s

Europe has now become a regular source of financing for British producers. With the help of British Screen, co-productions with European partners have been a steadily growing feature of British films between 1990 and 1996.

In 1990, the British Government made available £5m over the following three years to set up a Fund, the European Co-production Fund (ECF) to encourage British producers to work with their European partners. Since its inception in 1991, the British Screen-administered European Co-production Fund has been very influential in creating links with continental partners. From one co-production (Krzysztof Zanussi's *The Silent Touch*) in 1991 (of the eleven British Screen films started that year), the number of films supported by the ECF went to nine co-produced films in 1996 (of a total of nineteen British Screen films), four of which had French partners.

France is Britain's major European co-producer of films. The 1995 production figures give France as the main partner for British film-makers with sixteen films (eleven official co-productions), followed by Germany with eleven films, and Spain with five films. Producers from Belgium, Italy, Portugal, the Netherlands, Denmark, Sweden and Czechoslovakia were also involved in U.K. films that year.

Along with British Screen, the European Commission's MEDIA programme and the Council of Europe's Fund, Eurimages (between 1993 and 1995 for the latter) have also had a considerable impact on British involvement with European partners. Among the many programmes launched by MEDIA I, the European SCRIPT Fund (Support for Creative Independent Production Talent) has been particularly popular with British film-makers. A survey conducted between October 1989 and December 1995 showed that the U.K., which put in a staggering number of applications (2,598), was the major beneficiary of the Fund with 200 successful applications, followed by France (173), a record considering the number of films put into production in Britain during the same period (just over 400).

Unlike most EC countries, the United Kingdom only joined Eurimages in 1993 after years of lobbying by the British film industry. Two years later, in November 1995, the U.K. government withdrew 'for economic reasons'. The decision was unanimously condemned by the British film community which found the British Government's attitude 'arrogant' and 'incomprehensible', stressing that over a three-year period, Eurimages had contributed £14.5m to British production (sixty-five projects with majority or minority British participation) at the cost of an annual contribution of a mere £2m (the U.K. Government's contribution to the Fund).

The Council of Europe's Fund was set up in 1988 to develop the production and distribution of European films. A French initiative (France allocated half the initial budget), Eurimages supports cinematographic co-productions involving three partners from different member states. In 1996, the tripartite principle, the basic condition for project eligibility, was deemed to 'pose problems in certain cases, especially large budget films' by the Eurimages board which has now accepting the possibility of supporting bilateral co-productions, an historical development which is in sharp contrast with that of the cinematographic co-production Agreement between Britain and France.

British and French cinematographic co-productions

The original France-U.K. Agreement signed in 1965 only allowed bipartite co-productions but the new Agreement signed in November 1994 and ratified in February 1995 now sanctions tri-partite films and financial co-productions – films in which the minority partner's participation is purely financial (and limited to between 20 and 30 percent of the film's budget). An increasing number of co-producers/investors has become a characteristic feature of film production in general and of European co-productions in particular and the large budget British-French films of the 1990s are no exception. For a while now, multilateral co-productions and co-financed films have been made by British and French producers both outside and within the terms of the Agreement. In 1992, for example, officially-agreed co-productions such as *Sweet Killing, The Map of the Human Heart, 1492: Conquest of Paradise* and *The Plague* involved American investors and Canadian, Spanish and Argentinean partners respectively.

It is not the number of partners nor the size of the films' budget but the imbalance between French and British investments which led the CNC to take a cautious approach to co-productions in 1995 and to insist that the concept of 'reciprocity' or twinning be strictly applied. Yet, despite the CNC's demands, to date, only two pairs of films, co-produced by the same British-French team, have been made, *Victory* and *Une Femme Française*, and *Portraits Chinois* and *Downtime*. All other British-French films are traditional co-productions where the technical and artistic contributions are supposed to match the financial input of the British and French partners.

As far as twinning arrangements are concerned, the results, two years after the inception of the new Agreement, are mixed. On the one hand, the small number of agreed projects probably reflects more the difficulties of raising production finance for joint ambitious artistic and economic ventures than problems inherent in bureaucratic interference. On the other hand, the very fact that twinned films have been produced testifies both to the willingness of British producers to collaborate with European partners after a period of relative isolation and to the role played by national (the CNC and the ECF) and pan-European initiatives (*Victory* was backed up by Eurimages) in furthering international co-operation.

There is little doubt that, after less than a decade of renewed collaboration, British and French producers now have little difficulty in working together. Yet, the British-French films made so far – whether under the aegis of the official Agreement or outside the Treaty – show little inclination on the part of British and French film makers to tackle contemporary issues or explore intercultural exchanges. The few which do, tend to be shot abroad (Ian Sellar's *Prague*, Sally Potter's *Orlando*) and directed by 'foreign' film-makers (Vincent Ward's *Map of the Human Heart*, Elaine Proctor's *Friends*, Milcho Manchevski's *Before the Rain*, Jiri Menzel's *Chonkin*).

If the latter illustrates the positive – if somewhat small – impact that two countries like France and Britain can have on encouraging plurality in European cinema, the considerable budgets of several of the Anglo-French co-productions – most of them structured through multinational financial deals (*1492, Highlander III, The Serpent's Kiss*) – confirm that the major reasons to enter into co-production arrangements include, on the British side, access to European sources of finance and, on the French side, the possibility of entering the large North American anglophone market.

For such films, it may be fitting to paraphrase James Park's remarks on the involvement of British television companies in international projects in the 1980s and conclude:

'The international co-productions on which [British and French] companies are now concentrating their finances have no relevance to contemporary society and attitudes and in seeking to appeal to a mass audience in a relatively undemanding way, reflect no interest in any value other than simple-minded entertainment.'[17]

British broadcasters' involvement in European film co-productions

Encouraged by British Screen, European and pan-European initiatives and, above all, by the eagerness of continental producers to work on English-language projects, British film producers have willingly engaged in cinematographic co-productions with European partners. By contrast, British broadcasters have been more reticent to enter the field.

The reasons are multifold:

1. British isolation from the continent.
2. A different tradition as far as film and television work is concerned.
3. A different status for film on the French side.
4. No regulatory obligation to invest into films in the U.K.
5. A preference for the domestic products, traditionally more popular on television, particularly in Britain.

6. The reluctance of British audiences to watch dubbed or subtitled programmes.

Over the last fifteen years, Channel 4 has offered its occasional support to strong projects from abroad and has developed important links with other European television companies (Canal Plus, ZDF) and film producers (among them, Gaumont and MK2, the French company of Marin Karmitz which produced Kieslowski's trilogy, *Blue, White and Red*). However, as David Hancock remarked in 1996, 'for those who might have hoped that the broadcaster would have by now forged an umbilical cord across the Channel, they will be disappointed'. Hancock quoted David Aukin's difficulty 'to operate in another capacity than that of a financier due to the language barriers and the inability to get involved editorially'.[18]

Still, Channel 4 has been and continues to be working with European partners. Its ambitious slate in the mid-1990s included Ken Loach's *Carla's Song*, co-financed by Spain and Germany, the Merchant-Ivory film, *The Proprietor*, co-financed by France and Turkey, Mira Nair's *Kama Sutra*, co-financed by Germany, Spain, Italy, France, Japan and the U.S.A., and several officially agreed British-French co-productions (*Death and the Maiden, The Tango Lesson, Downtime, The Revenges' Comedies, Food of Love, Metroland* and *Woodlanders*).

Yet arguably, in Britain today, it is BSkyB which has become, through its deal with British Screen, the broadcaster most likely to be involved in European films. In 1994, BSkyB bought the rights to six co-productions (*All Men are Mortal, Antonia's Line, Letters from the East, Victory, The Young Poisoner's Handbook* and *Someone Else's America*). In 1995, they invested in only one film (*The Castle of the Monkeys*) but in 1996, BSkyB backed five European co-productions (*The Tango Lesson, The Fifth Province, Mrs Dalloway, Through the Day* and *House of America*).

In the early 1990s, the BBC showed no inclination to invest in European cinematographic co-productions, with one exception, *The Hour of the Pig*, a comedy set in France in the Middle Ages starring Colin Firth and directed by Leslie Megahey. However, in 1994, the BBC co-produced two feature films with European partners, the British-German film, *I.D.*, and Ken Loach's (Spanish-British-German) *Land and Freedom*. In 1996, the BBC made three films with France, *Metroland, The Revengers' Comedies* and *My Son the Fanatic* and was involved in three films made with other European and North American partners. By the mid-1990s, British broadcasters were even venturing – albeit on a very small scale – into foreign-language films.

British broadcasters' involvement in European film co-production

Despite David Aukin's earlier reservations on the language barrier, Channel 4 invested in three foreign-language films: the French co-financed Russian-language film of Czech director, Jiri Menzel, *The Life and Extraordinary Adventures of Ivan Chonkin,* the French-language first feature film of Québécois theatre Director, Robert Lepage, *Le Confessionnal,* and Marie Dugowson's *Portraits Chinois,* starring Helena Bonham Carter.

BSkyB has also invested in three ECF-aided foreign-language co-productions, *Antonia's Line, Before the Rain* and *Une Femme Française* (which have been subsequently dubbed for their television screening). To date, Channel 5 has no plan to either screen or co-produce foreign-language films.

The number of foreign-language films backed by British television companies is too small to draw a conclusion as far as the broadcasters' choices in terms of thematic concerns or artistic priorities are concerned. Overall, the few co-produced films tend to reflect the British-French output made under the cinematographic co-production Agreement between 1990 and 1996 (with the exploration of cross-cultural issues only visible in films directed by non-British and French film-makers and a strong preference for films set in the past).

For obvious economic reasons, continental broadcasters are more likely to get involved in English-language films than their British counterparts in films shot in another language than English.

Until recently, few European broadcasters had the resources to get involved in large-budget films but today's alliances and mergers are changing the European film financing scene and the number of broadcasters involved in U.K.-produced films has risen sharply in the 1990s.

In 1996, France's Canal Plus invested in five U.K.-produced films *(Amy Foster, The Serpent's Kiss, Metroland, Through the Day* and *Ma Vie en Rose),* Germany's WDR in three, Arte and Germany's WDR in two. France 2 Cinéma also co-produced two Anglo-French films, *The Serpent's Kiss* directed by Philippe Rousselot and *The Revengers' Comedies* made by Malcolm Mowbray. The channels which backed one U.K.-produced film include France's TF1 and M6, Germany's SDR, Belgium's RTBF, Ireland's RTE and KRO as well as the Czech Republic's Kopecky.

There is little doubt, however, that all this activity points more towards an internationalisation of European production – via English-language films – to compete in the global markets than to a Europeanisation of British film production.

Conclusion

In a recent article on the transnationalisation of the American film industry, Frederick Wasser noted that the economic history of Hollywood's transnationalisation was an important clue to the problem of why so many American films contributed so little to the social fabric of their country. 'American film makers', he concluded, 'have only sporadically addressed the American audience with artistic integrity and it will now be even more difficult to address the global audience in such a manner'.[19]

The concept of 'European cinema' as an alternative to Hollywood rests on the very notion of 'artistic integrity'. In the past, television had little to do with artistic integrity. However, in recent years, when national or bi-national broadcasters with a specific cultural remit have ventured into the domain of film production, not only have important contemporary issues for Europe been explored but also creativity has been allowed to flourish and artistic integrity respected.

In 1991 at British Screen, Simon Perry saw the introduction of the European Co-production Fund as 'an alternative to American funding on the one hand, and to excessive reliance on television finance on the other'.[20] It is ironic and no doubt a sign of the times that half a decade later, an increasing number of British films should be backed by American capital and, all British-Screen – and British Screen-administered ECF-aided films, co-financed by television companies.

In a very short time, European broadcasters have become major investors in the production of feature films. The distinction between films made for the cinema and those made for television has become blurred. The object of this chapter was not to discuss the limitations of television aesthetics or the less than benign influence of television on the film industry. Today, the specificity of film is less likely to be affected by 'an excessive reliance on television financing' than by the multiplex revolution. The arrival of multiplexes may have reversed the declining trend of cinema admissions but it has brought with it a uniformisation of the products on offer rather than an increase in the choice of films. In Britain, American blockbusters and, occasionally, their European English-language ersatz, dominate the multiplex scene where films co-produced by independent companies (in association with television channels) continue to be a rarity. The efforts of several broadcasters to secure a theatrical distribution for the latter have not proved successful. The art-house distributors – who dominate the sector of foreign-language films – are all battling for survival. Even British films have difficulties in getting a distribution deal in their domestic market.[21]

A 1997 Cinema and Video Industry Audience Report reveals that multiplexes are more likely to put 'big releases' on several of their screens at the same time than take a small-budget film, despite the fact that the regular cinema audience is widening (there were twice as many regular cinema-goers in the thirty-five-plus age-group and the 'fourteen and under' age groups in 1996 as there were in 1991) and the number of new customers for Art-films is growing (the thirty-five-plus made up 57 percent of the art-house audience in 1997).[22] The constitution of 'a mass audience' has an economic value within the system. Ien Ang rightly insists on the difficulty of understanding the audience because the entire business is run on the basis of ratings. As she points out, 'ratings are not pure knowledge but important sites of struggles within the institutional dynamics of the audiovisual industries'.[23] Market niches do exist and/or can be created, as the example of Arte shows. There is an audience in Europe for 'cultural' programming but at a time when new private/commercially-oriented channels are multiplying, the increasing trend of European broadcasters to invest in medium- to large-budget English-language films does not augur well for European plurality.

Europe's film and television industry is being told to open up in order to create more competition. However, the film industry does not operate in a free market and the free-marketeer mentality can have significant and damaging implications for the future of European cinema(s) and public service broadcasting.

Accusations that the so-called 'subsidy mentality leads to uniformity', that European films are 'made for the bureaucrats', abound in the anglophone press. Needless to say how little-substantiated such criticism can be when so few European films actually reach British and American screens (large and small). Anti-intellectual demagogy runs particularly high when what is at stake is an Art form which is also an industry with the largest potential growth forecast for the next century. European co-productions also have a bad press. What Anglo-Saxon film critics dismiss – a little too hastily – as 'Europuddings' are, more often than not, international co-productions made with European funding and with – or without – American stars and financing, depending on the size of the films' budget.

In their attempt to revise the definition of 'British film' at the beginning of 1997, the Department of National Heritage (DNH) came up with the notion of 'film of national interest'. Could MEDIA II consider 'films of European interest'?

At a time when cinematographic and television works are becoming indistinguishable, Arte's example, like Channel 4 before it, shows that commissioned work for television is not incompatible with innovation, creativity and artistic integrity. Broadcasters are set to play an increasing role in the future of cinema. Public broadcasters, like national institutions (British Screen and the BFI in

Britain, the CNC to a lesser degree in France) and European audiovisual support schemes have come under pressure to 'be commercially aware, if not commercially oriented' and are taking measures to 'improve the commercial potential of the films they help finance'. The schism between Channel 4 and British Screen over the BSkyB deal in the U.K., like the conflict between Canal Plus and TPS over cinema in France, illustrates too well the inevitable competitive pressures that the new media distribution outlets bring to bear on public broadcasters. One would agree with Stewart Till, Head of Distribution at Polygram Filmed Entertainment and member of the new British film industry committee, that 'a film needs to be good' and 'good equates marketable'[24] as long as 'marketable' does not only mean 'able to reach a worldwide mass audience', a distinction of vital importance and dangerously passed over by the controller of the European Commission's information technology and communications directorate, Martin Bangemann, when he stated that European film makers were 'largely disconnected from the market' because of their over-reliance on state subsidies.[25] The market is a social and cultural construct and economics cannot be dissociated from political and societal choices.

A comparison between the investments made in 'European cinema' between the larger 'commercial' players and public or semi-public organisations – broadcasters and national and European institutions – leaves little doubt about who is on the side of plurality and cultural diversity.

In a world where market forces dictate economic survival, the small independent players find it increasingly difficult to survive. Yet, in today's international audiovisual world, small market niches exist. Old markets can be revived and new markets can be created but as cinema enters its second century, the main questions remain unanswered: Will European policy-makers be bold enough to deploy cultural patronage and encourage and/or enforce broadcasters' expenditure requirements on new European fiction, or will they off-load economic risk onto the producers? (who will run the risk of becoming sub-contractors for prime-time products). Will the political will remain strong enough between France and Germany to continue to support the 'cultural channel' Arte? After it has achieved self-funding through advertising, will Channel 4 be able to maintain a film output as challenging as the one it helped produce in the last decade? Should some audiovisual issues remain within the purview of domestic regulation, will the national regulatory bodies be strong enough to guarantee the necessary degree of freedom and creativity to independent producers? As new broadcasters appear and disappear, and those who survive become more powerful, will they be willing to endorse – or comply with – national and European legislation?

The variety, plurality, quality, innovation, and ultimately the survival of European cinema seems to rest largely on the answers that European broadcasters – the principal financiers of European films today – are prepared to give to these questions.

Notes and References

1. *Screen Digest*, May 1997, 105. Statistics and the way they are collected fluctuate from year to year, and from one source of data to another. Methodological issues and other problems, such as allocating year of production and 'nationality' criteria onto a co-produced film or classifying a particular work as 'film' rather than 'television' or 'audiovisual' programme, explain the differences between the *Screen Digest* figures and those given by the European Audiovisual Observatory (451 films in 1990, 520 in 1996).
2. British Film Institute Report, *British Films, 1971-1981, Major Trends of the Seventies*, 1982.
3. I. Johns, 'Home View', *Films & Filming*, no. 411, January 1989, 17.
4. At the time, France was not the only large film producing country to resort to such interventionist measures. In America, television had become a dominant force in political, economic and cultural terms and the U.S. Federal government, lobbied by Hollywood, introduced tax shelters and regulatory measures for the three main television networks (ABC, CBS and NBC) to acquire programming 'to enable Hollywood studios to recover from the doldrums of the late 1960s'. Quoted in D. Puttnam, *The Undeclared War*, London, Harper Collins, 1997, 270.
5. D. Wood, 'Screen Heroes', *Broadcast*, 31 March 1995, 23.
6. Ibid., 25.
7. Figures from the CSA, 1997. The CSA data are based on information given in the channels' production statements, while the CNC data rely on the 'dossier d'agrément d'investissement', established for each film. The two sources differ on the allocation of the year of production. The CNC registers the year when the investment agreement is obtained, while the CSA registers the year the co-production contract (or pre-sale agreement) between the broadcaster and the production company is signed.
8. This may be partly due to the fact that TF1 recently chose to acquire the rights for two screenings rather than one.
9. J. Clément, Editorial, *La Sept Cinéma/ARTE*, Catalogue, May 1997.
10. C. Tesson, 'Arte de cinq à sept', *Cahiers du cinéma*, no. 461, November 1992, 14.
11. T. Leclercq, 'Fine Arte', *Television Business International*, June 1997, 43.
12. They include the Cannes Palme d'or and two Felixes – for best film and best actress (Emily Watson) – in 1996, and the 1997 César for best foreign film. The film financing was raised from twenty-seven organisations, two-thirds of which were national and European public broadcasters and/or institutions.
13. Leclercq, 'Fine Arte', 42.
14. D. Hancock, *Mirrors of our own, Eurimages*, Council of Europe, Strasbourg, 1996, 26.
15. T. Illot, 'U.K. Film, Television and Video: Overview', BFI Film and Television Handbook, London, 1997, 18.

16. Quoted in S. Clayton and J. Turner, 'The British Film Industry. Recovery on the table?', *Film and TV Technician*, July 1990, 12.
17. J. Park, *Learning to Dream the New British Cinema*, London, Faber & Faber, 1984, 19.
18. D. Hancock, *Eurimages*, 1996, 58.
19. F. Wasser, 'Is Hollywood America?' *Critical Studies in Mass Communications*, no. 12, 1995, 435.
20. S. Perry quoted in M. Le Fanu, 'New money leads British Screen nearer to Europe', *Screen Finance*, vol. 4 no. 9, 15 May 1991, 3.
21. Half the British films produced in 1995 had not found a distributor in 1996.
22. Caviar, Cinema and Video Industry Audience Research, London, 1997.
23. I. Ang, 'Response to Elizabeth Jacka', *Media Information Australia*, no. 77, 1995, 165.
24. Quoted in C. Pishiris, 'Team Manager', *Televisual*, August 1997, 25.
25. M. Bangemann, speech made to the European Parliament, June 1997.

CHAPTER 14

THE EUROPEAN UNION AUDIOVISUAL POLICIES OF THE U.K. AND FRANCE

RICHARD COLLINS

At a time when Europe, the cradle of western civilisation, loses control over one of the main areas in which contemporary culture is being made, the audiovisual, one can no longer react aesthetically to such liberal or ultra liberal ideologies. Reality demands that concrete steps be taken.[1]

Sometimes it is as if France, in remembrance of a once glorious past and in the name of a former universal cultural status, was attempting to fight against the overwhelming wave coming from across the Atlantic and was begging the Yankee ogre for mercy.[2]

Introduction

There are good reasons to study the European audiovisual[3] policies of France and the U.K., for, not only are the French and British audiovisual sectors more important economically than those of any other European Union Member States, but France and the U.K. represent, in their purest forms, the opposed visions and forces that have shaped EU audiovisual policy. The differences between the French and British visions are rooted in the different historical formations of the *frères ennemis* and are sharpened by the antagonists' pervasive mutual mistrust. For each, the other is the least trusted European Union partner.[4]

The European Union's, formerly the European Community's, audiovisual policy has been shaped by two contradictory dynamics: by promotion of, and resistance to, the integration and liberalisation of the EU's audiovisual markets. It would be too neat to state that the U.K. has been the principal proponent of liberalisation and

France the principal opponent, not least because, for the most part, the U.K.'s European audiovisual policy has been conspicuous by its absence! Better to state that the U.K. has gone with the flow of the policies of integration and liberalisation, which have been uppermost in recent EU history, whereas France has perceived such policies to be, at best, inefficient and, at worst, actively hostile to European interests. Accordingly, in the EU context Adam Smith's ghost has overshadowed Jean Baptiste Colbert's.

The U.K. has succeeded because of the requirement for unanimity on matters, such as audiovisual policy, which lie outside the provisions of the European treaties (with the qualified exception of the Maastricht Treaty). This, together with the coincidence of many U.K. interests with those of the great decider, Germany, Denmark's obdurate resistance to increased Community powers in the cultural domain, and the naked economic interest of Luxembourg in liberalisation of European audiovisual markets, have been sufficient to ensure success for the U.K. – a success which requires only maintenance of the status quo. France, on the other hand, requires change to achieve its economic, political and cultural goals.

In contrast to the U.K., France has a substantial deficit in its audiovisual trade balance. France invests far greater importance in the furtherance of European political union than does the U.K., a political union which, from the point of view of the dominant 'nationalist' assumptions which prevail in France can only be secured if polity and culture in Europe are made congruent through a 'Europeanisation' of the programmes shown on European screens.[5] Culture has, from this point of view, a central political importance. As the Member of the Senate Jean Cluzel stated: 'The construction of Europe forces one to go beyond the national context and to launch a European audiovisual policy ... while keeping the national production capacity which is essential to avoid losing the cultural identity of our own European space.[6]

Moreover, France, unlike the U.K., has characteristically seen U.S. film and television programmes – the presence of which has increased so strikingly following liberalisation of European audiovisual markets – as so much cultural pollution.

European Union policies and practices

There are four principal loci of European Union audiovisual policy.[7] First, the creation of a single European market for television – a Television without Frontiers. Second, the attempted establishment of common technical standards for European television, principally satellite television, so that viewers are not denied access to European television services because of differing technological standards and to protect European manufacturers from competition outside Europe. Third, establishment of subsidy and support for European film and television production and distribution via the MEDIA programme. And fourth, the measures taken by DG IV, the Commission's Competition Directorate, to establish a well functioning competitive broadcasting market and to countervail broadcasters' abuse of established dominant positions. These four initiatives have enjoyed very different levels of success. Broadly, the market opening initiatives – Television without Frontiers and the competition decisions of DG IV – have been successful and have dramatically changed European broadcasting, whereas the dirigiste initiatives – the MEDIA programme and the setting of satellite television transmission standards – have either failed or have had a weak impact.

Television without Frontiers

Perhaps the best known single EU initiative was Television without Frontiers. Creation of a single European broadcasting market was first proposed in the Television without Frontiers Green Paper and the Directive establishing the single market came into effect in 1991.[8] Television without Frontiers was presented as a measure to integrate the EU's broadcasting markets: to provide the EU with a home market comparable in size to the United States and to give European viewers access to broadcasting services from other Member States, thus promoting a shared European consciousness and culture. But the strengthening of European producers has been highly uneven. And, rather than fostering a shared European audio-visual culture, Television without Frontiers has increased and intensified competition within the distinct national, or more precisely linguistic, broadcasting markets of the EU.

Thanks to Television without Frontiers, Member States cannot lawfully block circulation of television signals originating in another Member State. Hence, broadcasters, formerly prohibited from establishment in or access to lucrative markets, have been able to establish new services and Europe has experienced an explosion in the number of commercial broadcasters. In 1982 there were four commercial television channels in Europe, in 1992 there were fifty-eight[9] and in 1997 there are more than 250. Massive expansion in the number of channels amplified demand for programming far beyond the ability of the European revenue base to fund new European works and thus created a large 'secondary market' where archive programming – often from the U.S.A. – was recycled.[10]

Indeed Jack Lang (and others such as Barzanti),[11] wrote: ' The countries of Europe, encumbered as they are with all sorts of historic, linguistic and sociological barriers, were more or less impervious to each other, while the European market – unified – existed only for the Americans'.[12]

France has consistently sought to countervail the effects of the single market. As President Mitterrand's principal official spokesperson and policy organiser, Bernard Miyet, put it: ' Building an integrated transparent, European market is an increasingly illusory project and free trade has some merits but can never be an unchallengeable sacred cow. Its straightforward application to the audiovisual sector would be economically unjustified, culturally damaging and undemocratic'.[13] France sought to translate into a European Union context its well established domestic policies of quotas and production support. It established the MEDIA programme and inserted a European content quota (Article 4) into the 1989 Directive and has consistently, but thus far unsuccessfully, sought stronger quotas in a new Television without Frontiers Directive.

The current Directive of 1989, which came into effect in 1991, imposes a 50 percent European television programme content quota. But the quota is gravely weakened because some types of programming are excluded from quota provisions and by the rider that quotas are required only 'where practicable'. The U.K. has interpreted the 'where practicable' provision liberally. A senior U.K. official stated that the U.K. did not think it 'appropriate' to require satellite film channels to conform to the Directive's European content quotas, and continued: 'We can't expect them to screen Jacques Tati films the whole time!'.[14] Describing France's part in the drafting of the 1989 Directive, the official stated that the U.K., Germany, Denmark, Ireland and Luxembourg opposed stringent quotas. Quotas have assumed a talismanic quality in the European audiovisual policy debate. As Noël du Payrat put it: 'quotas were, and remain, a point of crystallisation of opposing European audiovisual interest groups.[15]

The MEDIA programme

In a further response to the EU's growing audiovisual trade deficit with the U.S.A., a consequence of the demand unleashed by liberalisation of European audiovisual markets, the EU has fostered production and circulation of European audiovisual works by establishing the MEDIA programme, which originated from the 1980s proposals of the European Parliament and the Commission of the European Communities for measures to support the Community's audiovisual and broadcasting sectors. The first document issued by the Commission in which 'audiovisual' formed part of the title was the information release, 'The Community's Audiovisual Policy', which proposed a 'balancing' of the Community audiovisual market.

On the one hand, the market was to be integrated and the 'entangled underwood of national regulatory obstacles to admitting broadcasts from other Member States' swept away via Television without Frontiers. On the other hand, proactive measures to support and shape the film and television industries were to be adopted, notably the 'strengthening of the technological capacity of the Community's industry in the audiovisual and communications area'.[16]

In 1988 a pilot 'Action Programme to promote the Development of the European Audiovisual Industry', MEDIA, was established and in 1990 the Council of Ministers renewed the programme's mandate as MEDIA 1995.[17] But the funding for both phases is regarded, by MEDIA's proponents, as inadequate.[18] The MEDIA programme constituted a further cleavage between France and the U.K. Whereas France vigorously sponsored the MEDIA programme (and the Eurimages programme of support for European co-productions which, because opposed by the U.K. within the context of the Community, was established by 'European variable geometry' under the auspices of the Council of Europe) the U.K. opposed it. Indeed, the Whitehall official with U.K. responsibilities for the MEDIA programme described U.K. policy towards the MEDIA programme as 'to close it down'.[19] This provocative definition of U.K. policy was qualified and the official further stated 'we never wanted the MEDIA programme and we are trying to keep it on sensible lines'.

Satellite television transmission standards (the MAC Directive)

If Television without Frontiers and the MEDIA Programme concerned software, the third principal arena of European audiovisual policy, satellite television transmission standards, concerned hardware and creation, for reasons of electronics industrial policy, of an integrated Community satellite market. Just as European content quotas and the MEDIA Programme were conceived as instruments for the protection and stimulation of European audiovisual software, so the Directive on satellite television transmission standards and a subsequent programme for HDTV and wide-screen (16:9) television were conceived to protect and support the European television hardware industry. Here, too, France and the U.K. took different sides.

In 1986 the Community issued a Directive on satellite transmission standards to establish the MAC transmission standard as a Community norm.[20] It did so to ensure that new European television markets (notably satellite and cable) would develop as a single market rather than, as had terrestrial television, as a series of separate markets divided by incompatible PAL and SECAM transmission standards. It also hoped that a common European standard, protected by patents held by European firms, would enable Europe to reconquer the domestic television receiver market which had largely been lost to Japanese and Asian manufacturers. As France's Decaux report stated:

> There is a serious risk of European viewers eventually watching only American series on Japanese television sets.[21]

The Directive was poorly drafted and its provisions did not apply to the most vigorous and innovative delivery system – the Luxembourg-based Astra services (which included Rupert Murdoch's Sky channel). Astra-based services used PAL standard equipment which, because an old and proven technology, was cheaper and more reliable than the MAC-based systems mandated by the Directive. Although the Directive was revised and renewed in 1991, the U.K. (supported by Denmark, Spain and Ireland) successfully blocked France's, Germany's and the Netherlands' attempt to mandate the use of the MAC standard. A U.K. official, interviewed by the author on 10 February 1992, expressed satisfaction at the outcome of negotiations and commented, 'the U.K. did very well' in the negotiations over the new Directive. France, in contrast, recognised the outcome as *'une reculade française'* (a French back-down).[22]

DG IV and competition policy

In the fourth arena of Community audiovisual policy, the application of the competition provisions (especially Articles 85-90) of the Treaty of Rome to broadcasting, neither France nor the U.K. has actively shaped policy. Nor could they do so explicitly because the Competition Directorate, DG IV, has a considerable degree of independence and a quasi judicial status. However, the degree of vigour with which DG IV pursues competition issues seems to be related to the character of the Commissioner responsible for the Directorate. Unsurprisingly, pro-competition Member States strive to ensure that the Competition Commissioner reflects their values. There can be no doubt that Sir Leon Brittan, the U.K. Commissioner (and latterly Vice-President of the Commission) responsible for competition from 1987 to 1992, was particularly vigorous in striving to extirpate putatively anti-competitive practices in the audiovisual sector-notably in public service broadcasting. His Belgian successor, Karel van Miert, has been somewhat less aggressive but there can be no doubt that DG IV's impact has been to tilt the scales of EU audiovisual policy towards what Jacques Toubon described as *'la culture anglo-marchande'*[23] (the English shopkeeper mentality) rather than France's dirigiste interventionism.

If the outcome of a complex multidimensional policy process can be reduced to simple numerical values, France has lost either 3-0 or, depending on how one evaluates the importance of the MEDIA programme, 3-1 to the U.K. in EU audiovisual policy – in spite of playing a more active and committed game. There are no effective quotas in the Television without Frontiers Directive, no effective satellite transmission standards Directive, and a very effective pro-competition police force in DG IV. At best France has received an exiguous consolation prize in the MEDIA, HDTV and 16:9 production subsidy programmes. The U.K. has been fortunate in that its policies run with the grain of the Community's foundational economic values and, where faced by policy initiatives to which it is opposed, has been able to use the blocking minority and unanimous voting requirements provided in the Community's political arrangements[24] to secure its interests.

But to describe these events is to explain nothing. Why have France and the U.K. behaved as they have? Are the policies of the *'frères ennemis'* rooted in a well-founded apprehension of interests (whether national or European)? George has persuasively argued that the U.K.'s European policies are rooted in its domestic priorities and its European interests are, essentially, the projection of domestic interests onto a European stage.[25] His model is helpful in accounting for the European audiovisual policies of both France and the U.K. – with the qualifications that neither country has necessarily accurately translated its objective domestic interests into its European policies. How far does France's maximalism and the U.K.'s minimalism in European Union audiovisual policy correspond to their distinct economic and political formations?

International trade in films and television: France, the U.K. and the European Union

In 1986 the OECD published a study of global audiovisual trade which showed that, overwhelmingly, global trade flows were dominated by exports from the U.S.A. to the rest of the world. Second only to the U.S.A as an exporter, but a long way second, came the U.K. and after the U.K. came France.[26] INA confirms that there has been no change in the international pecking order and found 'France occupies an honourable second place among the top European exporting country just behind Great Britain'.[27] But, although the relative international trade positions of France, the U.K. and the U.S.A. have not changed, it is clear that the bilateral audiovisual trade balances of both France and the U.K. with the U.S.A. have worsened – as has the overall trade balance between the U.S.A. and the European Union. The EU's audiovisual deficit with U.S.A. has risen consistently since the mid-1980s to an estimated 3,500m Ecu in 1992 [28] and is likely to continue to rise as new television channels are established.[29]

The growing European trade deficit with the U.S.A. has borne unequally on European states. Although the U.K. is no exception to the European rule of growing film and television programme imports from the U.S.A., it maintained a positive 'visible' balance on the audiovisual trade account for the whole of the 1980s.[30] Although the U.K. went into 'visible' deficit, where for the most part it has remained, in the 1990s its deficit in film and television programmes has been more than balanced by net receipts deriving from other film and television services[31]. Moreover, unlike other EU states, including France, the U.S.A. is a significant audiovisual export market for the U.K.. As Hancock pointed out, 'the real winners in the US market ... have been English language films'.[32] Thus, the U.K. has no obvious interest in change to the European status quo which has permitted it to increase its exports to EU Member States, thanks to the opening of markets via Television without Frontiers, and maintain its access to the important US market.

In contrast, France, which has experienced a growing penetration of its audiovisual markets by US products without a compensating penetration of the US market by French productions, is passionately committed to change. For France has experienced increased import penetration from the U.S.A. without the exports to the U.S.A. enjoyed by the U.K. In the 1970s a particularly high proportion of the television programming screened in France was produced locally. UNESCO stated that 91.1 percent of French television programme output was of French origin in winter 1978-9.[33] Whereas a decade later the proportion of indigenous programming had fallen to (a still relatively high) total of 84 percent.[34] But in this period, between 1986 and 1988, there was a striking decline in the proportion of French programming in the key programme genre of fiction: 'French, or partially French (i.e. co-produced), fiction formerly accounted for 49 percent of broadcast fiction (on three channels) and now accounts for 25 percent (on five channels)'.[35]

This finding is consonant with the analysis advanced by Jack Lang, arguing that 'allowing market forces full play means accepting the disappearance of film production in time. It has long been accepted in France that protective measures are indispensable'.[36] The audiovisual trade statistics[37] of France and the U.K. for 1993 show the striking differences between the EU's two most important audiovisual traders and the extent to which France's experience is more representative of the EU as a whole.

The French market

By 1994 only 48.6 percent of programmes transmitted on French television were of French origin, 14.7 percent came from other EU states (of which 42 percent came from the U.K.) and 36 percent from non-EU states of which the U.S.A. was overwhelmingly the most important source of programmes, with 32.5 percent.[38] In two decades the national content of French television had declined from more than 90 percent to less than 50 percent. Furthermore, nearly 40 percent of programmes screened on French television emanated from anglophone states. The potential cultural impact of this transition needs no emphasis but it is also worth noting that its economic impact is far from negligible – France spends almost twice what the U.K. spends on television programme imports as a proportion of its total expenditure on television programming.[39]

A similar picture obtains in respect of cinema. In France in 1993, US films accounted for 57.7 percent of cinema admissions, French films 34.2 percent and films from other EU countries only 4 percent.[40] However, US penetration of the French film market was lower than for the EU as a whole and strikingly lower than for the U.K. In the EU as a whole American films accounted for 75 percent of cinema admissions and national productions 15 percent. And in 1993 American films accounted for 87 percent of cinema admissions in the U.K. where national productions accounted for only 4.7 percent of consumption.[41]

France's audiovisual exports go, for the most part, to Europe. In 1992 61 percent of French film exports went to Europe and only 14 percent to North America, producing total receipts of FF572m.[42] So too for television. North America accounted for 14 percent of French television exports and Europe 69 percent of a 1993 total export receipts of FF427m.[43] As Wallon stated: 'Europe remains our first market in terms of receipts ... the North American market remains almost completely closed to foreign film-making, and although French cinema occupies the first place in the American foreign market it is no exception to this rule.[44]

The U.K. market

In 1993 the U.K. had a positive balance of trade on the film account with receipts from exports (£336m) exceeding payments for imports (£257m) by £79m. For television in 1993, it had a trade deficit of £87m (receipts £181m, payments £268m) and thus an overall deficit on the 'visible' audiovisual account of £8m[45] offset by net receipts of £82m for other film and television services.[46] North America was the most important trading partner for the U.K., accounting for £181m of U.K. film exports (of a total of £336m) and £294m of payments for film imports compared to £95m receipts for film exports and £69m payments for film imports to the European Union.[47] The rise in U.K. film production rose from 67 features in 1993 to 127 in 1996[48] and is a further sign of health. Among these is a significant number of US 'transplant' productions such as *Evita, Mission Impossible* and the live-action version of *101 Dalmatians*.[49]

The European Union was the most important single television export market for the U.K., accounting for £78m of receipts (of a total £182m) in 1993 (whereas North America accounted for £49m of receipts). Payments in 1993 for television imports from North America totalled £199m (£31m for imports from the EU) of a total £268m. Other countries in Western Europe accounted for a further £12m in receipts and the same amount in payments.[50] The U.K. experience provides a strong contrast to the French experience of a closed United States market. Yet, like France, the U.K.'s film exports exceeded its television exports.

Domestic policy and the structure of audiovisual markets

The U.K. and France thus have pronounced differences in their economic interests in the audiovisual domain to which their European policies are approximately, but imperfectly, related. France underestimates the economic importance of television and the U.K. underestimates the economic health of its film sector. But both countries have creditable export records in spite of significant levels of import penetration-the apocalyptic scenarios often canvassed (see, *inter alia*, the citation from Lang which introduces this essay) are not supported by the evidence.

In film policy there is a neat congruence between the domestic and European policies of both the U.K. and France. France advocates European subsidy programmes to echo its domestic policies, whereas the U.K. abolished its main film support programme, the Eady Levy, and its U.K. content quota in the early years of the Thatcher governments. However, in television there is a remarkable contrast. Paradoxically, France – sceptical of liberalisation in an EU context – has, within a national context, more thoroughly liberalised its television market than has the U.K. And within France the Government has sponsored an expansion of the system which, in a European context, it has deplored as an engine of increased demand for American programming. France has privatised its flagship public service broadcaster, encouraged an increase in the number of television channels and actively supported the establishment of a commercial subscription channel, Canal Plus, on privileged regulatory terms; whereas the U.K. has created a new public service broadcaster – Channel 4 in 1982, only belatedly licensed a new terrestrial commercial channel – Channel 5 (which began transmissions in Spring 1997), and, in contrast to France, the U.K.'s chief commercial subscription service, BSkyB, was established in spite of official regulatory policy.[51]

Cathodon observed that an over-expanded French television encompasses a public sector of: 'three television channels (France 2, France 3, ARTE)' complemented by a strong private sector with three national terrestrial channels (TF1, Canal Plus, M6), thirteen local channels eight channels in the overseas territories ten thematic channels distributed by cable or satellite, a dozen of cable 'local channels', and more than two hundred cable networks'.[52] A major consequence of this explosion of capacity in France was a reduction in the average revenues available to fund each hour of programming screened, thus increasing demand for imports.[53] Cluzel judged this policy to have 'horrifying results' and placed the responsibility squarely at the door of the President of France: 'Unquestionably, François Mitterrand was responsible for the explosive growth of the French audiovisual landscape'.[54]

Cathodon persuasively argues that France's policy was distorted because its audiovisual policy makers have been captured by the film industry. He, or she, states, 'for example, the current regulation of cable television is an unconditional surrender to the film industry, and glossed the regulatory order to which s/he refers thus: 'the number and weight of the meticulously designed obligations imposed upon broadcast television (and now imposed upon cabled channels since the law of September the 1st 1992) are unparalleled elsewhere in the world'.[55] Furthermore, there is a pronounced disparity between the battery of institutions and support mechanisms for French film and the relative paucity of equivalents for television. The Centre National de la Cinématographie (CNC) was established in 1946 – no equivalent for television – and France has a host of aids for film production (though state aid to television, in the form of public funding for Antenne 2, FR3 and Arte should not be ignored).

France has an extensive range of subsidies available to film producers. Hypothetically, a producer drawing on the French support funds (Fonds de soutien, CNC selective subsidy, SOFICA) could defray up to 33 percent of the production costs of a film budgeted at U.S. $15m, whereas a U.K. producer could secure, at most, support for 20 percent of the production budget of a similar film.[56] However, it is easy to overestimate the importance of subsidy. France's subsidy, although more generous than the U.K.'s, pales into insignificance beside the subsidies potentially available to producers in Germany

(70 percent). Yet France is considerably more important than Germany as a film producer. Moreover, the cost of production is considerably higher in France (a fortiori in Germany) than in the U.K. for all major factors of production (crews, sound stage hire, catering, film stock, laboratory costs) except extras and post-production. Furthermore, cost comparisons do not tell the whole story. The source on which I have drawn for this information observes that, in qualitative terms: 'The U.K. has a wealth of all facilities and the reputation of the sector is second to none. Consequently producers often find it is, in the long run, cost-effective to locate in the U.K. even when the rate card shows another country may be cheaper'.

France has prioritised the cinema, in the U.K. relations are reversed. Yet, television is enormously more important than cinema[57] both economically and as a factor in cultural consumption. Nowhere in Europe does cinema attendance approach the number of hours devoted to television viewing. Cinema accounts for only 9 percent of European consumer expenditure on the audiovisual sector; television accounts for 72 percent.[58]

Americanisation

'In every country, the public prefers its own culture and is familiar with American culture. It is ignorant of the rest of the world'.[59]

Massive structural changes in European television, attributable to the growth of competition fostered by Television without Frontiers, have stimulated the increased proportion of exogenous, mainly American, programming on European television screens. Yet the impact of these changes has been very uneven and we must consider the distinct audiovisual histories of individual European countries if we are to understand European Union policy. Here too France and the U.K. are very different. The force of 'Americanisation' hit France and the U.K. at different times and, paradoxically, given the absence in the U.K. of the linguistic screen which separates France and the U.S.A., both film and television in the U.K. can be seen to have been strengthened by 'Americanisation', whereas in France the same forces have invariably been seen as destructive.

The Americanisation of French television is largely explained by the change in the structure of the French television market between the late 1970s and the mid-1990s: changes that had no parallel in the U.K. In 1974 France broke up the state broadcasting monopoly, the ORTF. This move 'induced the two companies [i.e., TF1 and Antenne 2 RC] to pursue the mass audience. The result was an effusion of American or American-style trivia'.[60] The privatisation of

TF1 in 1987 further reinforced the tendencies identified by Kuhn, as did the rapid, state-sponsored, growth in the number of terrestrial television channels in France. This government-sponsored, expansion of the French television system meant that the number of hours broadcast increased much faster than did the revenues broadcasters received. In consequence, the average expenditure per programme hour necessarily declined providing strong incentives to increase imports – to the extent that Cluzel acknowledged the impossibility of France's television channels meeting French quota requirements: 'Commercial television was thus forced to decide between two alternatives: to cheat or to die'.[61]

Clearly the number of U.K. television channels has also increased in the same period – but not by so much. Although there may formally be as many (or more) channels available to U.K. viewers as there are to French viewers, in the U.K., unlike in France, viewing, revenues and thus expenditure on programming are concentrated on two terrestrial channels, BBC1 and ITV, which together account for more than 60 percent of viewing, followed by two further terrestrial channels, Channel 4 and BBC2, and only then a sprinkling of cable and satellite channels. The state guided evolution of television in the U.K. and France has therefore followed radically different courses. In consequence, the U.K. television market is considerably less susceptible to import penetration than the French, not least because the 'Americanisation' of British television took place in the mid-1950s with the establishment of Europe's first commercial and first advertising-financed television channel and the closer approximation of television programming to popular taste.[62]

Commercial broadcasting in the U.K. began in 1955 (see chapter 3). The official history of the early days of Independent Television in Britain makes clear just how strongly committed were U.K. planners and regulators to establishing competition in broadcasting. As Sendall states, 'The dominant anxiety was to introduce competition between the contractors, as the Act required'.[63] This commitment resulted in a system better adapted to delivering the 'peoples' television, sought by Robert Fraser (the first Director General of the Independent Television Authority – the forerunner of the present Independent Television Commission) than was the public service monopoly which preceded it and which distinguished other European systems thereafter. Fraser's aspiration for ITV, though realised only in part, did succeed in establishing a distinctive 'streak of earthy vulgarity' in British television which has endured to this day.[64] Sendall makes clear how unusual was this British commitment to popular taste when compared to those of other contemporary European broadcasters; 'Nervous, not to say hostile, members of the European Broadcasting Union, whose governments (excepting Luxembourg and Monaco) were uniformly opposed to broadcast advertising, were to refuse to accept any ITV contributions to Eurovision unless they were 'clean feeds' protected from advertising'.[65] ITV's primary commitment, supported by the ITA, was to capturing an audience; its Chairman justified the commitment to entertainment programming by stating ,'You must capture an audience first of all. When you are established and secure you can gradually build up to a higher level'.[66] The success of ITV and the consequential catastrophic decline in the BBC's share of the U.K. television audience[67] led the BBC to follow many of the initiatives of commercial television.

In the U.K. a slow, early expansion and commercialisation of television strengthened the system as a whole and laid the foundations for the striking successes of British television drama in successfully combining demotic and élite culture; whereas in France, later and stronger commercialisation has subjected French television to much less healthy pressures. In the U.K. Americanisation was both positive and temporally distant – in France it is recent and destabilising. Moreover, its impact in France is amplified by the different linguistic and cultural formations of the two societies. France, and French television, is widely perceived to be more strongly governed than is the U.K. by high cultural values which, in spite of the fructifying influences of American cinema on the Nouvelle Vague and a host of other French cultural forms, perceive the influence of the U.S.A. (and U.K.) as uniquely malign. As Rigby and Hewitt state, 'cultural legitimacy in France is profoundly connected with exclusively *literary* ideas of culture'.[68]

Further, France's domestic policy emphasis, which has prioritised film so markedly, can only with difficulty be reconciled with the achievement of France's pan-European politico-cultural goals. A perverse emphasis, for, as Cluzel stated, television is more important:

> After the economic Europe, we are attempting to build the political Europe. However, the whole enterprise is vulnerable if we do not also realise a cultural Europe in a modern form, or more exactly a Europe of cultures. How can we do so? Television is unquestionably indispensable.[69]

Audiovisual policy, even in the age of the 'Information Society', is not simply a question of economic issues – of trade balances, matching of offer to demand, rates of innovation (aesthetic and in mode of production). It is also perceived – nowhere more than in France – to be a vector in the construction, or erosion, of collective identity, social solidarity and social cohesion. For much audiovisual policy is suffused with the nationalist presumption that polity and culture must be congruent[70] if political institutions are to be legitimate and stable. Such assumptions are so widely and deeply embedded in France that the vocabulary of French audiovisual commentators and policy makers is charged with military metaphors, few more eloquently than Jean Cluzel.

Language, culture and identity

> Over the centuries, the story of France's battles has been repeated. The military battle of France, of 1940, is only fifty years old, but a new one has been raging since the 1970s and this time, because it is part of a media war, it is French cultural identity which is at stake.[71]

Cluzel, as so often, succinctly epitomises views widely held in France by defining audiovisual policy as a matter of national survival. Cluzel's military metaphors are pervasive. For example, Jean-Pierre Landau (Director of the Department for Overseas Economic Affairs of the Economic Ministry of France) wrote, of audiovisual policy, 'in spite of having won a battle we have still to win the war'.[72] The Decaux report refers to 'a global offensive of the French audiovisual sector' and to 'the global battle of images'.[73]

Nowhere have military metaphors been more eloquently used than in Jack Lang's address to the 1982 UNESCO conference on cultural policy and cultural politics in Mexico City, where he asserted: 'Culture and economics: same battle'. French concern over the Americanisation (or anglo-saxonisation) of the audiovisual sector is but a subset, albeit a major subset, of a more pervasive concern over what a Council of Europe publication on French cultural policy named 'une anglophonie jugée envahissante' [an invasive English language].[74] Lang's own periods of ministerial office were neatly framed by two laws passed to defend the French language from the incursions of English: the Loi Bas-Lauriol of 31 December 1975 and the celebrated Loi Toubon of April 1994 – the Law for the use of French language.

The growing presence of American programmes on French screens, however plausibly they may be explained by Government-inspired changes to French television and by audience tastes, is the best known locus of French concern but other telling symptoms of anglophone hegemony come readily to hand. Moeglin, for example, observes that in 1990, of twelve transnational European television channels, five transmitted in English, another used English as one of its three languages, a seventh used no language and an eighth used several languages (including English). Moreover of ninety-six national and regional television channels in the European Community, twenty-four used English, more than used any other single language.[75]

The ascendancy of English is obviously assisted by the characteristics of audiovisual and other information markets. Films and television programmes (and indeed books and other printed works) are both non-rival products (consumption by one person does not exclude another from consumption of the same product) and are cheaply and easily reproduced and distributed. In consequence there are striking potential returns to economies of scale and strong incentives for producers to extend markets. Because the world population of English speakers is large and rich (markedly more so than the world population of francophones)[76] and because English is the world's dominant second language[77] all other things being equal, English language information goods and services will do better than their francophone equivalents. Hence, there less confidence among francophones in the merit of market outcomes; French recourse to the European Union as a source of allies in the construction of a bastion against the ingress of the invasion of English; and the endemic Franco-British squabbling over EU audiovisual policy.

Moreover, France has experienced a striking decline in the international power and prestige of the French language's virtually unchallenged European hegemony[78] to its present embattled status. In this context, what Mortimer described as the English's (sic) 'mistake of sharing their language with a great power outside Europe',[79] is of course profoundly threatening. The English language, the culture which it bears and the audiovisual media which deliver language and culture to Europeans, are therefore not only perceived to threaten European union but also European diversity. Hence France's recourse to the European Union, where 'French continued to strengthen its place in Community matters and France its influence in Europe',[80] and which France has consistently seen as a powerful potential support for its domestic efforts against an international anglophony perceived to be profoundly threatening. Hence the reciprocal anglophone perception (in this instance originating from an Irishman) that 'French thinking is nationalist at its core and federalist on the surface'.[81]

France's concerns about the erosion of linguistic and cultural hegemony are sharpened by France's distinctive experience of state building, an experience which again sharply differentiates France from the U.K. It is in France that an assumption of the intimacy of the connections between cultural and political identity, and between broadcasting and national identity, is most clearly to be found. As

Ritaine stated, 'in French political thought, the triad People-Nation-Culture is central. Culture is the foundation of the Nation'.[82] And Eugen Weber eloquently described the formation of the French state as indistinguishable from the creation of a strongly normative French national identity. Weber recounts how cultural and linguistic convergence was enjoined and enforced by the state apparatus in Paris. Indeed Weber goes so far as to claim that the creation of a modern national identity in France – achieved through a unified education system, universal military service and communication networks focused on Paris – was equivalent to colonisation: Fanon's account of the colonial experience is an apt description of what happened in the Landes and Corrèze. In France, as in Algeria, the destruction of what Fanon called national culture, and what I would call local or regional culture, was systematically pursued.[83]

Such strong charges have, of course, also been levelled at the metropolitan power of London and the predominance of England in a multinational U.K. But, my point is not to weigh in the balance the degree to which the balance of power in France and the U.K. has been more or less friendly to regional and national cultures, only to observe that the historical formations of France and the U.K. have been different. The U.K., contentedly or in teeth-gritting harmony, is based on recognition of difference – the semi official status of Welsh, the separate Scots legal and educational systems, for some time a separate Parliament in Northern Ireland – whereas France is a much more centralised state. In one national history acceptance of difference (within limits of course!) is the basis of the state, in the other difference has consistently been seen to threaten the state's integrity. Hence the different importance attributed to cultural difference, hybridisation, pluralism and pollution in France and the U.K.

If France represents a political history of the strong convergence between state and nation – of indissoluble coupling of cultural and political identity on a nationalist model[84] – then the U.K. represents a different aetiology. A rather functionalist[85] pragmatic association of political units with, relative to France, less concern for cultural unity and more for the evolution, however messy, of practicable working arrangements. Evidently these distinct visions, grounded in two successful histories of state building, point to different, and incompatible, strategies in and futures for audiovisual (and other) policies in the European Union. A U.K. oriented to the minimalism, as defined by its Foreign Secretary Douglas Hurd, of: 'a Europe that respects cultural and political diversity, which only does those things at the European level which need to be done at that level, which is outward-looking, free-trading, democratic and flexible: a partnership of nations working together to advance their national interests',[86] is unlikely to agree with a France enthusiastically fostering the 'ever closer union' prescribed in the preambles to both the Rome and Maastricht treaties.

Conclusion

The European audiovisual policies of France and the U.K. are thus both paradoxical and predictable. Predictable in that each country, *soit* Europhile *soit* Europhobe, has sought to make the European Union in its own image and in its own interests. In their European audiovisual policies France and the U.K. have sought (albeit with some significant inconsistencies and contradictions), to mirror their domestic regulatory and policy priorities and to reproduce, in a European context, their respective national experiences in state building, as well as to promote policies that favour their respective domestic interests. Interests that for the U.K. are almost wholly economic whereas for France, not only do similar economic considerations apply (albeit pointing to policies different to those of the U.K.), but the status and survival of the national language is perceived to be at stake. Moreover, France's and the U.K.'s different experiences of state building point to opposed conclusions: for France to a necessary congruence between polity and culture, for the U.K. to a looser, incongruent, politico-cultural formation. Paradoxical in that, in spite of its almost contemptuous attitude towards the European Union's audiovisual concerns, the U.K. has achieved considerably greater success in realising its policy objectives than has France for hers – in spite of France giving such matters a much higher priority.

One would look for a long time to find a U.K. Minister of National Heritage making so firm a commitment as did François Léotard when Minister of Communications: 'My priority is to make France the audiovisual centre of Europe'.[87] However, in spite of the salience of the audiovisual in France's European policy portfolio, it may be that its policies are fated not to succeed – as Cluzel uncomfortably acknowledged: 'in the cultural domain, Europe is a delusion'.[88]

The U.K.'s success is due to a combination of factors – the fundamental structure of the European Union which favours the operation of markets rather than dirigisme; the political structure of the Union which has allowed a minority of states to exercise power via blocking minorities or even through vetoes; the inherently greater strength of the U.K. audiovisual sector – itself due to a variety of factors including the inherent comparative advantage of the English language, the competitive advantages accrued from early and slow commercialisation of television and the absence of the over-expansion of the television sector which vitiated French television in the 1980s – a television perennially weakened by its subordination to the interests of the film sector.

However, the U.K. may yet pay a heavy penalty for its historic policies of abstentionism and obstruction. At best it is fated to respond to the agendas of others and thus to construct success solely as an ability to preserve U.K. television viewers from the torments of too many Jacques Tati films. At worst it may find itself outnumbered and outmanoeuvred by a successful French construction of a pan-European alliance of the other EU Member States, all of whose domestic audiovisual environments share, to a greater or lesser degree, the problems of the French and few of the advantages of the British.[89] As the *Financial Times*'s commentator on European Affairs, Ian Davidson, stated:

> The U.K.'s European policy has been a series of blunders based on a profound failure to devise a European strategy which can mesh plausibly with the other forces in place. And that failure in turn is the direct consequence of the defensive and adversarial vocabulary adopted consistently for the past forty years by almost the entire political class in Britain towards the European Community.[90]

The audiovisual sector is no exception to this general rule. The U.K. may yet pay a heavy price for indulging its perennial penchant of playing the awkward partner.[91] But, indisputably, the Franco-British dialogue of the deaf will continue at high volume even if future outcomes remain uncertain.

Notes and References

1. J. Lang, 'The Future of European Film and Television', in *European Affairs*, Vol. 2, No. 1, 12-20.
2. R. Chesnais, ' De la francomanie à la francophobie (1935-1815)', in *Medias Pouvoirs*, No. 33, 1994, 84-93.
3. I use 'audiovisual' here as a convenient synonym for film and television.
4. A telephone poll of respondents in all European Union states conducted in May 1994 showed that 27 percent of French respondents named the U.K. as the least trusted member of the Union – more than nominated any other Member State and that 44 percent of British respondents named France as the least trusted member of the Union – more than nominated any other Member State, *Financial Times*, 1 June 1994, 4.
5. E. Gellner, *Nations and Nationalism*, Oxford, Blackwell, 1983.
6. J. Cluzel, *Une autre bataille de France*, Paris, L.G.D.J., 1993, 7-8.
7. For an extensive discussion of EU audiovisual policy, see R. Collins, *Broadcasting and Audiovisual Policy in the European Single Market*, London, John Libbey, 1994.

8. Commission of the European Communities, *Television without Frontiers*, Green Paper on the establishment of the Common Market for broadcasting especially by satellite and cable, COM (84) 300 final, Luxembourg, 1984.
9. P. Hodgson, 'Foreword', in T. Congdon et al, *Paying for Broadcasting*, The Handbook, London, Routledge, 1992, vii.
10. Although the principal consequence of the increased demand for programming has been an increase in the volume of U.S. programming on European screens, it is not the only one. European producers have recycled old works (e.g., the BBC on U.K. Gold), low-cost production methods have been developed, new, low-cost European subject matter for programmes has been found, e.g., actuality footage of emergency services in action, recordings from security and traffic monitoring cameras, sports that were formerly not shown on television) and so on.
11. R. Barzanti, 'Audiovisual Opportunities in the Single Market', in *MEDIA 92 Newsletter*, Brussels, September 1990, 1.
12. J. Lang, 'European Film and Television', 18.
13. B. Miyet, 'La règle du plus fort', *Mediaspouvoirs*, no. 33, 1994, 60-62.
14. J. Cluzel, *bataille de France*, 46-50.
15. O. Noël du Payrat, 'Europe: l'intégration prioritaire à la place des quotas', in *Les cahiers de l'audiovisuel*, no. 9, September 1996, 15-21. A striking, and, from the French point of view, perverse consequence of Television without Frontiers was the requirement for France to weaken its own domestic television French language content quotas which discriminated against European works in languages other than French. Unsurprisingly France has perceived Television without Frontiers to disadvantage 'as seriously our producers as our broadcasters', in J. Cluzel, *bataille de France*,13.
16. Commission of the European Communities, *The Community's Audiovisual Policy*, Information Memo, COM (86) 146, Brussels, March 1986, 1-4.
17. Council of the European Communities, Decision concerning the implementation of an action programme to promote the development of the European audiovisual industry (MEDIA)(1991-1995), 90/685/EEC, OJL 380, 31.12.1990, 37-44.
18. R. Wangermée, 'What rules for transfrontier television?', in *Media Bulletin*, vol. 6, no. 2, 1989, 2. P. Moeglin, 'Télévision et Europe', in *Communication*, vol. 12, no. 2, 1991, 48.
19. Interviewed by the author on 10 February 1992. The U.K. Ministries responsible for European audiovisual policy had vigorously attempted to prevent the establishment of the MEDIA programme. However, the Foreign and Commonwealth Office counselled that a U.K. veto should not be exercised over a comparatively trivial Community issue.
20. Council of the European Communities, Council Directive on the adoption of common technical specifications of the MAC-packet family of standards for direct satellite television broadcasting, 86/529/EEC, OJL 311, 6/11/1986.
21. A. Decaux, *La politique télévisuelle extérieure de la France*, Paris, La Documentation francaise, 1989, 8.
22. J.Cluzel, *bataille de France*, 15.
23. Cited in P. Thody, *Le Franglais. Forbidden English, Forbidden American. Law Politics and Language in Contemporary France*, London, Athlone, 1995, 63.
24. The total votes required for decisions changes with the membership of the EU. Currently, with a fifteen member EU, a qualified majority requires 62 of the 87 votes in the Council of Ministers (European Council), a simple majority requires 44 votes and a blocking minority is 26 votes.

25. S. George, *An Awkward Partner*. Britain in the European Community, Oxford, Oxford University Press, 1990.
26. OECD Observer, No. 141, Paris, July 1986.
27. INA, *Observatoire de la création audiovisuelle*, Bry sur Marne, 1995.
28. A-P. Vasconcelos, *Report by the Think Tank*, DG X, Commission of the European Communities, 1994.
29. The European audiovisual Observatory estimated the European audiovisual trade deficit grew from US $2,100 in 1988 to US $6,300 in 1995.
30. CSO, *Overseas Transactions of the Film and TV Industry*, Newport, Government Statistical Service, 1991.
31. ONS, *Overseas Transaction of the Film and Television Industry*, London, 1996.
32. D. Hancock, 'Cinema in Europe a panorama', in *Communications et Stratégies*, no. 6, 1992, 148.
33. UNESCO, *Three Weeks of Television. An international comparative study*, Paris, 1982, 20.
34. P. Sepstrup, *Transnationalization of Television in Western Europe*, London, John Libbey, 1990, 23.
35. Personal communication to the author from R. Chaniac and J-P. Jézéquel, INA, 1996.
36. J. Lang, 'European Film and Television', 16. Lang's specific proposals for protection for the film industry were realised in Article 7 of the Television without frontiers Directive, for content quotas in Article 4 of the Television without Frontiers Directive, and for subventions in the MEDIA programme of the European Community and the Eurimages programme of the Council of Europe. The audiovisual Eureka was established following the Assises de l'audiovisuel in 1989.
37. The data cited should be used with caution. I make a snapshot comparison whereas trade statistics sometimes fluctuate significantly year by year. Moreover, there are difficulties of classification (use of different criteria). To my regret, I have not been able to secure statistics for French audiovisual imports comparable to those available for the U.K.. However, this data, although imperfect, is suggestive. It shows that, contrary to general belief, the U.K. film sector enjoys a more favourable trade balance than does the U.K. television sector, that the French television sector is a significant exporter, that, although the U.K. film exhibition sector has been considerably more completely penetrated by US productions than has either U.K. television or French film, it enjoys an export performance superior to either U.K. or French film and so on.
38. INA, *la création audiovisuelle*, 18-9.
39. A consultant's report shown to the author in confidence estimates that the U.K. spends 15 percent of its total television programme spend on imports whereas France spends 27 percent (and Germany 12 percent).
40. CNC info., No. 254, Paris, 1994, 13.
41. CNC info., No. 256, Paris, 1995, 63-6.
42. CNC info, No. 254, 7.
43. INA, *la création audiovisuelle*, 85-6.
44. D. Wallon, Editorial, in CNC, No. 254, 2.
45. ONS, *Overseas transactions*, Table 1. Throughout the 1980s the U.K. had a positive balance of audiovisual trade which went into deficit in 1990. The 1993 deficit was the lowest U.K. audiovisual deficit of the 1990s.
46. ONS, Ibid., Table 6.
47. ONS, Ibid., Table 2.
48. *Financial Times*, 11-12 January 1997, 4.

49. However, too much should not be made of changes in year-by-year levels of production – not least because a major factor in determining U.K. levels of film production is the £/$ parity.
50. ONS, *Overseas transactions*, Table 5.
51. The favoured child of the U.K. regulator, BSB, was ignominiously forced into an unequal merger with Sky Channel to form BSkyB.
52. Cathodon, (pseudonym of a senior government official), 'La législation de l'audiovisuel en France', in *Réseaux*, No. 59, 1993, p. 27.
53. A trend exacerbated by the 'freezing' of the French production archive in consequence of French copyright law and in spite of the new revenues generated by Europe's first and most successful pay-television service, Canal Plus.
54. J. Cluzel, *bataille de France*, 1993, 15-8.
55. Cathodon, 'législation de l'audiovisuel', 39-40.
56. These estimates are derived from a U.K. consultant's study made available to the author in confidence.
57. I make a categorical analytical distinction between film and television for convenience. Of course, firm distinctions are often hard to draw, not least because of the film's importance in television's programming strategies.
58. KPMG (Klynveld, Peat, Marwick, Goerdeler) estimated EU audiovisual expenditure in 1994 at 24,250m Ecu, of which cinema attendance accounted for 9 percent of the total, broadcast television 72 percent, with video rental accounting for a further 18 percent. The strikingly greater economic importance of television relative to film which the KPMG data suggests is misleading, in that KPMG consider here only the revenues from licence fee and subscription-funded television, whereas the television total should be increased by the revenues of advertising financed television.
59. J. Peskine, 'Les quotas, de l'incantation à l'analyse', in *Les cahiers de l'audiovisuel*, no. 9, September 1996, 23.
60. R. Kuhn, (ed.), *The Politics of Broadcasting*, Beckenham, Croom Helm, 1985, 58.
61. J. Cluzel , *bataille de France*, 18.
62. The successful adaptation of British television to the forces of commercialisation and Americanisation was not a peculiarly British experience. Rogers and Antola have claimed that, in spite of the economic advantages of American producers and the low prices of imported American programmes, television producers in Latin America have successfully domesticated their television schedules. They pertinently cite Pool's general proposition that 'domestic producers, as soon as they learn to produce the kind of attractive things that had come from abroad, have a distinct advantage in the competition for an audience' in explaining 'how telenovelas have come to replace imported US television programmes in Latin America . In fact, Rogers and Antola's findings extend forward an older established theoretical trajectory than they acknowledge. Pool, on whose work they draw, refers to Karl Deutsch's general proposition that introduction of exogenous information into a given context first provokes a decline in indigenous works but, second, tends to stimulate indigenous production. E. Rogers and L. Antola, 'Telenovelas: a Latin American Success Story', *Journal of Communication*, vol. 35, no. 4, Autumn 1985, 25-35. I. de sola Pool, 'The changing Flow of Television', *Journal of Communication*, vol. 27, no. 2, Spring 1977,139-49. K. Deutsch, *Communication and Social Integration*, Cambridge, MIT Press, 1953.
63. B. Sendall, *Independent Television in Britain*, vol. 1, 'Origin and Foundation, 1946-1962', London, Macmillan, 1982, 65. The regulators' aspirations were only partially fulfilled; the Peacock Committee justly described U.K. television in the early 1980s as a 'comfortable duopoly' and acidly remarked that 'the viewer's or listener's main function is to react to a set of choices, determined by

the broadcasting institutions' (Peacock 1986 para 577). However, my point is that in the U.K., although the system has been driven by broadcasters' definition of consumer choices, this supply-pushed set of options seems to have been closer to consumer demand than has been the case in other jurisdictions. I believe that this is due in important part to the early presence of competition, however imperfect, in the U.K. broadcasting order.
64. Ibid., 136-7.
65. Ibid., 100.
66. Ibid., 144.
67. Ibid., 249. In 1956 60 percent of London respondents polled expressed a preference for commercial television and only 16 percent for the BBC.
68. B. Rigby and N. Hewitt, *France and the Mass Media*, Basingstoke and London, Macmillan, 1991, 3. Also see S. Emanuel, 'Télévision et Culture en France. A la recherche d'une chaîne culturelle européenne', thesis presented for the Doctorat en Sciences de l'information et des Communications, Université de Rennes II.
69. J. Cluzel, *bataille de France*, 148.
70. E. Gellner, *Nations and Nationalism*, Oxford, Blackwell, 1983.
71. J. Cluzel, *bataille de France*, 11.
72. J-P. Landau, 'A la conquête des marchés étrangers', *CNC Info*, No. 254, December 1994, 4-5.
73. A. Decaux, *La politique audiovisuelle*, 7-8.
74. Council of Europe, Resolution (88)15, *Setting up a European Support Fund for the Co-production and Distribution of Creative Cinematographic and Audiovisual Works (Eurimages)*, Strasbourg, 1988, 43.
75. P. Moeglin, 'Télévision et Europe', 17.
76. See S. Wildman and S. Siwek, *International Trade in Films and Television Programs*, Cambridge, Ballinger, 1988.
77. See D. Crystal, 'The Language that took over the world', in *Guardian*, 22 February 1997, 21.
78. Thody sketches the decline of French thus: 'From 1714 onwards, with the Treaty of Rastadt, the French version of treaties took precedence over the Latin, and this remained the case until 1919, when French had to accept joint first place with English in the Treaty of Versailles. And in 1945 the French had to fight hard to have their language accepted alongside Chinese, English, Spanish and Russian as one of the working languages for the United Nations Organisation, only to see the Bandung conference of newly independent, uncommitted states conduct all its proceedings in English in 1955'. P. Thody, *Le franglais*, 90.
79. E. Mortimer, 'Searching for an elusive esprit de corps', in *Financial Times*, 26 January 1988, 19.
80. P. Thody, *Le franglais*, 95.
81. C. O' Brien, 'Pursuing a Chimera. Nationalism at odds with the idea of a federal Europe', in *Times Literary Supplement*, no. 4641, 13 March 1992, 3.
82. E. Ritaine, *Les Stratégies de la culture*, Paris, FNSP, 1983, 13.
83. E. Weber, *Peasants into Frenchmen. The Modernization of Rural France*, Stanford, Stanford University Press, 1976, 491.
84. Counter-indications can, of course, be found. For example, Lionel Jospin, in his inaugural speech to the Assemblée Nationale as Prime Minster on 19 June 1997, qualified his affirmation of French political sovereignty in Corsica, as an integral part of Metropolitan France, with recognition of the legitimacy of Corsica's linguistic and cultural distinctiveness. Jospin stated: 'In Corsica – as everywhere in France – the Government will safeguard the rule of law. The Government will encourage affirmation of Corsica's cultural identity and the teaching of its language', cited in *Libération*, 20 June 1997, 6.

85. D. Mitrany, *The Functional Theory of Politics*, London, Martin Robertson, 1975.
86. Commission of the European Communities, Background Report, The Intergovernmental Conference, B/2/97, January 1997, 1.
87. F. Léotard, *Culture: les chemins de printemps*, Paris, Albin Michel, 1988, 61.
88. J. Cluzel , *bataille de France*, 126.
89. But, whilst other EU Member States might appear to share France's concerns, appearances can deceive. For the European quotas, so vigorously espoused by France in its own and Europe's interest, turn the domestic audiovisual capacity to supply their domestic markets, into *chasses gardées* for European Union Member States with strong audiovisual sectors – for instance France and the U.K.. Moreover, quotas limit filmgoers' and television viewers' access to the American programming which, by and large, as Silj found, are preferred to rival offerings from other European Union Member States. Silj's pan-European research team, assembled by the Italian Council for the Social Sciences, analysed 'the contents and narrative structures of television fiction in European countries'. It found that 'national programmes occupy the top positions in the audience ratings, [but] the public's second choice never falls on programmes produced by other European countries. American is the lingua franca of the European market of television fiction' but that 'reality was much more diversified than we had expected'. A. Silj (et al), *East of Dallas, The European Challenge to American Television*, London, BFI, 1988. Or, as a Communist deputy stated in the April 1994 debate on the Loi Toubon in the Sénat, 'It's not America that invades us, it is we who adore it'. I. Renar in P. Thody, *Le franglais*, 81.
90. *Financial Times*, 12 December 1991, 3.
91. S. George, *An Awkward Partner. Britain in the European Community*, Oxford, Oxford University Press, 1990.

Select Bibliography

The following select bibliography is intended as a guide for further reading. It makes no claims to comprehensiveness, and is offered as an indication of the key texts used by the authors in the preparation of individual contributions. Texts are arranged according to section headings.

Part I: Regulatory and Political Structures

Achille, Y. and Bueno, J-I., *Les télévisions publiques en quête d'avenir*, Grenoble, Presses Universitaires, 1994.
Barnett, S. and Curry, A., *The Battle for the BBC*, London, Aurum Press, 1994.
Blumler, J. (ed.), *Television and the Public Interest*, London, Sage, 1992.
Bourdon, J., *Haute fidélité, pouvoir et télévision 1935-1994*, Paris, Seuil, 1994.
Brittan, S., 'The Fight for Freedom in Broadcasting', *The Political Quarterly*, vol. 58, 1987.
Chamard, M-E. and Kieffer, P., *La télé: dix ans d'histoires secrètes*, Paris, Flammarion, 1992.
Debbasch, C., *Droit de l'audiovisuel*, Paris, Dalloz, 1995.
Debbasch, C. and Gueydan, C. (eds), *La régulation de la liberté de la communication audiovisuelle*, Aix-Marseille, Economica/ Presses Universitaires, 1991.
Franceschini, L., *La régulation audiovisuelle en France*, Paris, Presses Universitaires de France, 1995.
Guilhaume, P., *Un président à abattre*, Paris, Albin Michel, 1991.
House of Commons National Heritage Committee, *The BBC and the Future of Broadcasting*, vol. 1, London, The Stationery Office, March 1997.
Jézéquel, J-P., 'Canal Plus... de privilèges', *Angle Droit*, no. 4, April-May 1991.

Jones, N., *Soundbites and Spin Doctors*, London, Cassell, 1995.
Jongen, F., *La police de l'audiovisuel. Analyse comparée de la régulation de la radio et de la télévision en Europe*, Bruxelles/Paris, Bruylant/L.G.D.J., 1994.
Miller, D., *Don't Mention the War: Northern Ireland, Propaganda and the Media*, London, Pluto Press, 1994.
Negrine, R., *Politics and the Mass Media in Britain*, 2nd edn, London, Routledge, 1994.
O'Malley, T., *Closedown? The BBC and Government Broadcasting Policy 1979-92*, London, Pluto, 1994.
Palmer, M. and Tunstall, J., *Liberating Communications: Policy Making in France and Britain*, Oxford, Blackwell, 1990.
Peacock, A., *Report of the Committee on Financing the BBC*, Cmnd 9824, London, HMSO, 1986.
Péan, P. and Nick, C., *TF1, un pouvoir*, Paris, Fayard, 1997.
Regourd, S., *La télévision des Européens*, Paris, IIAP/La Documentation française, 1992.
Robillard, S., *Television in Europe: Regulatory Bodies*, London, John Libbey, 1995.
Schlesinger, P. and Tumber, H., *Reporting Crime: the Media Politics of Criminal Justice*, Oxford, Clarendon Press, 1994.
Seaton, J., 'Broadcasting in the Age of Market Ideology: Is it Possible to Underestimate the Public Taste?', *The Political Quarterly*, vol. 65, 1994.
Taylor, P., *War and the Media*, Manchester, Manchester University Press, 1992.
Wolton, D., *War Game*, Paris, Flammarion, 1991.

Part II: Programming Structures

BBC *Annual Report and Accounts 1994/95*.
Bonnell, R., *La vingt-cinquième image*, Paris, Gallimard/FEMIS, 1989.
Brunsdon, C., 'Problems with Quality', *Screen* 31:1, Spring 1990.
Chancel, J. (ed.), *Les Ecrits de l'image*, no. 2, Spring 1994.
Collins, R., *Culture, Communication and National Identity: The Case of Canada*, Toronto, University Press of Toronto, 1990.
CSA, *Le cinéma à la télévision in 1990-1991*, Paris, CSA, 1992.
Emanuel, S., 'Télévision et Culture en France. A la recherche d'une chaîne culturelle européenne', Thesis presented for the Doctorat en Sciences de l'information et des Communications, Université de Rennes II, 1992.
_____,'Cultural Television: Western Europe and the United States', *European Journal of Communication*, vol. 8, 1993.
Mattelart, M., 'Education, Television and Mass Culture: reflections on Research and Innovation', in R. Paterson and P. Drummond (eds), *Television and its Audience*, London, BFI, 1985.
Mulgan, G. (ed.), *The Question of Quality*, London, BFI, 1990.
Wolton, D., *Eloge du grand public*, Paris, Flammarion, 1989.

Wyver, J., 'Representing Art or Reproducing Culture?-Tradition and innovation in British Television's Coverage of the Arts (1959-87)', in P. Hayward (ed.), *Picture This*, London, John Libbey, 1988.

Part III : The New Media

BBC, *The BBC's Fair Trading Commitment*, London, BBC, 1994.
Chamoux, J-P., 'Cinquante ans de télécommunications', *Médias Pouvoirs*, no. 39-40, 1995.
Chippindale, P. and Franks, S., *Dished! The rise and fall of British Satellite Broadcasting*, London, Simon and Schuster, 1991.
Council of the European Communities, *Council Directive on the adoption of common technical specifications of the MAC-packet family of standards for direct satellite television broadcasting*, 86/529/EEC, OJ L 311, 6.11.1986.
Council of the European Communities, *Directive on the adoption of standards for satellite broadcasting of television signals*, 92/38/EEC, 11 May 1992, OJ L 137, 20 May 1992.
CSA, 'Le câble français: vers de meilleures perspectives de rentabilité?', *La Lettre du CSA*, no. 81, June 1996.
Kuhn, R., *The Media in France*, London, Routledge, 1995.
———, 'France', in V. Macleod (ed.), *Media Ownership and Control in the Age of Convergence*, London, International Institute of Communications, 1996.
Thatcher, M., 'Telecommunications in Britain and France: the Impact of National Institutions', *Communications & Strategies*, no. 6, 1992.
Vittet-Philippe, P., *New Digital Services and the Information Society: Contribution to a Reflection in Progress*, Brussels, European Commission, DG XIII, February 1996.
———, *Electronic Commerce ; High Tech Crime and Secure Technologies*, Brussels, European Commission, DG XIII, April 1997.

Part IV : The Challenge of Europe

Barzanti, R., 'Audiovisual Opportunities in the Single Market', *MEDIA 92 Newsletter*, Brussels, September 1990.
Channel Four, 'Selling your Programmes Overseas: a guide', January 1986.
Chesnais, R., 'De la francomanie à la francophobie' (1935-1815), *Medias Pouvoirs*, no. 33, 1994.
Debbasch, C. and Gueydan, C. (eds), *Cinéma et télévision*, Aix-Marseille, Presses Universitaires /Economica, 1992.
Cluzel, J., *Une autre bataille de France*, Paris, L.G.D.J., 1993.
Collins, R., *Broadcasting and Audiovisual Policy in the European Single Market*, London, John Libbey, 1994.
Commission of the European Communities, 'Television Without Frontiers', Green Paper on the Establishment of the Common Market for broad-

casting especially by satellite and cable, COM (84)300 final, Luxembourg, Office for Official Publications of the European Communities, 1984.
Commission of the European Communities, *The Community's Audiovisual Policy*, Information Memo, COM (86) 146, Brussels, 1986.
Commission of the European Communities, *Commission Communication to the Council accompanied by two proposals for Council decisions relating to an action programme to promote the development of a European audiovisual Industry 'MEDIA' 1991-1995*, COM (90)132 final, 1990.
Commission of the European Communities, Green Paper, *Strategy Options to strengthen the European Programmme Industry in the context of the audiovisual policy of the European Union*, Brussels, 1994.
Commission of the European Communities, Background Report, The Intergovernmental Conference, B/2/97, 1997.
Council of Europe, Resolution (88)15, *Setting up a European Support Fund for the Co-production and Distribution of Creative Cinematographic and Audiovisual Works (Eurimages)*, Strasbourg, 1988.
Council of the European Communities, *Decision concerning the implementation of an action programme to promote the development of the European audiovisual industry (MEDIA) (1991-1995)*, 90/685/EEC, OJ L 380, 31 December 1990.
Decaux, A., *La politique télévisuelle extérieure de la France*, Paris, La Documentation française, 1989.
Dibbie, J.N., *Aid for Cinematographic and Audiovisual Production in Europe*, London, John Libbey, 1993.
European Parliament, Report on the European Film and Television Industry (the de Vries report), 09.01.1989, PE Document A2-03447/88, 1989.
Finney, A., *The State of European Cinema, a new dose of reality*, London, Cassell, 1996.
Gellner, E., *Nations and Nationalism*, Oxford, Blackwell, 1983.
George, S., *An Awkward Partner, Britain in the European Community*, Oxford, Oxford University Press, 1990.
Hancock, D., *Mirrors of our own, Eurimages*, Council of Europe, Strasbourg, 1996.
Hill, J. and McLoone, M. (eds), *Big Picture Small Screen: The Relations Between Film and Television*, Luton, University Press/John Libbey, 1997.
INA, *Observatoire de la création audiovisuelle*, Bry sur Marne, 1995.
Jäckel, A., 'European Co-production Strategies: The Case of France and Britain' in A. Moran (ed.), *Film Policy*, London, Routledge, 1996.
Lang, J., 'The Future of European Film and Television', *European Affairs*, vol. 2, no. 1, 1988.
Léotard, F., *Culture: les chemins de printemps*, Paris, Albin Michel, 1988.
Moeglin, P., 'Télévision et Europe', *Communication*, vol. 12, no. 2, 1991.
Noël du Payrat, O., 'Europe: L'intégration prioritaire à la place des quotas', *Les cahiers de l'audiovisuel*, no. 9, September 1996.
ONS, *Overseas Transaction of the Film and Television Industry 1995*, London, Office for National Statistics, 1996.

Peskine, J., 'Les quotas, de l'incantation à l'analyse', *Les cahiers de l'audiovisuel*, no. 9, September 1996.

Puttnam, D., *The Undeclared War*, London, Harper Collins, 1997.

Rigby, B. and Hewitt, N., *France and the Mass Media*, Basingstoke and London, Macmillan, 1991.

Sepstrup, P., *Transnationalization of Television in Western Europe*, London, John Libbey, 1990.

Silj, A. et al., *East of Dallas, The European Challenge to American Television*, London, BFI, 1988.

Tunstall, J. and Palmer, M., *Media Moguls*, London, Routledge, 1991.

UNESCO, *Three Weeks of Television, an International Comparative Study*, Paris, 1982.

Wangermée, R., 'What rules for transfrontier television?', *Media Bulletin*, vol. 6, no. 2, 1989.

Wolton, D., 'L'Europe, aux risques de la communication', *Médias Pouvoirs*, no. 33, 1994.

Notes on Contributors

Régine Chaniac is Director of Research at the Institut National de l'Audiovisuel. She has published extensively on audience behaviour and cultural television broadcasting and collaborates in the European Research group EUROFICTION.

Richard Collins is Senior Lecturer in Media and Communications at the London School of Economics and Political Science and member of the Comité Scientifique of the European Audiovisual Summer School. He has published widely on television and public policy within Europe, notably *Broadcasting and Audiovisual Policy in the European Single Market* (John Libbey, 1994).

Susan Emanuel was formerly Lecturer in Media Studies at the University of Bristol. She also worked as a producer of educational programmes for the BBC and recently completed a doctoral thesis entitled 'Télévision et Culture en France' at the Université de Rennes II.

Peter Goodwin is Senior Lecturer at the Centre for Communication and Information Studies, University of Westminster. He has published a number of articles on media policy in the U.K.

Hervé Isar is Lecturer in Public Law at the Université Jean Monnet, Saint-Etienne. His publications include *Le service public et la communication audiovisuelle* (PUAM-Economica, 1995).

Anne Jäckel is Senior Lecturer in French and Film Studies at the University of the West of England, Bristol. She has contributed numerous articles on European cinema to specialist journals, notably the *European Journal of Communication*.

Raymond Kuhn is Senior Lecturer in Politics at Queen Mary and Westfield College, University of London. He has published widely on British and French broadcasting policy in journals such as *Parliamentary Affairs, West European Politics* and the *Political Quarterly*. He is author of *The Media in France* (Routledge, 1995).

Monia Lecomte is Research Assistant at the University of the West of England, Bristol. She is completing a doctoral thesis entitled 'L' Européanisation de la télévision française', and has recently published an article entitled 'La libéralisation de la télévision des années Mitterrand' in *Modern and Contemporary France*.

Lucy Mazdon is based at the University of Southampton where she recently completed a doctoral thesis on 'Hollywood remakes of French cinema'. She is currently researching French and British television, specifically the place of the spectator in contemporary programming and the ways in which these programmes articulate and construct public and private spaces and identities.

Michael Palmer is Director of the Centre for Research on Information and the Media in Europe (C.R.I.M.E.), at the Université de la Sorbonne nouvelle, Paris III. He has published numerous books on broadcasting, notably *Liberating Communications: Policy Making in France and Britain* (Blackwell, 1990) and *Media Moguls* (Routledge, 1991).

Serge Regourd is Professor at the Université de Sciences Sociales, Toulouse where he is Director of the Institut du Droit de la Communication. He is also Expert-Advisor to the European Institute for the Media and has published extensively in the audiovisual field. His most recent books are entitled *La télévision des Européens* (La Documentation française, 1992) and *Le Droit de la communication audiovisuelle* (PUF, 1998).

Michael Scriven is Professor of European Studies and Director of the Centre for European Studies at the University of the West of England, Bristol. He has published extensively in the field of French and European intellectual history, culture and politics. His most recent book is entitled *Sartre and the Media* (Macmillan, 1993).

Jean-Claude Sergeant is Professor of English and American Studies at the Université de la Sorbonne Nouvelle, Paris III. He has contributed numerous articles on aspects of the British media, notably to *Medias Pouvoirs*. He has also published book chapters on the

French and British media and has recently completed a study of the media in Britain (Ophrys, 1998).

James Stanyer is Lecturer in Media and Communications at Cambridge University. He is completing a doctoral thesis on 'Political News Production' at the London School of Economics and Political Science.

Alex Taylor worked as presenter and producer of various programmes on French Television. As producer of 'Continentales', he won many awards such as Le prix de l'initiative européenne and le Grand Prix National du Ministère de la Culture for the best television programme in 1993. He is now Programme Director of Radio France Internationale.

Patrick Vittet-Philippe is Expert-Advisor at DGXIII in the European Commission. He recently co-drafted the Commission Communication on Illegal and Harmful Content on the Internet. He represents the Commission as an expert to the Carnegie Group of G7 Research Ministers and to the P8 Senior Experts Group on transnational high technology crime.

INDEX

Almodovar, P., 185
Americanisation, 64, 65, 69, 72, 76, 86, 88, 91, 92, 114, 116, 141, 205, 207, 209-212
Annaud, J., 187
ANOC, 111
Anti-concentration, 33, 41
Audience, 2, 3, 7, 8, 9, 32, 38, 39, 41, 46, 52, 60, 61, 63, 64, 71, 72, 73, 76, 79, 81, 84, 85, 118, 171, 185, 193-195, 211
Advertising, 2, 18, 22, 25, 33, 39, 41, 43, 51, 52, 59, 71, 85, 89, 125, 136
Aukin, D., 180, 191, 192
Averty, J-C., 86

Balle, F., 84, 88
Balladur, E., 6, 49
Bangemann, M., 195
Bellemare, P., 170
Berlusconi, S., 5, 32, 37, 84
Bertelsmann, 141, 151, 154
Bertolucci, B., 185
Besson, L., 187
BFI, 77, 90, 176, 186, 194
Birt, J., 54
Bourdieu, P., 184
Bourges, H., 53, 113, 182
Bouygues, F., 6, 38, 41, 150, 154
British Media Industry Group, 8

British Telecom, 4, 114, 116, 127
Brittan, L., 203
Broadcasting Act, 19
  1980, 79
  1984, 108, 113
  1990, 5, 6, 8, 21, 39, 40, 52, 60, 179
  1996, 9, 41, 42
Broadcasting Research Unit, 49
Brunsdon, C., 91
Buttes-Chaumont, 86

Cable, 3, 4, 5, 10, 26, 46, 48, 78, 95, 96, 102, 103, 107-119
Cable and Wireless, 116
Caisse des Dépôts, 112
Cameron, J., 186
Carignon, A., 13, 51
Carlton TV, 7, 35, 41
Carrière, J-C., 88, 89
Cavada, J-M., 84, 89
Censorship, 3, 11, 71
CGE, 9, 33, 35, 110, 112, 150, 154, 182
Chabrol, C., 183
Channel
  ARD, 58
  BBC, 3, 7, 10, 17, 21, 24, 25, 26, 28, 30, 37-39, 46, 50, 54, 61-63, 65-66, 68, 78-80, 87-90, 108, 156, 159, 161, 163, 164, 179, 191, 210, 211

Index 231

Bloomberg TV, 149, 155, 162, 163
C:, 125
Canal J, 118
Canal Plus, 4, 5, 7, 10, 32, 34-36, 39, 46, 50, 72, 74, 76, 85, 100-104, 109, 112, 125, 126, 133, 142-166, 175, 178, 181, 182, 185, 186, 191, 192, 207
Cartoon, 62, 109, 118
CBS, 155
Channel 4, 17, 30, 38-40, 46, 52, 61, 62, 79, 80, 84, 88, 171, 174, 177, 179-181, 191, 194, 195, 208, 210
Channel 5, 6, 9, 10, 17, 33, 35, 41, 42, 61, 179, 192, 208
Ciné-Cinémas, 74
Ciné-Cinéfil, 74
CNN, 141, 155, 156, 161-164
Controle televisa, 161
Disney channel, 117
Euronews, 163
Eurosport, 118
France 2/ A2, 7, 18, 26, 46, 51, 53, 60, 63, 64, 67, 73, 74, 76, 84, 85, 91, 171, 181-183, 192, 208, 209
France 3/ FR3, 7, 18, 26, 46, 51, 52, 60, 67, 74, 76, 85, 169, 178, 181, 182, 183, 208
France Television, 8, 10, 51, 53, 54, 102, 152, 154, 182
ITV/Channel 3, 6, 7, 9, 10, 17, 21, 30, 32, 33, 35, 38-42, 52, 58, 60-63, 65, 66, 68, 79, 80, 108, 177, 178, 210, 211
KRO, 192
LCI, 118, 155, 163, 164
La Cinq, 4, 6, 19, 32, 34, 35, 37, 46, 53, 60, 85, 109, 141
La cinquième, 6, 51, 60, 74, 83, 84, 89, 91, 172
La SEPT-ARTE, 6, 46, 50, 51, 60, 74, 83, 85, 86, 89, 91, 161, 171, 181-185, 192, 194, 195, 208

Live TV, 117
Monte Carlo TMC, 118
M6/ TV6, 4, 6, 19, 32, 34-36, 39, 41, 46, 51, 60, 64, 74, 102, 109, 118, 154, 155, 181, 182, 192
NBC, 161
Nickelodeon, 62
Paris Première, 118
Planète, 118
Playboy TV, 117
RAI, 169
Reuters TV, 133, 161
RTBF, 192
RTE, 192
RTL 9, 118
RTVE, 51
SDR, 192
S4C, 21, 39, 80
Sky 1, 118
Sky movies, 118
Sky news, 163, 164
Sky Sports, 118
Sport Wire, 117
TF1, 4, 6, 8, 10, 18, 19, 30-32, 34-39, 46, 51, 53, 54, 59-64, 67, 74, 76, 152, 154, 155, 158, 163, 170, 171, 178, 181, 182, 185, 192, 209, 210
The Movie channel, 118
TLM, 32
TLT, 32
TMB, 32
TNT, 109, 118
TV5, 169, 170
WDR, 171, 192
WebTV, 120, 133
ZDF, 58, 191
Chargeurs, 178, 182, 186
Children, 24, 40, 44, 62, 65, 66, 85, 87
Chirac, J., 4, 6, 12, 37, 51, 111
Ciby 2000, 185,186
Cinema, 25, 71-81, 86, 175-196, 206, 209
Clément, J., 183
CLT, 32, 35, 41, 101, 102, 118, 151, 153, 154, 182

Cluzel, J., 164, 199, 208, 210-212, 215
CNC, 176, 181, 189, 195, 208
Code of Advertising standards and practice, 25
Code of Practice, 24
Code of Programme sponsorship, 25, 43
Columbia/Tristar, 153
Commercial television, 5, 9, 26, 30, 33, 38, 46, 68, 84, 215
Convergence, 4, 120-137, 140, 165
Copyright, 87
Craxi, B., 37

D2 MAC, 85
De Caune, A., 174
Decree
  26 January 1987, 75, 76
  9 September 1988, 75
  17 January 1990, 25, 178
  9 May 1995, 25
De Gaulle, C., 10, 11, 18, 177
DGT, 107-110
DHN, 23, 194
Digital, 4, 7, 28, 46, 53, 54, 94, 102, 104, 118, 120-137, 151-154, 182
Directive
  Legal Protection, 136
  Licensing, 134
  MAC, 202, 203
  Television Without Frontiers, 40, 78, 85, 140, 200-202, 204, 209
Drucker, J., 165

EBU, 133, 158, 160, 211
ECF, 187-189, 192, 193
Eco, U., 90
Education, 83, 84, 87-89, 168-170
  Children's, 87
  Schools, 87
  Continuing education, 87
  The Open University, 87, 89
Elkabbach, J-P., 53, 54
Eurimages, 188, 189

European Union, 5, 28, 49, 58, 120, 133, 140, 175, 176, 198-216

Fabius, L., 13
Falklands war, 17, 37
Film, 10, 44, 66, 68, 71-81, 153, 170, 175-196, 200, 207, 208
France Télécom, 4, 107, 112, 113, 154, 182
Franchise/Licence, 6, 7, 26, 30, 34, 35, 36, 37, 42, 44, 127
Frankfurt school, 86

GATT, 5, 55
Gaumont, 178, 182, 191
Good taste and decency, 24, 43, 61, 66, 68
Granada, 7, 41, 176, 179
Green paper
  1984, 140, 144
  1996, 134
Guardian Media Group, 8
Guilhaume, P., 7
Gulf War, 12, 141, 142, 156, 157, 169

Hachette, 32, 149
Hancock, D., 191
Havas, 112, 142, 143, 149, 150, 151, 154
HDTV, 147, 204
Hersant, R., 32, 37, 141
Hill, J., 73, 79
Hollywood, 72, 73, 74, 77, 141, 149, 153, 186, 193
Hurd, D., 214

INA, 58, 85, 204
Internet, 119, 122, 123, 124, 129, 136
ITN, 30
ITP, 30

Job, P., 146
Johnnson, U., 71
Jospin, L., 12

Kassovitz, M., 184
Kirch, L., 151
Kohl, H., 171, 183
Kuhn, M., 168

Lang, J., 175, 178, 200, 207, 212
Law
  11 March 1957, 73
  4 February 1959, 17
  27 June 1964, 18
  3 July 1972, 18
  7 August 1974, 18
  31 December 1975/Loi Bas-Lauriol, 212
  29 July 1982/Loi Fillioud, 4, 35, 55
  30 September 1986/ Loi Léotard, 4, 18, 19, 23, 30, 35, 41, 75
  27 November 1986, 141
  18 January 1992, 25
  1 February 1994/ Loi Carignon, 9, 28, 36, 37, 42
  April 1994/ Loi Toubon, 212
Leigh, M., 91, 180, 185
Léotard, F., 141
Lescure, P., 146, 147, 150
Licence-fee, 2, 10, 47, 49-53, 55, 61, 89
Loach, K., 91, 178, 180, 191
Local opt-out, 33, 52, 64, 65, 155
Lobby, 11, 141
Lynch, D., 185
Lyonnaise des Eaux, 9, 42, 110, 154

Mai Group, 35, 41
Malle, L., 187
Malraux, A., 177
Martin, J., 53
Mattelart, M., 89
Maxwell, R., 141
MCA/Universal, 153
MEDIA, 188, 194, 200-204
Mercury, 114, 116
Meridian Broadcasting, 35, 41
Messier, J-M., 112
Microsoft, 126, 163

Ministry of Information, 11, 18
Ministry of Communication, 141, 215
Ministry of Culture, 177, 178
Minitel, 110
Mirror Group, 9
Mitterrand, F., 4, 6, 12, 36, 37, 89, 109, 143, 149, 153, 171, 178, 183, 201
Miyet, B., 201
Multimedia, 4, 5, 42, 125, 131, 140, 141
Murdoch, R., 7, 8, 9, 98, 99, 101, 104, 141, 145, 151, 163, 203

Nethold, 153
News, 30, 64, 65, 68, 155-165, 169, 171
News agencies
  AFP, 142, 160, 162, 164-166
  ANSA, 162
  EFE, 162
  Arabvision, 164
  AVN, 164
  Reuters, 142-166
News agenda, 10, 11, 12, 13
News Corporation, 8, 9
Nynex, 116, 117

Ockrent, C., 174
Oftel, 6, 120, 124, 134
Onwership, 8, 9, 141
ORTF, 18, 47, 84, 178
Orwell, G., 146

PAL, 202
Pathé, 151, 178, 186
Pay-TV, 4, 8, 10, 95, 101, 103, 104, 117, 124, 149, 151, 152, 166, 182
Pay-per-view, 102, 118, 182
Pearson, 8, 35
Pialat, M., 183
Pilhan, J., 12
Polygram, 195
Pluralism, 91, 132
Poivre d'Arvor, P., 158
Pompidou, G., 47

Postman, N., 90
Privatisation, 4, 19, 29, 30, 38, 46, 53, 59
Production, 2, 10, 26, 27, 59, 69, 74, 76, 77, 80, 175-196
Programme code, 24, 25
Programmes, 62-69, 72, 87-89, 92, 145, 146, 158,168-174
Programming, 24, 25, 26, 27, 32, 33, 38, 58-69, 85, 95, 99
Public Service, 3, 34, 38-40, 47, 50, 51, 55, 68, 84

Quality, 23, 34, 40, 83-85, 87, 89-92, 127, 166, 185, 196
Quotas, 9, 25, 40, 75, 76, 78, 85, 113, 181, 185

Regulatory Bodies
  Board of Governors, 17, 18, 21, 22, 24-26, 53
  BCC, 21, 23, 28, 42
  BSC, 5, 21, 23, 24, 25, 42, 43, 91
  Cable Authority, 5, 19, 108, 113,115
  CSA, 6, 18, 22, 23, 25-27, 36, 43, 44, 53, 75, 109, 111, 113, 181, 182
  CNCL, 6, 18, 19, 22
  HACA, 6, 18, 22
  IBA, 5, 17, 21, 30, 34, 38, 40, 79, 108
  ITA, 17, 210, 211
  ITC, 5, 6, 7, 17, 23, 24, 25, 26, 28, 30, 34, 35, 38, 39, 40, 41, 42, 43, 115, 116, 210
  RA, 21, 23
Report
  Annan, 52
  Bredin, 32
  Decaux, 203, 212
  Hunt, 107, 108
  Peacock, 4, 50
RFI, 142, 156
Rights of Authors, 73
Rousselet, A., 36, 109, 143, 146, 149, 150

Royal Charter, 17, 19, 21, 22
RTF, 17, 18, 47

Sannier, H., 146
Satellite, 3, 4, 26, 46, 48, 50, 68, 85, 94-104, 118, 124
  ABSat, 118, 152
  Astra, 98, 113, 116, 118, 129
  BSB, 7, 98, 99, 113, 179
  BSkyB, 5, 7, 8, 10, 61, 98-104, 113, 116, 118, 145, 179, 180, 191, 195, 208
  Canalsatellite, 102, 118, 148, 152-154, 162
  Eutelsat, 118
  TDF1-2, 7
  Telecom 2, 118
  Telepiù, 151
  TPS, 102, 118, 152, 154, 182, 195
Scheduling, 10, 27, 38, 52, 58-69, 170
Scorsese, M., 185
SCRIPT, 188
SECAM, 202
SLII, 18
Société générale, 113, 150
Sofica, 178, 181, 208
Spin doctors, 12
Sponsorship, 25, 51
Sport, 10, 67, 117, 118, 145, 153
State Monopoly, 2, 4, 19, 29
Statutory Obligations/Cahier des charges, 40, 48, 51, 59, 66, 68, 74-76
Stone, O., 186
Subtitling, 169, 191
Sunrise TV, 35

Tati, J., 201, 216
Taxes, 77, 78, 177, 207
Telecommunications, 5, 19, 22, 114, 124, 132, 134-136
Telecracy, 11
Telegraph group, 8
Teleshopping, 25, 160, 170
Television Producers' Association, 77

Telewest, 115, 117
Thames TV, 35
Thatcher, M., 3, 4, 10, 11, 17
Time Warner, 35, 54, 113, 114
Toubon, J., 203
TSW, 35
Turner, T., 118, 141, 163
TV AM, 35
TVS, 35

UGC, 178
United Artists Entertainment company, 115
United Newspapers, 9

Van Miert, K., 203
Vichy, 17
Vidéopole, 114
Vidéotron, 116
Visnews, 157, 165

Wallon, D., 206
West Country TV, 35
White Paper
   1988, 37, 50
   1990, 114
   1995, 9
Wiehn, P., 66
Wolton, D., 55, 91
Wood, D., 180, 181
WRAC, 97
WTN, 158-165
WTO, 131
Wyver, J., 87

Yorkshire TV, 41

Zapping, 72, 86

Now Available

POSTMODERNISM IN THE CINEMA
Edited by **Cristina Degli-Esposti**

"Postmodernism" is a widely used catch word and its concepts are frequently discussed in cultural studies, political thought, and the arts, yet the subject continues to confound, not in the least because there is not one but several definitions of postmodernism – each pointing to different states of questioning, remembering, interpreting, or representing.

Postmodernism in the Cinema presents new strategies for reading and understanding postmodernism and opens up the horizons of investigation to address the dynamic relationship between the art of moving images and complex concepts of postmodern theory. Organized according to specific themes such as auteurism, meta-cinema, national cinema, and the parodic, this anthology of essays examines films such as *The Player, Aladdin, Singles, Reality Bites, Wayne's World, Tampopo, A Room with a View, Barton Fink, Akira Kurosawa's Dreams, Drowning by Numbers, Coup de torchon,* and *Querelle.*

Cristina Degli-Esposti is Assistant Professor at Kent State University where she teaches courses in Italian Studies and Film Studies. She is co-editor of *Perspectives on Frederico Fellini* and has contributed to *Italica, Cinefocus,* and *Cinema Journal.*

ISBN 1-57181-105-2 hardback
ISBN 1-57181-106-0 paperback

Berghahn Books
55 John Street, 3rd Floor, New York, NY 10038, USA
E-mail: BerghahnUS@juno.com • Tel: (212) 233 1075 • Fax: (212) 791 5246
3, Newtec Place, Magdalen Road, Oxford, OX4 1RE, UK
E-mail: BerghahnUK@aol.com • Tel: (01865) 250 011 • Fax: (01865) 250 056

Upcoming Titles from Berghahn Books

DEFA
East German Cinema 1946-1992

Edited by **Seán Allan** and **John Sandford**

East German culture has not lost any of its fascination for Western scholars, even after unification. It is cinema in particular that continues to attract interest. This volume traces the development of the main institution, the state-sponsored Deutsche Film-Aktiengesellschaft (DEFA), that was responsible for film production in the former GDR starting in 1946 and ceasing to exist in 1992.

Although largely ignored outside the former GDR, DEFA produced a number of excellent films and scriptwriters that are examined here for the first time and presented to a wider readership. The themes covered by the contributors include the representation of fascism and anti-fascism in the cinema of the 1940s and 1950s, the conflicts between the state and the film makers of the 1960s, and the social-political criticism in the 1970s and early 1980s. Other chapters focus on key issues such as the representation of women, the concept of "Heimat," the reception of the classical heritage, documentary film making before and after unification, and the relation of DEFA cinema to other European film traditions. The comprehensive bibliography makes this volume an indispensible tool for students and scholars of the media alike.

ISBN 1-57181-943-6 hardback
ISBN 1-57181-753-0 paperback

Berghahn Books

Upcoming Titles from Berghahn Books

Beyond Caligari
The Films of Robert Wiene

Uli Jung and **Walter Schatzberg**

Although *The Cabinent of Dr. Caligari* became an international film classic, its director Rovert Wiene was disparaged and forgotten. Wiene's oeuvre exhibits a surprising versatility and quality, as expressed in *Raskolnikov*, an adaptation of Dostoevsky's novel, *INRI*, a monumental Bible epic, *Orlac's Hands*, a psychological thriller, and *Der Rosenkavalier*, an ambitious opera film. With painstaking research of the major European film archives, the authors' detailed portrait reveals a career far more differentiated than hitherto acknowledged.

As the field of film studies rediscovers film history and the value of historical context for the analysis of films, monographs on film makers provide an invaluable tool for scholars and students of film history and cultural studies. Through the provocative and prolific career of Robert Wiene, a wider, more dynamic view of fantasy production in the Weimar Republic is revealed, enabling the reader to better appreciate the complex shapes of Weimar cinema, its inimitable blend of modernism and mass culture, of avant-garde enterprise, and generic production.

ISBN 1-57181-156-7 hardback
ISBN 1-57181-196-6 paperback

Berghahn Books

Now Available

From World War to Waldheim
Culture and Politics in Austria and the United States

Edited by **David F. Good** and **Ruth Wodak**

The growing internationalization of the world poses a fundamental question: through what mechanisms does culture diffuse across political boundaries and what is the role of politics in shaping this diffusion? This volume offers some answers through a case study that examines the relationship between two quite different states during the cold war era – Austria, a small neutral country, and the United States, the reigning superpower. The authors of this volume challenge naive notions of cultural diffusion that posit the submission of small peripheral areas to the dictates of hegemonic powers at the core. "Americanization" has no doubt taken place since 1945 in Austria; local forces, however, crucially shaped this process, and Austrian elites enjoyed considerable leeway in pursuing "Austrian" political objectives.

At the same time, with the expulsion of Vienna's cultural and intellectual elite after the *Anschluss*, the United States, more than any other country, became heir to the rich cultural legacy of "Vienna 1900," which profoundly shaped politics and culture in postwar America. The relationship climaxed and came full circle with the unfolding of the Waldheim affair, which forced Americans and Austrians to reinterpret the meaning of the Nazi era as a confrontation with the "other."

ISBN 1-57181-103-6 hardback

Berghahn Books

www.ingramcontent.com/pod-product-compliance
Lightning Source LLC
Chambersburg PA
CBHW071155070526
44584CB00019B/2796